D1562226

# Being Female

# World Anthropology

General Editor

SOL TAX

*Patrons*

CLAUDE LÉVI-STRAUSS
MARGARET MEAD
LAILA SHUKRY EL HAMAMSY
M. N. SRINIVAS

MOUTON PUBLISHERS · THE HAGUE · PARIS
DISTRIBUTED IN THE USA AND CANADA BY ALDINE, CHICAGO

# Being Female

*Reproduction, Power, and Change*

*Editor*

DANA RAPHAEL

MOUTON PUBLISHERS · THE HAGUE · PARIS
DISTRIBUTED IN THE USA AND CANADA BY ALDINE, CHICAGO

# General Editor's Preface

Being a male, the General Editor is surprised that until now anthropology has never devoted a book exclusively to either males or females. However, as the present book explains, the male-bias in anthropology is just now beginning to be recognized as a stumbling block in our undertaking of human behavior. This book therefore is a welcome contribution for the statement it makes that the former anthropological reports have been lopsided; that females essentially have been overlooked in the ethnographic literature; that most ethnographies were by males and about male activities; that the viewing of the world from a male vantage has distorted our understanding and slowed our science; that the present volume which is skewed predominantly to looking at female interests clearly does not claim to right all these distortions, but only to start to balance the scale as one necessary step in the evolution of our science.

Like most contemporary sciences, anthropology is a product of the European tradition. Some argue that it is a product of colonialism, with one small and self-interested part of the species dominating the study of the whole. If we are to understand the species, our science needs substantial input from scholars who represent a variety of the world's cultures. It was a deliberate purpose of the IXth International Congress of Anthropological and Ethnological Sciences to provide impetus in this direction. The *World Anthropology* volumes, therefore, offer a first glimpse of a human science in which members from all societies have played an active role. Each of the books is designed to be self-contained; each is an attempt to update its particular sector of scientific knowledge and is written by specialists from all parts of the world. Each volume should be read and reviewed individually as a separate volume on its own given subject. The set as a whole will indicate what changes are in store for anthropology as scholars from the developing countries join in studying the species of which we are all a part.

The IXth Congress was planned from the beginning not only to include as many of the scholars from every part of the world as possible, but also with a view toward the eventual publication of the papers in high-quality volumes. At previous Congresses scholars were invited to bring papers which were then read out loud. They were necessarily limited in length; many were only summarized; there was little time for discussion; and the sparse discussion could only be in one language. The IXth Congress was an experiment aimed at changing this. Papers were written with the intention of exchanging them before the Congress, particularly in extensive pre-Congress sessions; they were not intended to be read at the Congress, that time being devoted to discussions — discussions which were simultaneously and professionally translated into five languages. The method for eliciting the papers was structured to make as representative a sample as was allowable when scholarly creativity — hence self-selection — was critically important. Scholars were asked both to propose papers of their own and to suggest topics for sessions of the Congress which they might edit into volumes. All were then informed of the suggestions and encouraged to re-think their own papers and the topics. The process, therefore, was a continuous one of feedback and exchange and it has continued to be so even after the Congress. The some two thousand papers comprising *World Anthropology* certainly then offer a substantial sample of world anthropology. It has been said that anthropology is at a turning point; if this is so, these volumes will be the historical direction-markers.

As might have been foreseen in the first post-colonial generation, the large majority of the Congress papers (82 percent) are the work of scholars identified with the industrialized world which fathered our traditional discipline and the institution of the Congress itself: Eastern Europe (15 percent); Western Europe (16 percent); North America (47 percent); Japan, South Africa, Australia, and New Zealand (4 percent). Only 18 percent of the papers are from developing areas: Africa (4 percent); Asia-Oceania (9 percent); Latin American (5 percent). Aside from the substantial representation from the U.S.S.R. and the nations of Eastern Europe, a significant difference between this corpus of written material and that of other Congresses is the addition of the large proportion of contributions from Africa, Asia, and Latin America. "Only 18 percent" is two to four times as great a proportion as that of other Congresses; moreover, 18 percent of 2,000 papers is 360 papers, 10 times the number of "Third World" papers presented at previous Congresses. In fact, these 360 papers are more than the total of ALL papers published after the last International Congress of Anthropological and Ethnological Sciences which was held in the United States (Philadelphia, 1956). Even in the beautifully organized Tokyo Congress in 1968 less than a third as many members from developing nations, including those of Asia, participated.

The significance of the increase is not simply quantitative. The input of scholars from areas which have until recently been no more than subject matter for anthropology represents both feedback and also long-awaited theoretical contributions from the perspectives of very different cultural, social, and historical traditions. Many who attended the IXth Congress were convinced that anthropology would not be the same in the future. The fact that the next Congress (India, 1978) will be our first in the "Third World" may be symbolic of the change. Meanwhile, sober consideration of the present set of books will show how much, and just where and how, our discipline is being revolutionized.

The present book is ably complemented in this series by Ruby Rohrlich-Leavitt's *Women cross-culturally*, which describes the position of women today, especially in developing countries. Other books in *World Anthropology* which will also be of special relevance to the present one deal with primatology, ethnicity, migration, medical anthropology, mental health, adolescence, the family, and so on.

*Chicago, Illinois*                                                                              SOL TAX
*July 14, 1975*

# Acknowledgments

Not only I, but almost all female anthropologists owe Margaret Mead a measure of gratitude. A volume on "women" by anthropologists seems a most appropriate place to recognize her contributions.

Margaret Mead was calling for a woman's view in anthropology long before most anthropologists even guessed that what we were writing and reading about in most societies was predominantly male-centered.

Hers is a constant voice requesting that the female dimension be added to our perspective. Not surprising then, once feminization took hold within our discipline, she was one of the first to remind us not to throw out the males or their point of view either.

Not only was Mead the catalyst for legitimizing the study of female concerns, but she was instrumental, above all others, in bringing females into anthropology. I, like many of my same-sex colleagues, might not have considered this discipline had it not been for her precedent and her very presence which gave us leave to work on those subjects most interesting to us. The courage it took so many decades ago to present material about women has been a good example for us. On the other hand, she never let us, her graduate students, use a cultural bias toward male interests as a crutch. When we offered complaints instead of accomplishments, she would retort, "Never mind that, just get to work."

I want also to thank those women who came to my rescue in Chicago during the IXth International Congress with such willingness when I was caught with too little time, too many papers, and the chaos that such a marvelous and huge undertaking inevitably creates.

I refer to Rounaq Jahan, Lucile Newman, Anke Ehrhardt, Marilyn Hoskins and Lola Hanson.

Marion Cardozo, so helpful in editing this material, deserves much praise and many thanks.

One last thought. In a section of acknowledgments, even though it seems redundant — a bit of gratitude that goes without saying — I should like to mention the encouragement, unique foresight, and enormous durability of Sol Tax. To me his open invitation for innovation has become a new platform in anthropology.

DANA RAPHAEL

# Table of Contents

# Introduction

DANA RAPHAEL

This volume on the acts and actions of females doesn't pretend to represent all of womankind, all female problems — human and non-human, or even all the areas about females that social and biological scientists are investigating. It represents research interests of those who attended the IXth International Anthropological Congress, September, 1973, and though basically concerned with human beings maintains the anthropological tradition of including other primates as well.

The sample of concerns presented have three major foci: REPRODUCTION, POWER and SOCIAL TRENDS. A contrapuntal theme running through all the papers is that of CHANGE. The scholars represented include a psychologist, a physician, a neuroendocrinologist, a political scientist, a musicologist, a public health administrator, a primatologist, and a variety of professors and students of anthropology.

The content reflects a preoccupation by the world's females with the processes of pregnancy, childbirth, lactation and abortion. In fact, most women spend most of their adult lives either pregnant or lactating or worried about being or not being either pregnant or lactating. And, contrary to popular opinion, most women in non-Western cultures do not find their lives unrewarding, frustrating, or a waste of time. In fact, concern with family/infant/child matters appears to be at least as satisfying to the female as the male role is to her father, husband and sons.

The rather pejorative argument that lack of exposure means women are happy where they are and thus don't want to change, is as questionable as suggesting that modern Western women ought to be dissatisfied with their lot because they don't know how swell it is going to be in the year 2074. No doubt many women are not content with some dimensions of their lives but non-female roles are not the answer either. They want their lives improved, their hunger abated, their children educated, and they want a general increase in the variety of their options. Individual freedom and self-determination appear to be related to the number of choices and options that are open. An extension of choices rather than a denial of current roles is a central concern of today's women.

Noticeably absent from this collection are any papers on sexual behavior. There were none offered. Though this may be regrettable, it comes as a surprise only to those who think of human female reproductive behavior as synonymous with sexual behavior.

The first section of this book deals with those aspects of the reproductive cycle which are exclusively female — childbirth, lactation and mothering. However, as Margaret Mead mentioned during her discussion of these papers at this session, even such an intimate experience as breastfeeding should no longer be examined in the limited light of a mother/infant interrelationship. Intrinsic to that activity is someone to feed that mother who feeds the child, someone to care for the needs of that mother and someone to give status and community to that child. The social unit of the breastfeeding pair must include a male (probably father of the child or husband of the mother) and several supportive others (probably mother's mother) and other females. Without such mothering of the mother, without such supportive help, even such a natural process as breastfeeding is affected and the infant's life is endangered (Raphael 1973).

It is particularly in those areas which have a biological base that the broad view of anthropology can make a most valuable] contribution. Throughout this section, the presence of the larger networks of influence and the idea of a continuity of human behavior with that of other mammals has been emphasized.

Fundamental questions are raised in the first section. What is maleness and femaleness? What is the frequency of abortion in primates? What American childbirth practices are considered aberrant in other cultures? Are there universal patterns in the *rites de passage* of matrescence, becoming a mother? What are the nutritional needs of human females during pregnancy? What are the attributes of an alliance called "marriage?" What needs of the new mother determine the choice of "matridomiparas"[1] residence? What other factors determine matrilocal residence?

The second section focuses on a non-male view of power. Domestic power is separated from public power. Females are depicted primarily and

---

[1] This term was coined by Conrad Arensberg to express the return of a primiparas female to her own mother's (and father's) home with or without her spouse during the perinatal period.

dominantly involved with decisions and authority in the home sphere but having a large influence as well on public decisions and power. Several strategies are described of how women exert their influence in the public arena. Since women are hardly ever in the public/political scene, even in those cultures where matrilineality/matrilocality is the dominant pattern, what is it that prevents them from being there? where are they? and what are they doing?

We know the average female spends most of her waking hours reproducing and rearing children, so more than likely she would not be available for other commitments until she is done with her reproductive years. But how about the women who fail to reproduce at all? One could ask why these females are not trained or permitted to learn the role-requirements for leadership. One answer is that the non-reproducing female is not identified as such until she is an adult.

The women who have become political figures in their own right have done so either after their reproductive years were over or because certain unique life situations have permitted them access to the kinds of information and experiences which could be transformed into active political behavior. Apparently, human beings did not find it economically feasible until recently for people in any culture to train both males and females to assume power roles and child-rearing roles.

Our responsibility as social scientists, then, is not to define power as public, domestic, male or female, and then to put a prejudicial value on such a definition, but to look at where people are and what they do with the time and the resources available to them. We are not suggesting that interactional analyses of power relationships have not been made. They have. We are saying that little has been done to adjust the criteria so that the power roles of women are more clearly understood.

The last section introduces general trends of change in female life patterns as they have been subjected to such forces as urbanization, educational accessibility, food supply, and family planning or lack of it. Many trends are highlighted here. The similarities in content are overshadowed by the variety of results as each culture responds to new challenges in different ways, depending on the history and current stage of economic development of each.

It is sad but true that anthropologists had to wait to obtain information about women until enough female ethnographers were trained who could enter, observe and describe the inside scene so often not available to men. The focus on women, stimulated by the women's liberation movement in the United States, has also been helpful. The movement has encouraged women to study other women.

An impression that women have been hidden behind the veil and are now coming out is too simplistic. More realistically, one can see that many avenues have opened to women with the adoption of Western economic influences and patterns. Far greater choices of activity exist, or are potentially available.

Since we propose adding a female perception to a view of the world, the reader might question whether we too are not distorting reality by this new female-centered approach. Certainly we are and yet we forge ahead, not unaware of the difficulties, because we sincerely believe that this is a necessary next step in the development of our science. We hold that the proper unit for anthropological investigation must include males/females/children/others within a given environment.

There are several new and controversial arguments introduced in this book. For instance, a much broader continuum of normal "male-type" behavior in the female is proposed. Concepts of power are reevaluated. A division into public and domestic spheres is defined within which male/female contributions are seen as interaction on a multidimensional plane mutually influential. The position of women in terms of power is argued as largely related to the time-consuming reproductive and child-rearing functions. One conclusion is that female power to determine the lot of each generation is as great if not greater than the male/political input.

The contributors to this section also persuasively contend that a woman's matrescence, heretofore ignored in the literature, may be her most dramatic *rite de passage*, that a definition of marriage needs the criterion of many factors not just one, that friendship can be substituted for kin, that affectional and instrumental functions can be delegated to different individuals, that women change occupational roles with more ease and less disruption in non-Western cultures, and that policies of "unequalness" favoring working women during pregnancy and the early years of child rearing might be in the offing.

On the whole, it seems that the female perspective throughout this book offers new explanations and insights for phenomena which to date have never been satisfactorily or adequately analyzed. By adding a biological basis of universal dimension based on real problems with real people (including female people) we are getting nearer the truth.


## REFERENCES

RAPHAEL, DANA
    1973  *The tender gift — breastfeeding.* Englewood Cliffs, N.J.: Prentice-Hall.

# SECTION ONE

*Reproduction*

# Reproduction: Introductory Notes

LUCILE NEWMAN

This session on the status of women addresses itself to a major aspect of female role behavior — reproduction.

Status is a social rather than a biological term, and yet we as women are continually beset by cultural differentiations of status rooted in biological differences. Equality is not identity, and social equality should not require biological identity. We approach the female here precisely at the point of biological differentiation from the male — her reproductive role — and attempt to assess what this capacity means, or could mean, in terms of status.

Academic interest and scientific research in many of these areas has been sparse. We know more about lactation in the cow than in the human, more about nutrition in the chicken than in most mammals. We know much more about abstract kinship than about the experiences of mothering and fathering and growing up in a family. We know so very little about the diverse aspects of human reproduction and what they mean for the status of the female. We feel the researchers whose works are included here are contributing new understanding to this dual relationship.

Anke Ehrhardt, a neuroendocrinologist, discusses the effect of maternal sex hormones on the fetus in the prenatal period and the potential effects of such hormones on postnatal behavior. The scope of laboratory experimentation on the effects of human sex hormones is necessarily limited. Ehrhardt has worked with individuals exposed to high levels of androgen (male sex hormones) before birth.

"The evidence," claims Ehrhardt, "reveals that genetic females who were exposed to high levels of androgen, either due to maternal intake of masculinizing drugs or to their own hyperactive, erroneously working

adrenal cortex in a medical condition called the adrenogenital syndrome...
show... consistently similar behavior profiles. These individuals exhibit a
high energy expenditure in outdoor athletic and 'rough-and-tumble'
activities throughout childhood and a reduced interest in dollplay and infant care-taking. Their fantasy and play rehearsal of marital and maternal
adult roles are far lower than those relating to work away from home."
She notes, however, that these androgenic hormones do not reverse gender
identity. They do not cause the affected individual to identify as male.

Ehrhardt's studies were consistent with earlier studies of hermaphrodites by John Money which showed that the one most important
variable in determining a person's self-image as a female or a male is the
sex in which the individual is raised as a child. The study group of prena-
tally masculinized females showed social behaviors within the range of
accepted female behavior in our society but clustered toward "tomboyish"
activities. Hormonal factors certainly have an effect on some social
differences between males and females as well as variation among females
and males. Ehrhardt suggests that there are hormonally based variations
in inclination toward maternal behavior.

Poirier's study of the socialization process of other primates supports
these findings. Males show more aggressive behavior, more rough and
tumble play, more peer group interaction. Females tend to be more gentle,
more interested in infants and, unlike the males who are actively "pushed
out," they remain in close proximity to the mother. From the very beginning the sexes are handled differently and dissimilar rhythms in the interactional patterns between them and adults result. He suggests that origina-
tion of these patterns is in the differential behaviors emanating from the
infant due to the presence of either male or female hormones. The pervasiveness of the "facts" of maternity is as dominant and apparent in the
activity and character traits of nonhuman primates as it is in the food
production actions or power roles of human females.

Anthropology has in the past suffered less than many other disciplines
from Platonic ideal types and has focused instead on diverse models
within which patterns were sought. Now evidence is emerging of a biologically based diversity within the two gender groups themselves refuting the
concept of ideal femaleness and maleness which so frequently leads to
status and hierarchical distinctions. Ehrhardt's (and Poirier's) findings
support and strengthen the argument that a variety of social roles, each
equally acceptable and respectable, should be available to members of
both sexes.

Just as Ehrhardt's paper reveals that biological factors influence without
determining behavior, Dana Raphael's concept of the *rite de passage* of

matrescence, of becoming a mother, suggests that biology is not enough. Giving birth to a child does not automatically unleash a previously contained flood of maternal behavior. Nor, as she shows, does it determine when a woman becomes a mother, a decision that varies from culture to culture by months, even years. The process of matrescence includes a subtle, supportive process of socialization into motherhood. In many cultures and for most women becoming a mother is their most dramatic life crisis.

The emphasis on marriage in the Western anthropologists' own culture may have been responsible for blinding us to this fact. Raphael's work serves to remind us that culture and biology are inextricably interrelated and interacting. In our complex, dehumanized society, it should come as no surprise that voluntary organizations outside the family, such as La Leche League, should arise to fulfill the supportive role traditionally played within the family. Such voluntary associations appear to be cultural artifacts of an urban age.

There has been far more theoretical work dealing with the difficulties of defining marriage than in considering motherhood. Dillingham and Isaac contend that a definition of marriage must be inclusive of all sorts of alliances, including female-female "marriage". They suggest three criteria: the legitimization of children, the establishment of jural (kin) relations, and a public verification of the union by proclaimed public act.

Next to come under close scrutiny is the nutritional status of women during pregnancy and the effects of inadequate nutrition on the offspring and on society. John Robson calls for evaluative field work to supplement present laboratory studies on the way nutrition affects reproductive performance. Such studies should include observations of the mother before, during, and after pregnancy; descriptions of food habits; measurements of food intake; and objective assessment of nutritive value. A significant advance toward a method of obtaining nutritional information in the field is anticipated with publication of *The ethnographic field guide to human reproduction* by Dana Raphael.

An example of the kind of data which Robson considers ought to be gathered is provided by Judit Katona-Apte. Her ethnographic study demonstrates, among other things, selective attention to male children in the distribution of food, differential and better health treatment of males, and the nutritional deprivation of pregnant females at a time when they most need sufficient diets.

Anthropological literature has long recognized that the circumstances under which birth takes place vary greatly from society to society. How others give birth — their peculiar customs in relation to birth — has always invited investigation. Papers by Suzanne F. Wilson and Niles Newton suggest that anthropological investigations of birth practices do more than focus on quaint customs. They enlarge the possible choices and suggest that women question present practices in light of a cross-cultural perspective.

Suzanne Wilson conducted a cross-cultural study to test Raphael's hypothesis that in many societies socialization to motherhood takes place usually in the home of the woman's *own* mother. She reviews the extent of the custom which holds that a woman return to the supportive environment of her natal home to give birth to her first child no matter what her residence pattern. A new term "matridomiparas" was coined by Conrad Arensberg to describe where the parturient female stays — with or without her spouse — during the critical perinatal period.

Another researcher (Divale) deals with factors determining matrilocality. The paper was included here as an interesting contrast to the Wilson paper. The hypothesis is based on factors totally unrelated to biological or reproductive functions.

Ying-Ying Yuan's paper describes how American women use each other in temporary friendship relationships to fill the supportive functions necessary during the reproductive years. With the lessening role of the kin group, friendship becomes important. The women questioned by Yuan admitted they would prefer to ask close kin for help with child care, a pattern which is common around the world. However, in the United States kin tend to be too far away to fill this role. Instead, temporary friendship relationships are established which function for short term assistance and daily companionship, answering the new mothers' mutual daily needs. Friendliness, not friendship, characterizes the quality of their relationships.

Yuan separates this instrumental, functional pattern of interaction from the affectional arrangement between BEST FRIENDS. Best friends are usually formed during the critical teenage period. However, since these friends do not usually live near each other, they are not available to help with day to day problems. They serve an entirely different function from the helping acquaintance-friends. It is these latter neighborly friends whom most American middle class women call upon for support during their matrescence.

Niles Newton discusses the negative impact of obstetrical professionalism on the conditions of birth. In particular, Newton questions two of the "modern" practices characteristic of American medicine — the standard practice of performing an episiotomy (making an incision in the perineum which is said to be performed to avoid a tear) and withholding nourishment during labor, a custom which introduces a sense of deprivation when the physical and emotional needs of the woman in labor are acute. Her paper suggests that women should be able not only to seek a gratifying birth experience but also to avoid potentially threatening practices.

Ethel Nurge continues the anthropological tradition of seeing *Homo sapiens* and other primates as subject to many similar biological processes. Her discussion of spontaneous abortions stresses our animal heritage. Deliberate or induced abortion is strictly a human phenomenon and one of the oldest. Nurge presents statistics showing that whenever women are given the chance, many of them opt to terminate some of their pregnancies. Unfortunately, only at a few places and during certain times in history have women had the freedom to make this decision with the consent of their society and safe methods. Even when the option is nominally available, far too often the power of decision-making lies with pro-natalist groups such as the family, state, or religious authorities. Where legal abortion has been available, women have used it. Where it has been unavailable, illegal abortion practices have resulted in a high death rate among pregnant women.

Where choices are open, practice can be improved. Nurge cites the use of menstrual extraction (also called menstrual induction or minisuction) as an early and safe method of abortion. The availability of menstrual extraction, a procedure performed before conclusive evidence of pregnancy is available, has important implications for the status of women seeking health care.

The practice suggests a new locus for decision-making power around therapeutic interventions. It has traditionally been the prerogative of the physician to diagnose and to recommend therapy. With abortion, a woman after a pregnancy test decides on therapeutic intervention and seeks a physician who will perform it. With menstrual extraction, which Nurge terms "the pregnancy test for those who don't want to be pregnant," the woman herself identifies a potential pregnancy without diagnostic help from a physician. Early abortion, therefore, becomes an occasion for a woman to exercise autonomy. As such it becomes a problematic issue in health care, for it challenges traditional notions about who is in charge.

We have gathered here new and essential information, some of which has related reproduction to biosocial factors. We have suggested there may be a normally-based variation in an inclination toward maternal behavior. We have proposed that becoming a mother is not simply a biological process but a bio-social process. In preparing to give birth, we advocate that women should be able to seek supportive services and avoid damaging ones. Finally, we found that abortion is sought whether or not it is legal, whether or not there are drastic consequences. An important theme recurrent throughout these papers is the need to recognize a wide variety of behaviors as being within the limits of normal femaleness and normal reproductive behavior.

# Socialization of Non-Human Primate Females: A Brief Overview

FRANK E. POIRIER

Most non-human primates are socialized and learn the life-ways and traditions of preceding generations within a social group. There an animal learns to express its biology and adapt to its surroundings. Differences in primate societies depend not only upon biological factors but upon the circumstances and setting within which individuals live and learn. The composition of the social group, and the particular balance of inter-animal relationships, determines the nature of the social environment within which the young learn and mature.

One of the most exciting lines of research in socialization studies deals with the diverse handling of males and females in the rearing process. A direct relationship exists between the socialization and learning processes of infants and their subsequent adult roles (Poirier 1972, 1973, 1974; Poirier and Smith 1974). Goy (1968) notes the high level of hormones circulating in the blood of newborn rhesus and suggests that during fetal or neonatal life these hormones may act on the undifferentiated brain cells to organize certain circuits into male or female patterns. And, they may act to produce or influence behavioral patterns. For example, hormonal influences at a critical developmental period may affect later sensitivity to certain stimuli. Such a situation could account for the varying reactions of males and females to infant natal coats. Hormones may also reinforce some behavioral patterns and not others. A female may derive pleasure from hugging an infant to its chest, whereas a male may prefer the large muscle movements and fast actions involved in play-fighting and aggressive behavior (Lancaster 1972).

Gender differences in role patterns are partly due to the dynamics of group social interaction. Social roles in animal societies, as in human societies, are not strictly inherited (Benedict 1969). Laboratory studies, for instance, indicate that primates without social experiences lack marked sexual behavioral differences (Chamove, et al. 1967). Studies of the mother-infant interactional dyad in pigtail (Jensen, et al. 1968) and rhesus macaques (Mitchell and Brandt 1970) clearly show that there are sexual differences in the development of independence from the mother. The effects of such early behavioral trends are apparent later in adult life (Poirier 1972, 1973).

Differential treatment occurs right from the beginning due perhaps to the mother's reactions to dissimilar behavior in the male and female young. Developmental studies of laboratory-reared rhesus (Mitchell 1969; Mitchell and Brandt 1970) and the provisioned Cayo Santiago colony (Vessey 1971) show that mothers threaten and punish their male infants at an earlier age and at more frequent intervals than female infants, whom they restrain, retrieve and protect.

A major differentiating feature of male primates is the larger amount of aggressive output they exhibit (Poirier 1974). The infant male's characteristic predisposition toward rougher play and rougher infant-directed activity is subtly supported by both the mother's behavior and the observation of other mother-infant interactions (Mitchell, et al. 1967).

In a recent study of nursery school children, Knudson (1971) found similar gender-related differences in play and aggressive behavior. Boys engaged in a higher total frequency of dominance behavior than did girls. Boys showed more physical dominance behavior while girls exhibited a significantly higher proportion of verbal dominance. The frequency of rough-and-tumble play was significantly higher and the establishment of dominance rankings far easier for boys than for girls.

Another early behavioral difference between male and female pigtail macaques was described by Jensen, et al (1966). They found that, where an adult male was missing in a deprived laboratory environment, the behavior of the male infant was more adversely affected than the female's. Nash (1965) reviewed much of the literature relevant to the role of the human father in early experience and indicated that the father's absence is more harmful to the later behavioral development and role playing of boys than of girls.

Early differences in maternal behavior quite clearly affect the infant's socialization and the learning of adult roles. The mother's early rejection of the male infant forces the infant into earlier contact with other male infants, usually in the form of peer play groups. They are often found in age-graded play groups which move farther and farther from the mothers as they age. Young females, however, usually remain with the adults.

Macaque and baboon play groups generally include more juvenile males than females. In hamadryas baboon groups the ratio is about 8 to 1. Young females remain with the adult females of the family group but the young males join the play groups. Sociographic analyses show that male juveniles interact in larger groups. Females for the most part prefer to associate with only one partner. Preliminary sociographic results reveal a similar pattern in human children (Kummer 1971).

A recent study of feral baboons shows that there are consistent differences in the expression of the mother-infant relationship and peer interactions as early as 2 or 3 months (Ransom and Rowell 1972). By the time the transitional period to the juvenile stage occurs, sexual differences in the frequency, initiation, withdrawal, duration and roughness of play bouts are present. These differences increase with age until, by the time their mothers again give birth, young males have joined relatively permanent peer play groups where they spend much of their time. Young females, however, avoid rough and prolonged peer group interactions and most of the time remain with the mother's subgroup. During the next four or five years, males continue to interact mostly with each other. They cluster on the periphery of the group and are generally avoided by mothers and other females. In this same period, females maintain close proximity to adult females. Gender role learning through experiences with older individuals of both sexes differ markedly.

Other behavioral differences in nonhuman primates become pronounced early in life. Vessey (1971) found that the most striking qualitative difference between male and female rhesus infants was the occurrence of mounting behavior in males and its absence in females. Among baboons, females are more consistently involved in close associative behaviors such as grooming, and are usually in closer proximity to other animals than are males. Males, however, begin the process of peripheralization earlier in life (Nash and Ransom 1971).

In studying socialization and learning processes characteristic of male and female non-human primates it is very important to relate them to adult roles. The role a female must learn is that of BEING A MOTHER. Field and laboratory studies have consistently shown that females (even by the juvenile stage) are more closely attached to the mother, show more interest in young infants (Spencer-Booth 1968; Chamove, et al. 1967), and are gentler (less aggressive) in their social relationships than are males. Field reports note that (most, perhaps all) adult females have experience in caring for young even before they themselves give birth. It seems reasonable to conclude that playing a mothering role as a juvenile contributes to the success of the primiparous mother. See, for example, Lancaster's (1972) study of vervet play-mothering.

This does not mean that all maternal behavior patterns are inborn, for we know that a total lack of social experience leads to the development of very infantile and aggressive mothers. A laboratory study by the Harlows, Dodsworth, and Arling (1966) found that motherless mothers raised in semi-isolation, or females deprived of peer interaction, responded to their first infant with active rejection and hostility. However, they also found that social experience with an infant, no matter how minimal, affected maternal behavior. The same females who rejected their first infant often accepted the second.

Although some basic patterns of maternal behavior may be relatively inborn, learning plays an important part in the development of skills in performing them. Many studies note that young juvenile females are inept in handling infants, but when they reach adulthood they can carry and handle infants with ease and expertise (Jay 1962; Lancaster 1972; Struhsaker 1967). The dynamics of the maternal learning process occur under the mother's watchful eyes. Instances of carelessness, clumsiness, or real abuse are punished. Through a simple conditioning process, juvenile females learn appropriate behavior patterns with their reward being the continued presence of the infant. Laboratory studies support the idea that this early experience may be a kind of "practice" for adult maternal behavioral patterns (Seay 1966).

CONCLUSION

Learning is an important process in acquiring the primate social roles. In large part, rather than inheriting their behavioral patterns, males and females learn them at an early age. Mothers and other group members soon discern sex differences and react to them. Thus very early in life males and females are reared differently. Males are soon forced away from their mothers into peer groups. They learn to be assertive, aggresive individuals. Females, on the other hand, remain closely attached to their mothers and learn to interact with other females. Most importantly, they learn how to care for infants. The socialization and learning processes of the male and female non-human primate, although overlapping, differ in important respects. The processes for the female seem to be geared toward producing a healthy, effective mother. The human situation, however, greatly differs in that females have many options and alternatives concerning the assumption of their biological role of motherhood. This is an important point.

# REFERENCES

BENEDICT, B.
1969   Role analyses in animals and men. *Man, Journal of the Royal Anthropological Institute* 4:203–214.

CHAMOVE, A., H. HARLOW, G. MITCHELL
1967   Sex differences in the infant-directed behavior of preadolescent rhesus monkeys. *Child Development* 38:329–335.

GOY, R.
1968   "Organizing effects of androgen on the behavior of rhesus monkeys," in *Endocrinology and human behavior.* Edited by R. Michael, 12–31.

HARLOW, H., M. HARLOW, R. DODSWORTH, G. ARLING
1966   Maternal behavior of rhesus monkeys deprived of mothering and peer associations in infancy. *Proceedings of American Philosophical Society* 110:58–66.

JAY, P.
1962   Aspects of maternal behavior among langurs. *Annals of the New York Academy of Science* 102:468–476.

JENSEN, G., R. BOBBITT, B. GORDON
1966   Sex differences in social interaction between infant monkeys and their mothers. *Recent Advances in Biological Psychiatry* 9:283–293.
1968   "The development of mutual avoidance in mother-infant pigtailed monkeys, *Macaca nemestrina*," in *Social communication among primates.* Edited by S. A. Altman, 43–55. Chicago: University of Chicago Press.

KNUDSON, M.
1971   "Sex differences in dominance behavior of young human primates." Paper presented at American Anthropological Association, New York City.

KUMMER, H.
1971   *Primate societies.* Chicago: Aldine.

LANCASTER, J.
1972   "Play-mothering: the relations between juvenile females and young infants among free-ranging vervet monkeys," in *Primate socialization,* Edited by F. E. Poirier, 83–101. New York: Random House.

MITCHELL, G.
1969   Paternalistic behavior in primates. *Psychological Bulletin* 41:399–417.

MITCHELL, G., G. ARLING, G. MOLLER
1967   Long-term effects of maternal punishment on the behavior of monkeys. *Psychonomic Science* 8:197–198.

MITCHELL, G., E. BRANDT
1970   Behavioral differences related to experience of mother and sex of infant in the rhesus monkey. *Developmental Psychology* 3:149.

NASH, J.
1965   The father in contemporary culture and current psychological literature. *Child Development* 36:261–297.

NASH, L., T. RANSOM
1971   "Socialization in baboons at the Gombe Stream National Park,

Tanzania." Paper presented at the American Anthropological Association, New York City.

POIRIER, F. E.

1970a "Nilgiri langur ecology and social behavior," in *Primate behavior: developments in field and laboratory research,* volume one. Edited by L. Rosenblum, 251–383. New York: Academic Press.

1970b Characteristics of the Nilgiri langur dominance structure. *Folia primatologica* 12:161–187.

1970c The Nilgiri langur communication matrix. *Folia primatologica* 13: 92–137.

1971 "Socialization variables." Paper presented at American Anthropological Association, New York City.

1972 "Introduction," in *Primate socialization.* Edited by F. E. Poirier, 1–28. New York: Random House.

1973 "Socialization and learning among nonhuman primates," in *Learning and culture.* Edited by S. Kimball and J. Burnett, 3–39. Seattle: University of Washington Press.

1974 "Colobine aggression: a review," in *Primate aggression, territoriality and zenophobia.* Edited by R. Holloway, 123–157. New York: Academic Press.

POIRIER, F. E., E. O. SMITH

1974 The socializing functions of primate play behavior. *American Zoologist* 14:275–287.

RANSOM, T., T. ROWELL

1972 "Early social development of feral baboons," in *Primate socialization.* Edited by F. E. Poirier, 102–144. New York: Random House.

SEAY, B.

1966 Maternal behavior in primiparous and multiparous rhesus monkeys. *Folia primatologica* 4:146–168.

SPENCER-BOOTH, Y.

1968 The behavior of group companions towards rhesus monkey infants. *Animal Behavior* 16:541–557.

STRUHSAKER, T.,

1967 Behavior of vervet monkeys, *Cercopithecus aethiops. University of California Publications in Zoology* 82:1–74.

VESSEY, S.

1971 "Social behavior of free-ranging rhesus monekys in the first year." Paper presented at American Anthropological Association, New York City.

# Prenatal Hormones and Human Behavior: Implications for the Status of Women

ANKE A. EHRHARDT

One of the basic tenets of the recent feminist movement in the United States has been a rejection of the concept of any physiological difference as a basis for sex role differences. This is a very understandable position for a movement which aims at changing sex inequalities, for physiological factors, as opposed to culturally conditioned or environmentally acquired characteristics would be the first targets taken as grounds to dictate sex roles in society. The reasoning usually is — if there is a physiological basis for sex differences, good, then it is "nature's own plan." The argument continues, if all women and all men have to fulfill a stereotyped role at home, on the job-market, and in politics, so be it!

I would like to propose a somewhat different point of view by suggesting that prenatal and postnatal hormones may play a role in the development of sex differences without producing any basis for sex discrimination in any of society's prescribed social roles.

As of today, there have been relatively few studies on the possible role of biological variables, such as hormonal effects in human psychosexual differentiation. The reasons are easily understood if one considers on the one hand the complexity of interaction between constitutional and social-environmental factors in all behavioral sex differences, and on the other, the relatively recent advances in biochemical and neurohormonal methodology.

There are two developmental periods during which dramatic hormonal

Research support by a grant from the United Health Foundation of Western New York (# CL–10–CH–71); The Human Growth Foundation; the Variety Club of Buffalo, Tent No. 7; and the Erickson Educational Foundation.

changes occur — one is before birth and the other is at the time of puberty.[1]

This paper deals with the prenatal period, examining the effects of sex hormones on the differentiating nervous system which in turn mediates some aspects of postnatal behavior.

Sex hormones, in particular androgens (male hormones) are of paramount importance for the differentiation of external genitalia. The testes in the male fetus start producing testicular hormones soon after gonadal differentiation, as early as the first trimester of pregnancy. The presence of androgens in sufficient amounts, at a critical time when the body is ready to respond to their action, determines whether the same bipotential primitive anlagen in the genetic male or genetic female embryo will develop into a penis and a scrotum or a clitoris, a vagina and labia. If something goes wrong with the production of male hormones in a genetic male fetus or if the ability of the cells to respond is impaired, he will be born with female-looking external genitalia, inharmonious with his male genetic and gonadal status. On the other hand, if a genetic female fetus is exposed to a high level of androgens from an endogenous or exogenous source, the baby will be born with male-looking genitalia.

Experimental research on animals suggests that not only sex organs but also parts of the developing brain are organized in a sexually dimorphic fashion by the action of prenatal sex hormones. Thus, these hormones effect sex-specific behavior postnatally. For example, at a critical time around birth in rats, mice and rabbits, the presence of androgens in males mediates such sex-related activity as mating and aggressive behavior; the absence of sufficient androgens during this critical time of differentiation has a long-term effect on female mating patterns, on the degree of aggression and on some aspects of maternal behavior.

In the rhesus monkey, an animal more closely related to the human being, a long-term study was designed to test out the effects on female behavior of the presence of excessive androgen (Goy 1970). Pregnant rhesus monkeys were treated with testosterone (male hormone). Their female offspring were born physically masculinized externally with a penis and empty scrotum though their internal organs were normal. Play behavior in the fetally androgenized female was found to be more similar to normal male monkeys than to normal female monkeys, especially rough-and-tumble play, fear grimacing and dominance behavior. Adult behavior in the fetally androgenized female monkeys also differed from normal females. There was a higher degree of aggressiveness which suggested that prenatal

---

[1]   The time between birth till puberty appears to be one of relative dormancy during which the sex hormone output between normal girls and boys does not differ significantly (Boon, Keenan, Slaunwhite, and Aceto 1972).

hormones had a long-term masculinizing effect on the rhesus brain, modifying childhood and adult behavior (Eaton, Goy, and Phoenix 1973).

## HORMONAL EFFECTS ON HUMAN SOCIAL BEHAVIOR

Though no equivalent experiments have been done on human behavior, we can use research data on extreme cases (outside of the normal range of variations and within clinical populations) to shed light on normal sexual differentiation. Such clinical groups as those with a known history of prenatal hormonal imbalance ranging from an excess of fetal androgens in genetic females to a cellular insensitivity to androgen in genetic males were studied (Money and Ehrhardt 1972). In the case of genetic females, the evidence revealed that those exposed to high levels of androgen, either due to maternal intake of androgenic drugs or to their own hyperactive, erroneously working adrenal cortex in the androgenital syndrome, have in two different hospital populations[2] consistently shown similar profiles. These individuals exhibit a high energy expenditure in outdoor tomboyish activities throughout childhood and a reduced interest in doll play and infant caretaking. Their fantasy and play rehearsal of marital and maternal adult roles are far lower than those relating to work away from home.

This profile is significantly different from their mothers (Ehrhardt and Baker 1974), from their unaffected female siblings (Ehrhardt and Baker 1973), or from matched normal control females (Ehrhardt 1973; Ehrhardt, Epstein, and Money 1968; Ehrhardt and Money 1967). Behavior differences between the clinical and control groups were found unrelated to any other postnatal difference, such as sex of rearing (female), postnatal androgen levels (controlled by medication), appearance of external genitalia (corrected by plastic surgery), internal organs (normal for a female), or IQ (matched in control group comparison and documented as no different from their siblings and parents) (Baker and Ehrhardt 1974). This strengthens the hypothesis that the fetal hormonal imbalance in these clinical groups was one of the factors contributing to a specific pattern of social behavior.

If the presence of androgenic hormones in fetally androgenized females is responsible for the specific pattern of behavior typically identified as tomboyism and the low interest in maternalism, the effects are clearly not dramatic in the sense that they do not reverse the girls' sense of gender identity or make them unhappy and dissatisfied with their sex role. This

---

[2] This research was done at The Johns Hopkins Hospital in collaboration with John Money and at the Buffalo Children's Hospital with Susan W. Baker.

response to sex indentification is similar to the pattern found in studies on hermaphrodites which showed that the one most important variable in determining a person's self-image as female or male is the sex in which he or she is raised as a child (Money 1955; Money, Hampson, and Hampson 1955).

Fetal hormones may, however, modify a person's temperamental set of energy expenditure and goal orientation which in turn may affect the threshold level of responsiveness to small infants. For example, girls with a high level of prenatal androgen showed social behavior which some normal girls occasionally exhibit. Their conduct was clearly within the wide range of accepted female behavior in our society. However, as a group, they tended to manifest one cluster of behavior at one end of the male/female spectrum more frequently than in a random group of girls matched in age, social class, and IQ. These findings raise the possibility that somewhat similar hormonal factors may have an effect on some social differences between normal males and females and may even be responsible for variation within the female sex (Rossi 1973).

## PRENATAL HORMONES AND THE STATUS OF WOMEN

If we assume that prenatal androgens influence social behavior and temperamental differences between the two sexes and within the same sex, we can suggest certain ideas about the prescription of social roles and the status of men and women in Western culture. For instance, a higher level of prenatal androgen in men may be responsible for a low interest and minimal response to the very young. Thus, they may be less inclined to take care of infants, in fact their energy may be more oriented to behavior and roles antagonistic to child rearing. The fact that some boys and men like caring for infants, although their reactions to them are possibly less intense and less frequent than those of most women (Ehrhardt and Baker 1973), can be explained by the fact that sex differences in response to small infants have a variable threshold and are not an "all-or-none" phenomenon.

Western society typically magnifies this sex difference by reinforcing childhood maternalism and adult caretaking behavior in females and not in males. But, to say that it may be somewhat easier and more pleasurable for most women to fulfill the maternal caretaking role than for most men to do so, is not to conclude that only women are able to be good caretakers and homemakers or that women are abnormal if they do not like all or even most aspects of rearing children.

The physiological sex difference caused by prenatal androgens does not carry with it a sign saying "homemaker" for the female or "provider away from home" for the male! Furthermore, if prenatal hormones are ONE of the factors which in fact do account for the wide range of temperamental differences and role aspirations within the female sex, then this fact could enhance the women's liberation movement's argument which states that women are capable of and thus should be allowed to choose freely between a variety of social roles. Some women find their greatest enjoyment and fulfillment in the home as a wife and mother. Others may enjoy a combination of the homemaking and maternal role as well as a part-time professional role. Still another group may prefer a full-time career unrelated to a married or maternal role. And though prenatal hormones do not dictate adult role decisions, they can certainly be understood as one facilitator interacting with a multitude of postnatal socioenvironmental factors.

If children and adolescents are offered a choice of a great variety of adult roles, each of which is equally acceptable and respectable and each of which can be aspired to without any sex discrimination, the society as a whole will benefit. Such liberation and flexibility will allow individuals to choose the most appropriate social role for their specific personality, temperament and abilities. And this should result in a higher degree of individual fulfillment and better informed and equipped candidates for either the parental and/or occupational roles in our society.

## REFERENCES

BAKER, S. W., A. A. EHRHARDT
  1974  "Prenatal androgen, intelligence and cognitive sex differences," in *Sex differences in behavior*. Edited by R. C. Friedman, R. M. Richart, and R. L. VandeWiele, 53–76. New York: John Wiley & Sons, Inc.
BOON, D. A., R. E. KEENAN, W. R. SLAUNWHITE, JR., T. ACETO, JR.
  1972  Conjugated and unconjugated plasma androgens in normal children. *Pediatric Research* 6:111–118.
EATON, G. G., R. W. GOY, C. H. PHOENIX
  1973  Effects of testosterone treatment in adulthood on sexual behavior of female pseudohermaphrodite rhesus monkeys. *Nature New Biology* 242:119–120.
EHRHARDT, A. A.
  1973  "Maternalism in fetal hormonal and related syndromes," in *Contemporary sexual behavior: critical issues in the 1970's*. Edited by J. Zubin and J. Money, 99–115. Baltimore: Johns Hopkins Press.

EHRHARDT, A. A., S. W. BAKER
1973   "Hormonal aberrations and their implications for the understanding of normal sex differentiation." Paper presented at the Society for Research in Child Development. Philadelphia. March 31.
1974   "Fetal androgens, humans CNS differentiation and behavior sex differences," in *Sex differences in behavior*. Edited by R. C. Friedman, R. M. Richart, and R. L. VandeWiele, 33–51. New York: John Wiley & Sons, Inc.
EHRHARDT, A. A., R. EPSTEIN, J. MONEY
1968   Fetal androgens and female gender identity in the early-treated andrenogenital syndrome. *The Johns Hopkins Medical Journal* 122: 160–167.
EHRHARDT, A. A., J. MONEY
1967   Progestin-induced hermaphroditism: IQ and psychosexual identity in a study of ten girls. *The Journal of Sex Research* 3:83–100.
GOY, R. W.
1970   Experimental control of psychosexuality. *Philosophical Transactions of the Royal Society of London* 259:149–162.
MONEY, J.
1955   Hermaphroditism, gender and precocity in hyperadrenocorticism: psychological findings. *Bulletin of The Johns Hopkins Hospital* 96:253–264.
MONEY, J., A. A. EHRHARDT
1972   *Man and woman, boy and girl. The differentation and dimorphism of gender identity from conception to maturity*. Baltimore: Johns Hopkins Press.
MONEY, J., J. G. HAMPSON, J. L. HAMPSON
1955   An examination of some basic sexual concepts: the evidence of human hermaphroditism. *Bulletin of The Johns Hopkins Hospital* 97:301–319.
ROSSI, A. S.
1973   "Maternalism, sexuality, and the new feminism," in *Contemporary sexual behavior: critical issues in the 1970's*. Edited by J. Zubin and J. Money, 145–173. Baltimore: Johns Hopkins Press.

# Spontaneous and Induced Abortion in Human and Non-Human Primates

ETHEL NURGE

## 1. SPONTANEOUS ABORTION IN HUMAN AND NON-HUMAN PRIMATES

This study concerns two types of abortion: SPONTANEOUS (often called miscarriage), and INDUCED (popularly known as "abortion"). Both are worldwide in distribution, the former is involuntary and the latter voluntary.

Spontaneous abortion occurs in at least 10% of human pregnancies. Some estimates place it at 25% or even higher (Newman 1972:8). Spontaneous abortion also occurs among our nearest relatives, the Pongidae and Cercopitheoidae. Anatomically and physiologically, monkey, ape, and man share systems so similar that it is no surprise to find similarities of disease and reproductive disorders.

Genito-urinary disorders have been found in aged laboratory primates but are rare in young laboratory animals, a pattern similar to that in human females. Laboratory primates show spontaneous vaginal infections, one of the reasons for spontaneous abortion in women and other female primates.

Disorders of pregnancy among laboratory primates from a primate colony in the city of Sukhumi in the U.S.S.R. between 1928 and 1952 were found to decrease between the first and fourth pregnancies and increase with the subsequent pregnancies, reaching a maximum between the ninth and eleventh. Among laboratory born monkeys complications of pregnancy were more common than among feral monkeys. Complications of pregnancy occur most often in the cold months, January through April, and least often in the late spring and summer. Miscarriage in the last days of pregnancy or stillbirths accounted for termination of about 22% of the pregnancies occurring at the Sukhumi colony between 1952 and 1957. The causes of stillbirth included face or breech presentation, aspiration of masses surrounding the fetus, twisted umbilical cord, and intracranial hemorrhage. Laboratory primates also had difficulties during delivery, as for example, when the skull was too big for the pelvic opening (Ruch 1959: 451–457).

Further data come from reports on the capture and shipment of animals in recent years. Trappers try to capture pregnant rhesus monkeys, for they are greatly needed for research. However, the stress of capture and shipment result in a high incidence of abortion and stillbirths (up to fifty percent) (M. N. Wardall, private communication).

In a four year attempt to establish a breeding colony of *Macaca mulatta*, captive pregnant and laboratory impregnated females were compared for fertility and fecundity (Valerio, et al. 1968:589–595). The rate of spontaneous abortion in captive pregnant monkeys was high and more of the imported pregnant monkeys died than the non-pregnant imported. Abortions or stillbirths for the imported pregnant was 59% as compared with 12% for the laboratory bred animals. Curiously a significantly higher proportion of female fetuses were spontaneously lost, especially in those monkeys who became pregnant in captivity. Despite their initial history on entering the breeding colony, in subsequent pregnancies, all the monkeys did equally well in producing live offspring (Valerio, et al. 1968: 589–595).

*Spontaneous Abortion in the Hominidae*

The human female has ten thousand ova in each ovary. All these ova are present at birth. In a reproductive span of about thirty years, less than four hundred ova will leave the ovary and only twenty or so could give rise to offspring (Corner 1970:5).

Many fetuses are not viable but it is not always possible to recognize a fetal death. Many miscarriages occur during the first month of pregnancy and are unrecognized. One study estimated that one-third of all fertilized ova are shed before the first missed period and nearly one-quarter of the remainder are lost later. These fractions "suggest 49% zygotes perish naturally between fertilization and confinement" (Westoff 1971:31). Since not all fetal deaths are registered, accurate statistics on fetal mortality are difficult to obtain and can only be estimated. One such estimate for the United States suggests "natural fetal death" (as opposed to induced abortions) of 295 deaths for every 1,000 pregnancies (Westoff 1971). Other studies, based on known pregnancies, show that the rate of losses, through miscarriage, ranged from 120 to 142 fetal deaths per 1,000 women. This is a rate of 12% to 14% and probably expresses a minimum for the United States. A downward trend occurs as prenatal care improves (Westoff 1971:30) and the quality of prenatal care in different communities can be deduced from the fact that twice as many Negroes have miscarriages as do whites (Westoff 1971:32).

Studies among women who have ever been pregnant show that 25% had a miscarriage. Among those who had been pregnant four times, almost 50% had a miscarriage; and 60% of those pregnant six times or more reported miscarriage. Risk to the fetus varies with the age of the mother. Fetal deaths are more frequent for women under 20 than for those in the 20–24 group, and the risk rises with age. In one study the fetal death rate for women age 35 and over was 219 per 1,000 pregnancies (Westoff 1971: 31). And as shown above, risk also rises with the number of pregnancies. Added risk occurs with multiple fetuses. "There are 15 deaths per 1,000 pregnancies for a single fetus, 42 deaths per 1,000 for twins and 51 deaths per 1,000 for triplets or other multiple pregnancies" (Westoff 1971:32).

## 2.  UNWANTED BIRTHS AND INDUCED ABORTION IN SEVERAL COUNTRIES

*Unwanted Births*

There always have been, and there are today, unwanted births. The "unwantedness" of births is beginning to be a concern of demographers and others interested in population growth and dispersion. The question of whether the couple, and, especially, the woman, wants a pregnancy is receiving deserved attention. The number of unwanted pregnancies is difficult to ascertain. When estimates are made, they may be for whole countries, or geographical units as small as counties, making comparison difficult.

In the United States, research relating to how many women needed family planning but were economically unable to secure it, indicated a wide range of estimates between researchers and in the numbers of women reported. Estimates ranged from approximately 1.2 million to 5 million (*Family Planning Digest* 1973a:6f.). Estimates for the total population were 196,560,000 in 1966 and 198,712,000 in 1967.

Aristotle, Plato and other writers discussed population problems. They recommended a one child family and condoned abortion and infanticide. Plato believed that the age of childbearing should be regulated by law — 30–35 years for the male and 20–40 years for the female. Aristotle approved of abortion and abandoning deformed infants (Himes 1963:79).

Norman Himes, a sociologist who wrote a medical source book on contraception, believed that preliterates did not use contraception as frequently as abortion and infanticide. This may account for the presence of more information on infanticide than on abortion in the ethnographic literature. The search for and use of contraceptives, abortion, and infanticide have been going on for millennia.

... Primitive women are as sensitive about such matters as are modern women. There is reason to believe that many of them realized that it was easier on them, more economical of their energy, to prevent pregnancy than repeatedly to abort themselves at great cost of pain and discomfort. Such women are, moreover, anxious to do justice to their children according to the mores of their particular group. ... *The desire for control is neither time nor space bound. It is a universal characteristic of social life* (Himes 1963:54f.).

Devereux, a psychological anthropologist writes:

... there is every indication that abortion is an absolutely universal phenomenon, and that it is impossible even to construct an imaginary social system in which no woman would ever feel at least impelled to abort (1954:98).

His sample included 350 societies: tribes, rudimentary states and 20 pre-industrial states.

Ralph Linton argued that infanticide is more effective than abortion because the desired sex could be augmented, e.g. a hunting group may want more males, an agricultural group may want more females (Himes 1963:52).

Techniques for abortion are many: hard work and overwork, rhythmic movements of the pelvis such as squatting on the ground and grinding corn on a stone slab, lifting or carrying heavy objects, climbing, jumping, jolting oneself, and diving into the sea. Sympathetic magical techniques are used such as grasping the woman by the hips from behind and shaking her. Other practices include pouring hot water on the belly, placing hot ashes on the abdomen, applying hot wrapped coals just above the uterus, rubbing warm stones on the belly, lying on a heated coconut husk and steaming the belly. Skin irritants like leaves, beetles and ants are tried. Another approach is to weaken the woman by starvation or bleeding.

Mechanical abortion, which Devereux defines as an attempt to damage the fetus through the abdominal wall, includes rolling around, leaning the belly against the edge of a box, and planting a stick in the ground and leaning and rolling against it. Weights may be applied and various forms of constrictions and squeezing devices are used, including pulling a woman through a forked tree.

There are also massage and rubbing, pressure with a pointed object, or with the thumbs and fingernails, pinching and twisting of the belly, grasping and twisting of the uterus through the abdominal wall or hitting the fetal head with a stone.

Gross traumatization of the belly includes having someone kneel on it or put a plank across a woman's belly and have another woman hop up and down on it until blood spurts out of the vagina but these methods are usually used only after other attempts have failed.

Many instruments are inserted into the vagina. The Hawaiians had a god for abortion called Kupo. They reproduced his likeness in the form of a wooden stiletto and attempted to dislodge the fetus with it. Other instruments reported include sticks, the rib of a large and heavy leaf, a pointed root, a hook, a knife made of thinned down seal or walrus rib wrapped in a tanned sealskin tube and manipulated with reindeer sinew.

Drugs and other esoteric products, taken internally and applied externally were also used. These abortifacients were primarily herbs and plants, but insects (pounded ants made into a paste), animal secretions (foam from a camel's mouth or musk), animal products (tail hairs of a deer chopped and ingested in bear fat; goat dung), and seawater and sulphur spring water were also tried (Devereux 1967:121–133).

## Modern Approach to Unwanted Births

Himes develops a thesis that birth control knowledge was always available to the upper classes, but diffusion of this knowledge to the other classes, a process which he calls "democratization," only recently occurred (Himes 1963:210, Part 5). Access to some forms of birth control and contraception as well as the practice of some types of abortions is limited by social class. Membership in the higher social classes is not necessary to secure an abortion, but it makes it easier and safer (Lee 1969).

An increasing awareness of the worldwide population crisis has led many national governments to institute vigorous family planning programs available to a wide spectrum of their population (Newman 1972:14). On one end of the scale, countries like Canada put a premium on child-bearing and pay families a subsidy for the support of children. This is understandable because they have uninhabited land and they need people to develop it. The Biblical injunction "be fruitful and multiply" is more than a religious shibboleth. It reflects many social orders in which the fertility of women was everybody's desire. But when births are unwanted both by the women and the government, choice becomes a constant consideration.

A most dramatic example of birth limitation and wide freedom of choice comes from the U.S.S.R. in the years immediately following the revolution. In the 1920's Russia was the first country to legalize abortion, in line with one of the aims of the revolution which was to obtain equal rights for women. Lenin insisted that no woman be forced to continue pregnancy against her wish and that women should be guaranteed the right of "deciding for themselves a fundamental issue of their lives" (cited in Lader 1966:121).

This policy is reflected in the Communist states of eastern Europe. Some statistics from those nations will illustrate. Bulgaria, Hungary, Poland, and Romania legalized abortion in 1956, Czechoslovakia in 1957, and Yugoslavia in 1960. In these countries, abortion was primarily for married women; the same was initially true when the countries of western Europe legalized abortions. In Hungary abortion on demand to terminate a pregnancy up to three months was available, and abortions numbered 16,300 in 1954 and 170,000 in 1962. In the same period the abortion death rate declined from 5.6 per 100,000 in 1957–1958 to 1.2 per 100,000 in 1962–1963 (Hordern 1971:221). In Romania a legal abortion rate of 24.7 per 1,000 population in 1965, which was considered too high, led to a reversal and more restrictive laws (Hordern 1971:222). In Czechoslovakia 723,833 legal abortions were performed between 1958 and 1968. During the same period there were 2 million live births (Hordern 1971:67). The figures for one Yugoslavian university hospital show that dilation and curettage accounted for 7,833 abortions in 1965–1968 (Hordern 1971: 93f.). In 1969 the newer, safer, less painful suction curettage technique terminated 10,586 pregnancies.

In several countries the statistics indicate that illegal abortions decrease in number when legal abortions are available. This was so in Hungary and Poland. When the Czechoslovakian government restricted the number of hospital abortions in 1962, the number of illegal abortions rose. In East Germany, with strict limitation on the number of legal abortions, the number of illegal procedures soared (Lader 1966:129f.). Of course, with a reduction in the number of illegal operations comes a decline in the number of deaths due to abortion (Hordern 1971:67). The benefits of widely available legal abortion affect the society as a whole and not just the women caught in pregnancy.

Great Britain passed an abortion act in 1967 partly because the number of illegal abortions had become a serious problem (Hordern 1971:x). The subsequent history of liberalized abortion laws has been well documented (Hordern 1971; Baird 1970). Before 1967 an estimated 35,000 women per year entered National Health Service Hospitals as a result of attempts at illegal abortions. It is estimated that this figure represents only a third of the number of illegal abortions (Hordern 1971:1ff.).

Sweden passed a liberal abortion act in 1938 and further extended it by permitting abortion on medico-social grounds eight years later (Hordern 1971:9). The number of legal abortions was 400 in 1939 and 6,300 in 1951. There was a decline between 1953 and 1963 but the number rose again to an estimated 9,000 in 1967 (Hordern 1971:220). The rate per live births was 7.9 (Hordern 1971:223).

Judging by the increase in the numbers of women who seek legal abortion whenever it becomes available, we can only conclude that when choice is permitted, many women opt to terminate pregnancy. Yet in many advanced societies women still have very limited or no opportunity for legal abortion, while many preliterate and contemporary societies do permit choice against maternity. And, depending on class or economic status within a society, a woman may be helped or hindered from getting an abortion. She may be pressured toward, or protected from, personal trauma. For example, in some contemporary societies a primary organizing principle is the legal system, and therefore abortion may be prohibited despite the fact that compulsory maternity reflects an older social order rather than the ongoing dynamic present.

*The Factor of Choice*

Devereux (1967) writes that the decision to abort (step one on a multiple decision path) may be made (1) by the woman herself; (2) by a person powerful or persuasive enough to exert his or her will or influence on the woman; or (3) by society as a whole. Impersonal representatives from social agencies or the amorphous but powerful mass media are also influential.

The woman is forced to make a choice between two kinds of stress, one of which she must deem less painful or destructive. As for abortion to alleviate stress, it is often rationalized as therapeutically indicated. The degree and kind of stress deemed sufficient for therapeutic abortions differ from society to society and even in the United States from state to state. There are also variations in who may be stressed other than the mother. For example, in Dobu where a man's sister's children are his descendants

and heirs, one man was repeatly unconcerned about his wife's many aborted pregnancies, but he beat his sister's daughter when she aborted his
potential heir. People thought his action appropriate (Devereux 1967:100).

Sometimes, the choice is left to the individual. Devereux cites the example of an old Germanic rule that holds a girl's body is her own and concludes that what she does with it is her own affair. However, anyone helping
her abort is punished (Devereux 1967:144). Elsewhere, abortion is a FAMILY
MATTER. In the summer of 1970 a Navaho woman with five children was
asked if she would like a tubal ligation. She indicated that she would but
first had to ask her mother, the lineage head. The old lady said, no, she
wanted more children. The young mother obeyed. Further, the decision
for or against abortion may be a STATE MATTER. The political unit, whether
it be as small as the Cheyenne tribe or as large as the U.S.A., may determine
a woman's fate by enacting legislation permitting abortion or by demanding punishment for it. Both possibilities occur, often consecutively, depending on the philosophy and needs of the times.

There are also decisions on abortion which involve RELIGIOUS sanctions.
In these cases the consequences of abortion are often clothed in mythical
terms, whether they be American Indian or American middle-class white
(Devereux 1967:145).

Choice may have to be secretive, as among the Keisar where women
abort without the husband's knowledge or consent. However, among the
Crow and the Assiniboine, husbands urge their wives to abort, but not
openly. Among the Omaha, a husband candidly and frankly advises his
wife to abort. There is no attempt at concealment. Among the Buin,
abortion should have the consent of both partners (Devereux 1967:109ff.).

*Frequency of Abortion*

Anthropological data on the frequency of abortion are rare and, for the
most part, unreliable. A few more carefully conducted studies are available;
for example, in Formosa there was a unique group where all women aborted all pregnancies until they were 34–37 years of age. Some of these
women had as many as 16 pregnancies. The reproductive histories from
three Chukchee women record two abortions, five living children and two
dead from the first woman; three abortions, seven living children, three
dead from the second; and, two abortions, six living children and two dead
from the third woman. Among the Alorese, 10.5% of 121 pregnancies
resulted in spontaneous or induced abortions (Devereux 1967:120).

Jane Goodale (1971) studied the Tiwi of Melville Island, North Australia. She reports that women practiced abortion, and everyone past puberty knew the method. Many have multiple abortions. Young females induced abortions if they became pregnant before they had decided whom they would marry. Goodale thinks the commonness of abortion is more frequent in recent times than in the past when a woman gained status in the society only by becoming a mother.

The earliest deciphered records indicate there has always been control (or attempts at control) of natality by physical and chemical abortions. A Chinese herbalist of 5,000 years ago wrote of using mercury as an effective abortifacient, and the Greeks were recording procedures for producing abortions 3,500 years ago (Guttmacher 1967:175).

## A New Method

One apparatus promising a significant increase in an individual's control over her fertility is the menstrual extractor. This instrument, also called the endometrial aspirator, is a device credited to Harvey Karman, a psychologist who reasoned that gynecologists need not work with metal instruments when plastics were available. The plastic menstrual extractor which he developed is softer, more flexible and considered by many to be safer than the older metal instruments. The device includes a cannula (a tube) attached to a vacuum syringe. Pumps can be used but are not necessary. The tube is gently inserted into the uterus; the end is slowly rotated in a full circle while a light suction pressure extracts the endometrium, (the lining of the uterus which is normally shed in menstruation.) Menstrual aspiration can be performed from two to fourteen days after a menstrual period is due. One speaker phrases it as a "bridge between contraception and abortion."

Extraction takes two minutes. When performed in a midwestern state hospital, the procedure costs between U.S. $30. to $50. The disposable cannula will soon be marketed for under U.S. $2.00. The disposable speculum, which expands the vaginal canal, is already available. Women are performing menstrual extraction on each other. One self-help group proposes that a woman buy her own speculum and extractor, keep them sterile and use them repeatedly. Several groups train women in the use of the apparatus.

Some physicians protest against women using the menstrual extractor. They say it is not safe and list such complications as infection, perforation of the uterus, and hemorrhage, the very same dangers which exist no matter who does the procedure. Whether self-help groups have a higher incidence of accident than do others, including physicians, is a question to be researched. It is likely that in the future women using the extractor will perform as well in this function as they do in all the other operations for which they are professionally trained. It is known that women performing as nurse physicians or physicians' assistants are well accepted by the patients, and that patients come back more frequently than to male physicians (*Family Planning Digest* 1973b).

While the aspirator may not, as one exuberant woman put it, be "the greatest invention since the wheel," it does have important implications. The first is that with minimum training and maximum care women can perform abortions on each other very easily, very simply and with little expense and risk. Menstrual extraction can hardly be compared with the dangerous techniques of illegal abortion of earlier days. It is cheap, immediate, private, safe, and almost inevitably successful. Though the aspirator is still unknown to the older generation, many young people have incorporated it already as a part of their cultural inventory, part of the way they cope with life, indeed, a safeguard to their experimentation with new life styles. At one university, endometrial aspirations (colloquially called "bobbings") are performed on the average of five a week.

The second implication in the use of the aspirator is that by eliminating the possibility of pregnancy the question of "abortion" need never arise. Some women already think of the endometrial aspirator as a means of avoiding the inconvenience of the menses. If they "bob" they have no mess or fuss that month. The choice and freedom that the endometrial aspirator gives to women is enormous. And, they are responding.

The trends are for women to take more responsibility for their reproductive functions and to learn more about their bodies. They will be aided by technological inventions and changing legislation. Self pregnancy testing is on the way. The "morning after" pill is currently prescribed by some physicians and will no doubt become non-prescription. Abortion is covered by insurance in some areas and in some cases is paid for by Medicaid. In the future, it may well become chargeable as any other medical expense.

Women's choices in reproduction are increasing in an era dedicated to the attempt to increase everybody's choices. The choice to have fewer or no children will do much to decrease over-population and ameliorate many of the problems that stem from it.

# REFERENCES

BAIRD, SIR DUGALD

1970 The Abortion Act 1967: the advantages and disadvantages. *Royal Society of Health Journal* 90 (November-December): 6.

CORNER, GEORGE W.

1970 "An embryologist's view," in *Abortion in a changing world.* Edited by R. E. Hall. International Conference on Abortion, Hot Springs, Virginia, 1968, volume one. New York: Columbia University Press.

DEVEREUX, GEORGE

1967 "A typological study of abortion in 350 primitive ancient and pre-industrial societies," in *Abortion in America.* Edited by H. Rosen. Beacon Paperback. (First published as *Therapeutic abortion*, 1954.)

*Family Planning Digest*

1973a *Family Planning Digest* 2(3): 6, 8, 9.

1973b *Family Planning Digest* 2(4): 1–6.

GOODALE, JANE C.

1971 *Tiwi wives.* Seattle: University of Washington Press.

GUTTMACHER, M. S.

1967 "The legal status of therapeutic abortions," in *Abortion in America.* Edited by H. Rosen. Beacon Paperback. (First published as *Therapeutic abortion*, 1954.)

HIMES, NORMAN E.

1963 *Medical history of contraception.* New York: Gamut Press.

HORDERN, ANTHONY

1971 *Legal abortion: the English experience.* New York: Pergamon Press.

LADER, LAWRENCE

1966 *Abortion.* Indianapolis: Bobbs-Merrill.

LEE, NANCY HOWELL

1969 *The search for an abortionist.* Chicago: University of Chicago Press.

NEWMAN, LUCILE F.

1972 *Birth control: an anthropological view.* Addison-Wesley Module in Anthropology 27. Reading, Massachusetts.

RUCH, THEODORE C.

1959 *Diseases of laboratory primates.* Philadelphia: W. B. Saunders.

VALERIO, D. A., K. D. COURTNEY, R. L. MILLER, A. J. PALLOTTA

1968 The establishment of a *Macaca mullata* breeding colony. *Laboratory Animal Care* 18(6): 589–95.

WESTOFF, LESLIE ALDRIDGE, CHARLES F. WESTOFF

1968-1971 *From now to zero: fertility, contraception and abortion in America.* Boston: Little, Brown.

# Birth Rituals in Cross-Cultural Perspective: Some Practical Applications

NILES NEWTON

Margaret Mead has pointed out that one of the values of studying other societies is that it gives us a new perspective on our own (1967). This may be particularly helpful in viewing behavior that involves reproduction and other life cycle events that trigger strong emotions, because when these are aroused particularly rapid learning may take place. Thus, elaborate and persistent rituals may proliferate, which may be far removed from the biological substrate of behavior. Cross-cultural comparison may be particularly helpful under these circumstances.

Let us illustrate these points by analyzing patterns of behavior at birth, a dramatic event in reproductive biology that stirs human feelings. In particular, let us examine two American birth customs in cross-cultural and historical perspective. Both are sufficiently common so that most female anthropologists who have had a hospital delivery in the United States or Canada in the last thirty years will probably have experienced these patterns. The first involves the practice of cutting the vagina just before the baby is born, and the second involves the taboos on food and drink in labor.

Episiotomy is a Western medical term for the practice of making an incision into the perineum as the baby descends the birth canal, which widens the passage and speeds the delivery. This operation results in appreciable blood loss, which has been measured to be even greater than when tears of the vaginal tissue occur in multiparae (M. Newton, et al. 1961). It also leads to discomfort from surgical stitches used to hold the wound together, a frequent maternal complaint in the postpartum period. Pain on resumption of intercourse is sometimes experienced, which may be related to the fact that the birth cut severs muscles and erectile tissues involved in sexual response.

The current North American belief is that unless such cuts are made, the mother will tear, causing even more injury, and that some gynecological problems of middle age may be forestalled by this vaginal incision. However, the research literature indicates that well controlled studies demonstrating these beliefs do not appear to have been done. Thus, episiotomies may meaningfully be viewed as a product of social patterning in keeping with the prevailing culturally determined philosophy of LABOR SPEEDING (Newton 1964; Mead and Newton 1967).

Cross-cultural information indicates that birth cuts or tears during delivery are not biologically inevitable. Delivery with an uninjured perineum is the usual occurrence in the Netherlands. Neither severe tears or episiotomies are common. Along with this the Dutch maintain some of the best maternal child health records in the world.

In November 1971, I visited the University of Amsterdam's obstetrical service to observe their birth customs. Other related practices in managing labor appear to help make it possible to preserve the vagina. General relaxation of the mother is encouraged by not subjecting her to a move as birth climax approaches. She delivers on the same bed she used during labor with her husband almost always sitting soothingly at her side. She pushes the baby out in the curved back position with head and shoulders elevated. This facilitates expulsion. Attendants hold her legs which are not spread so wide apart so that the perineal area is unduly taut at delivery. The baby is delivered slowly so that the birth area has time to stretch in the usual mammalian manner.

Although birth passage cutting is not a biological necessity, it has occasionally been appealing to birth attendants at other times and places long before it was given the surgical term of episiotomy. Ould in 1742 and Michaelis in 1810 advocated cutting the vagina during labor under certain circumstances (De Lee 1913). Early records of Hottentot deliveries indicated that the perineum was sometimes deliberately torn to help the baby exit (Schultz 1907). The Chagga also are reported to have developed a technique of cutting the birth passage to facilitate delivery when birth was greatly delayed in primiparae (Gutmann 1926).

Thus a cross-cultural, historical view of the birth cut indicates that although this ritual has occasionally appealed to preliterate and historic peoples as well as current Americans, it is not a biological necessity. Vaginal injury can usually be avoided during labor by patterns that emphasize relaxation and the support of physiologic mechanisms operative in normal parturition.

The prohibition of food and liquid during labor is another recent American custom which illustrates the extremes of patterning that can develop around events that arouse strong emotions, and which can be helpfully viewed in cross-cultural perspective.

Recently a friend told me how throughout labor in a communal American labor room her neighbor kept begging for just a little drink of water. The taboo against liquid was so strong that no nurse or obstetrical aid dared give it to her. This American taboo usually covers food and beverages. Sometimes ice chips are allowed.

Like the birth cut, this custom may have psychological and physiological reactions. The deprivation of a cup of coffee in the morning, or a light snack when hungry, or water when thirsty can be an added emotional stress to the mother already facing a major life crisis. Then too, on the physiological level, deprivation of food and beverage may bring on low blood sugar and dehydration at a time when the body needs maximal efficiency for the strenuous prolonged muscular activities of labor.

The taboo against food and water is enforced by the belief that if something goes wrong and general anesthesia is given, then if vomiting occurs, the mother may inhale her own vomitus, a serious condition sometimes leading to death.

However, just as in the case of the custom of cutting the birth passages before delivery, the limitation of nourishment has also occurred among preliterate peoples. Here too it is accompanied by the strong belief that something bad will happen to the mother who breaks the taboo.

The Yumans (Spier 1933) and the Pawnee (Dorsey and Murie 1940) were reported to have developed a strong prohibition against drinking water in labor; it must cease with the first labor pain. Maternal death could be ascribed to the breaking of this taboo. The Bahaya of Africa (Moller 1961) were permitted to drink during labor, but prohibited from eating.

However, cross-cultural materials indicate that the taboos on all food and drink may be extremely unusual. For instance, the British customs in this regard are summarized in a recent popular obstetrical text (Baird 1969). In normal cases, three meals a day during labor are recommended. Breakfast is to consist of tea, thinly cut and lightly buttered toast, "jelly" marmalade, and egg if the patient wishes. Lunch includes strained chicken broth, sieved meat or fish with no fat, sieved fruits (except citrus fruits). Supper is to be like breakfast. When general anesthesia is anticipated, the women in early labor are still permitted strained chicken soup, sieved fruit, tea, toast, lightly boiled egg and fruit juice.

While in Amsterdam, I mentioned the American custom of withholding food and water in labor. The instantaneous reply was, "But labor is sometimes long. Women need nourishment!"

The food and drink taboo in American culture is of fairly recent origin. An early nineteenth-century obstetrical text (Merriman 1816) urges nutritional supplementation in labor as follows: "She should be supplied from time to time with mild bland nourishment in moderate quantities. Tea, coffee, gruel, barley water, milk and water, broths, etc., may safely be allowed."

Currently the taboo against nourishment is being broken by a few obstetricians and midwives in the United States who take their cues from the biological substrate. One obstetrical department makes food and drink available to the laboring mother as well as to her husband or other family members. If an unusual emergency arises so that the mother does need comprehensive anesthesia, she is given conduction anesthesia (such as spinal or epidural) to eliminate the possibly of inhaled vomitus during inhalation anesthesia. Unfortunately, hospital authorities requested that their name be withheld in describing their system, because it was felt most American medical personnel do not have sufficient cross-cultural perspective to accept this breaking of the food and drink taboo without reacting negatively.

American birth patterns in regard to limitation of nourishment in labor and cutting of the vagina before delivery seem quite exotic to those not immersed in our cultural presumptions. These procedures serve as a good illustration of the type of extreme customs that are quite likely to develop when strong emotions are aroused by reproductive events, thus reinforcing any behavior patterns that may have developed.

Cross-cultural and historical scholarship make it possible, however, to get a new and different view on such strongly entrenched customs. It is not necessary to accept them as biological necessities when, in fact, they are actually culturally determined.

## REFERENCES

BAIRD, D.
  1969   *Combined textbook of obstetrics and gynecology* (eighth edition). Edinburgh: E. and S. Livingston.
DE LEE, J. B.
  1913   *The principles and practice of obstetrics*. Philadelphia: W. B. Saunders.
DORSEY, G. A., J. R. MURIE
  1940   "Notes on Skidi Pawnee society," in *Field Museum of Natural History, Anthropology Series* 27(2):65–119. Chicago: Field Museum Press.
GUTMANN, B.
  1926   *Das Recht der Dschagga*. Munich: C. H. Beck.

MEAD, M., N. NEWTON
1967 "Cultural patterning in perinatal behavior," in *Childbearing: its social and psychological aspects.* Edited by S. A. Richardson and A. F. Guftmacher. Baltimore: Williams and Wilkins.

MERRIMAN, S.
1816 *A synopsis of the various kinds of difficult parturition, with practical remarks on the management of labours.* Philadelphia: Stone House.

MOLLER, M. S. G.
1961 Custom, pregnancy and child rearing in Tanganyika. *Journal of Tropical Pediatrics* 7:66–80.

NEWTON, M., L. M. MOSEY, G. E. EGLI, W. B. GIFFORD, C. T. HULL
1961 Blood loss during and immediately after delivery. *Obstetrics and Gynecology* 17:9–18.

NEWTON, N.
1964 Some aspects of primitive childbirth. *Journal of the American Medical Association* 188 (June 8):261–264 (rear numbered pages).

SCHULTZE, L.
1907 *Aus Nanaland und Kalahari.* Jena: Gustav Fischer.

SPIER, L.
1933 *Yuman tribes of the Gila River.* Chicago: University of Chicago Press.

# The Relevance of Nourishment
# to the Reproductive Cycle
# of the Female in India

JUDIT KATONA-APTE

This paper indicates that the low-income rural Indian female who represents the majority of the female population is undernourished, especially during the reproductive period of her life. Much of the literature surveyed, as well as my fieldwork in both Maharashtra and Tamilnad, support this statement. This can be seen in the following brief description of the reproductive period of such females.

A female infant in a low-income household in India begins life with a handicap. She is a financial liability in regions characterized by the dowry system. While female infanticide is not extensively practiced as it once was, female infants are not cared for as well as are male infants. A female infant is nursed, but not as long as the male. She is less likely to have supplements such as powdered milk added to her diet. She will not be taken to the hospital as quickly when ill. She is generally not fussed over as her brothers are. In a 1901 census report the following observation is made:

But if the practice of doing away with female infants is now confined to a limited area ... there is little reason to doubt that in most parts of India, female infants receive far less attention than males. It is almost universally the case that, whereas male offspring are ardently desired, the birth of a female child is unwelcome. It is especially so where the securing of a husband is a matter of difficulty and expense and where there are already several female children in the family. Consequently, even if there is no deliberate design of hastening a girl's death, there is no doubt that, as a rule, she receives less attention than would be bestowed on a son... she is also probably not fed as a boy would be and when ill her parents are not as likely to make the same strenuous efforts to insure her recovery (Risley and Gait 1901:115).

The situation does not seem to have changed much in the sixties.

... while the risk of male deaths at most ages seem to have steadily decreased, ... there has been no corresponding improvement in female deaths... a larger proportion of boys than girls seem to be born in this country than in the West ... girls, in the first few years of their life, still seem to suffer from greater neglect than boys, as a result of which Nature's balancing action of taking away more boys than girls in the first years of life does not properly come into play, and the survival of girls never seems to draw even with that of boys ... (*Census of India* 1962:xvii).

There are some interesting statistics to support the above statement. In the first week of life, 61.9 of the male and 58.9 of the female infants per 1000 die. But by the end of the first year, 172 male and 182 female babies per 1000 have died (Agarwala 1970:122).

But the number of infant deaths under one year of age due to disease in the latest available year for the four major cities of India is 6,191 for males and 5,164 for females (Chandrasekhar 1972:173-175). These figures probably come from hospital records and may indicate that female infants do not receive medical attention as readily as males.

The ratio of females to males is as low as 719:1000 in some areas (*Census of India* 1962:xviii). The figure for all of the U.S. is 1030:1000 (*U.N. Demographic Yearbook* 1965). The life expectancy figures for females in India is 40.55 years, for males 41.89 years. In developed countries the figures for male life expectancy are considerably lower than the female. U.S. figures, for example, are 66.90 (males) and 73.70 (females) (*U.N. demographic year book* 1965).

Marriages in India are based more on socioeconomic factors than on companionship. Total devotion by the wife to her husband is demanded since according to the Laws of Manu — ancient Indian code of behavior — eternal salvation for women is attained only through worshipping the husband while on earth. Thus she does not look upon herself as her husband's equal, indeed does not address him directly or by name and does not question why her wishes and opinions may not be asked for when important decisions are made.

A woman generally becomes pregnant within a year of her marriage. For the first time she has an opportunity to justify her existence. If she gives birth to a male offspring, her status is elevated as befits the mother of a son. If she has only daughters, her status drops to just above that of a barren wife. Barrenness is the worst affliction for a female. Although the fathers of daughters are pitied, the mothers are blamed for "not having any sons in them."

As a wife and mother, a woman works hard. The preparation of food is complicated and time consuming. All grains and legumes (these are the staples) have to be picked, cleaned, and often ground by hand. Cooking is done on a smoky burner. Women sometimes cart water from a long distance. They collect fuel such as cow dung or twigs, clean and wash cooking and eating utensils, clean the house, care for and worship at the "god's corner," and play a major part in raising children. They often work in the fields along with their husbands and tend the garden around the house. There is very little, if any, time for recreation for a lower class rural housewife.

At meals, the wife feeds her husband first, then the children, boys before girls; only then does she eat. Often she eats separately with her daughters. If available, the major portions of such nourishing foods as meat, fish, egg, or milk, and sweets, are served to the males, because it is believed that they need it for strength or growth, and often not much is left over for the females. It is not unusual to find households where the women are vegetarian but the males are not. Vegetarianism among females may be rationalized on religious grounds, thus leaving more (or all) of the high protein foods for the males.

If a woman dies before her husband, she is considered fortunate. If her husband dies before she does, it is believed to be the results of HER sins, either in this or a previous life. As a widow she is dependent upon a son's kindness for her support and can be relegated to the status of servant in her son's home. A widow eats sparingly, only one meal a day, because it is said to be unhealthy to eat much in this state of life. Even at the death feast the female is treated in an inferior manner. The food served does not consists of staples (as it is for the male) but only of snack items (lower status). For example, instead of clarified butter (very high status), water (low status) is used for the preparation of certain items.

The major part of an adult female's life in rural India is spent in some stage of the pregnancy, childbirth, and lactation cycle. Since infant mortality is still very high — in 1965 the number of registered deaths for infants was 65 per 1000 as opposed to 25 per 1,000 in the U.S. (WHO Report 1967) — often several pregnancies are necessary for each child who survives to adulthood.

In spite of the fact that the most important function for a female in India is reproduction, a girl is not given any formal sex education and is rarely aware of the connection between sexual intercourse and conception. Girls are seldom taught anything about puberty or about sex. The first menstrual period is often a horrifying and frightening experience to them. Even after reaching menarche the connection between menstruation and conception is not explained, though they are given special foods for a few days "to strengthen the waist," presumably for future pregnancies. As they near marriage, girls are not prepared for the physical aspects and the first act of intercourse can be, and often is, a shocking and painful experience.

A woman learns sexual activity from her husband, who is often inexperienced himself. She is expected to provide sexual satisfaction for her husband. A pregnant woman traditionally goes to her father's house[1] for her confinement. Sometimes she uses this occasion to stay away from her husband and his family as long as possible.

In Hinduism, wifehood equals motherhood. To be a mother gives meaning to the life of all women. To be pregnant is considered both honorable and auspicious. Women have little status until they have had a child. It is not surprising that motherhood — not womanhood — is considered to be the most sacred state.

The caloric intake of the pregnant women is far below Western standards. In the lower economic classes in India, is between 1300 and 1700 calories (Chandrasekhar 1972:217). In Tamilnad, South India, a pregnant women's nutrition was affected by a belief that too much and very nutritional foods were not good for her and harmful to the fetus. A pregnant woman may be still nursing a previous child and thus have further restrictions on her diet.

The restrictions on newly delivered mothers were strict even sixty years ago:

... all nourishment is denied to her and for five days she is to live upon a stuff made up of molasses, gum acacia, and ajawan ... (Bose 1913:324).

The situation has not changed. Last year in South India I found women living *post partum* only on coffee for three days or more. After this initial period they are still denied certain foods which are considered improper to eat while lactating. For as long as six weeks, the new mother eats only one instead of the accustomed two meals per day. Even that meal is lacking in foods considered important by Western standards, such as vegetables, milk products, meat, fish, eggs, etc. (Katona-Apte 1972). Lactating mothers are permitted all the coffee or tea and bread they want. Interestingly, these are the same foods that are considered proper for sick persons.

A mother's intake of nutrients is also restricted by the infant's state of health. When a child is ill, rather a common occurrence in developing nations, the illness is blamed on the mother's milk, and thus on the foods she consumes to produce the milk. Just as garlic is believed to help the production of milk, other foods are believed to be harmful to the infant, and she is expected to avoid them, further limiting her diet and reminding

[1]    "Matridomiparas residence," (see page 2). — *Editor.*

her that she may cause harm to the child by overindulgence or gluttony. The connection between nutrition and the physical well-being of the infant unfortunately is a negative one.

The nursing woman is the least well-fed member of the household. The number of restrictions on her diet is extensive. Yet the Indian mother:

... continues to nurse her baby into the second and often into the third year ... she continues to nurse the first baby until the new one arrives and occasionally even after the birth of the new baby. The Indian woman is thus in an almost continuous state of lactation – however meagre – throughout the child-bearing period of her life (Chandrasekhar 1972:219).

A woman is considered impure during her menstrual periods and her confinement. During these times she is isolated and is not expected to touch anything or anyone, or to sleep near her husband. She is barred from the kitchen and can eat only what is given to her. Since she is not working during this period, she is often given less food, which affects her health in general.

After delivery, confinement may last from ten to forty days. The impure woman often stays within a small poorly lit and ventilated area in the house, reserved for such occasions. She is considered to be dirty and defiling.

Fasting is often a burden for the Hindu woman. Whether pregnant, lactating, healthy, or ill, a woman is expected to fast several times a week, either to appease certain selected gods, to bring about good events, or to avoid bad ones. Woman fast to obtain male offspring, to gain long life for their husbands, and to assure themselves that they will get the same husband again in the next rebirth. They fast on the eves of holidays, and on days declared sacred by astrologers. In the lower economic classes even staples are in short supply. This added to the fasting means that much of the time women go without food (Katona-Apte 1974).

We can speculate that a chronic shortage of food forces people to make choices as to who is to get which foods and how much of them. In India, this choice favors those who are expending visible physical energy. Rationalization for not feeding a woman very much after delivery is that she is not expending energy and so would not be able to digest the food. The same is true while she is lactating. Since she is not visibly contributing any labor, she may be viewed as an economic burden on the family. It is likely that the dietary restrictions are related, amongst other things, to a lack of economic contributions to the family.

The Indian female has a difficult time. She is underfed, overworked and her body is constantly supporting a fetus or breastfeeding infant:

... a heavy toll of female lives is taken in the earlier reproductive age, i.e. between the ages of 15 and 34. The toll is so heavy that the difference between the male and female population grows remarkably rapid and wide and this gap is never made up in the middle or old age. What is more, proportionately greater deaths occur among females even between the ages of 35 and 54 than is commonly believed (*census of India* 1962:xvii).

The Indian female's short life expectancy, 40.55 years (U.S. female 73.70 years) is largely due to malnutrition, especially during the strenuous reproductive years, and to various sociocultural restrictions just described. It is a vicious circle — poor maternal nutrition contributes to the unhealthy state of infants who often do not survive. This in turn causes repeated pregnancies which drain the mother. There is no question that improved nutrition would provide healthier infants and longer life for the female.

## REFERENCES

AGARWALA, S. N.
1970    *A demographic study of six urban villages.* Bombay: Asia Publishing House.
BOSE, K. C.
1913    "Infantile mortality: its causes and prevention," in *The proceedings of the second all-Indian sanitary conference held in Madras, 1912,* Volume II. Simla: Government Central Press.
*Census of India*
1962    Final population totals, Paper No. I.
CHANDRASEKHAR, S.
1972    *Infant mortality, population growth and family planning in India.* London: George Allen and Unwin.
KATONA-APTE, JUDIT
1972    *The relevance of socio-cultural factors to malnutrition.* Paper presented at the meeting of the American Anthropological Association in Toronto, December.
1974    "Dietary aspects of acculturation: meals, feasts, and fasts in a minority community in South Asia," in *Gastronomy: the anthropology of food habits.* Edited by M. Arnolt. The Hague: Mouton.
RISELEY, H. H., E. A. GAIT
1903    *Census of India*, 1901. Vol. I, Part I: report Superintendent of Government Printing, Calcutta.
*U.N. Demographic Yearbook*
1965    New York.
WHO
1967    *Epidemiological and vital statistical reports.* Geneva.

# Nutrition and Pregnancy

JOHN R. K. ROBSON

Little is known of the nutritional status of mothers during pregnancy or the effect of inadequate nutrition on their offspring and ultimately, the society as a whole. Field studies are needed to evaluate the effects of nutrition on reproductive performance. Studies should include observations of the mother before, during, and after pregnancy, descriptions of her food habits, measurements of intake and the utilization of nutrients, and an assessment of the nutritive value of the foods.

Restrictions or prohibitions of dietary components during pregnancy are well known. The most appropriate diet during this important period is still largely a matter of conjecture and empiricism. Perfectly normal, fully developed, healthy infants have been born to mothers who, during pregnancy, consumed a variety of diets comprising a wide range of nutrient intakes. Despite this, there is evidence that physical growth, development, and viability are adversely affected by inadequate nutrition. A grossly inadequate maternal diet has been associated with subsequent infertility. Lesser degrees of nutritional insult have been associated with abortion, prematurity and low birth weight. Fetal abnormality has been attributed to specific nutrient deficiencies (Smith 1947; Antonov 1947; Osofsky 1969).

In animals there is evidence that deprivation of nutrients results in a reduction of the number of cells in fetal organs including the brain (Winick 1968). The timing of the insult is important, thus, malnutrition imposed on animals and humans when the cells are increasing in size rather than number, results in a reduction in the cell mass (Winick 1969). Recovery is possible on refeeding (Winick 1966). Anatomical changes and reduction of cell numbers do not necessarily mean that function is impaired, but reduction in brain lipids and enzymes (Chase, et al. 1971) suggest such dysfunction may occur.

In human infants, the neurones of the nervous system are organized very early in pregnancy, and by the end of the sixth week following conception, reflex function has been established. Development and differentiation of the various parts of the brain, including the myelin sheath of nerves and supporting tissue, takes place from the fourth month of pregnancy through the second year of postnatal life. Thus, dietary deprivation, both early in pregnancy when the foundation of the nervous system is being laid, and later when the higher centers are being formed may have deleterious effects on the nervous system. These may include disturbance in function such as impaired learning ability. Whereas, a group may be physically handicapped if a large proportion of its members have received an inadequate diet, these disadvantages will be compounded if they also suffer from impaired learning ability. Thus, the successful development of a society must begin with adequate maternal nutrition.

## MEASUREMENTS OF REPRODUCTIVE PERFORMANCE

Indices of effective reproductive performance might include the prevalence of amenorrhea not associated with pregnancy, or infrequent scanty menses. This would be especially significant between the ages of twenty and thirty-five years of age. Age of menarche and marriage are important, too. In pregnant women, an obstetrical history including details of prior fetal loss through unintentional abortion should be collected. Successful and unsuccessful attempts at intentional abortion should also be noted. The description and recording of fetal abnormalities, physical deformities and development anomalies in the infant are important as they may be related to maternal nutrition. Birth order and birth weight should be ascertained and correlated to duration of gestation. Body length, head, arm and chest circumference and the thickness of subcutaneous fat should be measured (Jelliffe 1966). Signs of intrauterine growth failure should be noted. These include decreased weight for length, peeling and wrinkling of the skin. Where sophisticated facilities for biochemical studies exist, diagnosis of fetal malnutrition may be made from an examination of the cord blood.

## OBSERVATIONS OF THE MOTHER

Early fetal development also depends on the nutritional status of the mother before she becomes pregnant. Therefore, the health of the mother and her diet prior to pregnancy should be reported. Debilitating diseases such as malaria, severe upper respiratory tract infections, intestinal parasites, especially hookworm, may all influence the reproductive performance. Body weight, the thickness of the subcutaneous fat over the triceps and subscapular regions and careful records of physical activity may be used to evaluate energy balance. If the mother expends more energy than she consumes in her food, there is likely to be interference with proper fetal growth; this is especially important at adolescence. Thus, estimates of energy intake from the food intake, and energy output from physical activity and increases or decreases in subcutaneous fat, and body weight during and after pregnancy (Taggart, et al. 1967) will indicate whether the mother is maintaining her energy balance. If possible, measurements should be made of blood pressure, pulse rates and biochemical indices including serum transferrin, hemoglobin, and changes in the relative proportions of plasma and corpuscles in blood as measured by an hematocrit. All of these measurements could be made by anthropologists, provided they were given the necessary training. Such data would provide valuable information on the circulatory and hemapoeitic system on which fetal respiration and nutrient transfer depends.

## FOOD HABITS

Quantities of foods consumed, and condiments which may have an important role in protein sparing (Townsend, et al. 1973) and in providing trace elements and vitamins, should be carefully measured. The method of selection of the food from the plant in the field or in the market, the method of preparation and cooking should be described in detail. Analysis of the foods in the raw state and "as consumed" is vital to the understanding of the nutritive value of diets, and overcomes many of the inadequacies of Food Composition Tables (Robson, et al. 1972). In addition to recording food restrictions and prohibitions, the mother and relatives should be questioned on the diet in pregnancy. Supplemental foods may be reserved specially for the mother who eats them "to promote the prenatal growth of the baby," to ensure that the child will be "intelligent" or to reduce "the risk of obstetrical difficulties of physical abnormality" (Ferro-Luzzi 1974).

In evaluating the data, due note should be taken of other nutrients which may affect the specific nutrient being measured. Thus, protein adequacy cannot be estimated without taking into account energy intake. Similarly, vitamin A levels in the blood are dependent on protein, and thiamine needs on the carbohydrate source of energy. Consideration of a single nutrient in isolation causes us to overlook important side effects resulting from synergism or antagonism between nutrients or even the food supplying those nutrients.

Anthropologists should be able to make significant contributions to nutritional knowledge and collaboration between researchers in nutrition and anthropology should provide much needed information on maternal nutrition and its influence on development.

## REFERENCES

ANTONOV, A. M.
  1947   Children born during the siege of Leningrad in 1942. *Journal of Pediatrics* 30:250.
CHASE, H. P., C. S. DABIERE, N. NOREEN WELCH, D. O'BRIEN
  1971   Intrauterine undernutrition and brain development. *Pediatrics* 47:491.
FERRO-LUZZI, G. E.
  1974   Food avoidances of pregnant women in Tamilnad. *Ecology of Food and Nutrition* 2:259.
JELLIFFE, D. B.
  1966   *The assessment of nutritional status of the community*. W. H. O. Monograph 53. W. H. O. Geneva.
  1970   *Maternal nutrition and the course of pregnancy*. Washington, D. C.: Nation Academy of Sciences.
*Nutrition Review*
  1971   Chemical diagnosis of fetal malnutrition. *Nutrition Review* 29:160.
OSOFSKY, H. J.
  1969   Antenatal malnutrition, its relationship to subsequent infant and child development. *American Journal of Obstetrics and Gynecology* 105:1150.
ROBSON, J. R. K., F. A. LARKIN, A. M. SANDRETTO, B. TADAYYON
  1972   *Malnutrition – its causation and control*. New York: Gordon and Breach.
SMITH, C. A.
  1947   Effects of maternal undernutrition upon newborn infants in Holland (1944–1945). *Journal of Pediatrics* 30:229.
TAGGART, N. R., R. M. HOLLIDAY, W. Z. BILLEWICZ, F. E. HYTTEN, A. M. THOMSON
  1967   Changes in skinfolds during pregnancy. *British Journal of Nutrition* 21:439.
TOWNSEND, P. K., J. E. KONLANDE, SHU-CHUNG LIAO
  1973   Nutritive contributions of sago ash used as a native salt in Papua, New Guinea. *Ecology of Food and Nutrition* 3:65.
WINICK, M.
  1968   Retardation in cell division in organs of fetal rats after severe maternal undernutrition. *International Congress on Pediatrics*, Mexico City.

WINICK, M., A. NOBLE
1966 Cellular responses in rats during malnutrition at varying ages. *Journal of Nutrition* 89:300.
WINICK, M., P. ROSSO
1969 Head circumference and cellular growth of the brain in normal and marasmic infants. *Journal of Pediatrics* 74:774.

# Defining Marriage Cross-Culturally

BETH W. DILLINGHAM, BARRY L. ISAAC

In a well-known article entitled "The Nayars and the definition of marriage," E. Kathleen Gough defines marriage as "...a relationship between a woman and one or more other persons, which provides that a child born to the woman under circumstances not prohibited by the rules of the relationship, is accorded full birth-status rights common to normal members of his society or social stratum" (Gough 1959:32). This definition is designed for cross-cultural research: "... for most if not all of the societies for which we now have information, including the Nayar, marriage as I have defined it is a significant relationship, DISTINGUISHED BY THE PEOPLE THEMSELVES FROM ALL OTHER KINDS OF RELATIONSHIPS. My definition should therefore enable us to isolate marriage as a cross-cultural phenomenon..." (Gough 1959:33; emphasis added). Judging by the frequency with which her article has been reprinted and her definition adopted, it would appear that Dr. Gough's criteria are considered adequate by a great many other researchers interested in the cross-cultural study of marriage and the family.[1]

However, an attempt to apply Gough's definition cross-culturally results in an inability to isolate marriage as "a significant relationship, distinguished by the people themselves from all other kinds of relation-

The authors thank Ivan Brady, Elman Service, and Raymond Wilder for their criticisms of the manuscript. Dillingham also thanks the Department of Anthropology, University of California at Santa Barbara, for providing work space for the completion of the final draft.

[1] The article appears in the Bobbs-Merrill Reprint Series in Anthropology (A-378) and is also included in five recent "readers": Bell and Vogel (1960:72–92), Bohannan and Middleton (1968:49–71), Graburn (1971:365–377), Hammond (1964:167–180), and Spradley and McCurdy (1971:126–144).

ships."[2] Take, for example, the *sore* custom of the Hottentots, as described by Schapera:

Nowadays the Hottentots are ostensibly monogamists. But where there are no children to the marriage or only daughters, the custom is still sometimes exercised by which the husband enters into the *sore* relationship with a girl, who becomes his concubine. This *sore* relationship in no way debars the girl from subsequently marrying another man, if she wishes to, but her marriage results in the ending of all intimacy. THE CHILDREN BORN OF THIS RELATIONSHIP REMAIN WITH THEIR NATURAL FATHER, AND HAVE THE SAME RIGHTS OF INHERITANCE AS THE CHILDREN OF A PROPERLY-MARRIED WOMAN (Schapera 1930: 252; emphasis added).

According to the Hottentots, this relationship is not a marriage, but a *sore*. According to Gough's definition, however, it would have to be classified as marriage, in spite of the fact that marriage and *sore* are regarded as different types of relationships by the Hottentots themselves.

We find a similar situation in our own Judeo-Christian heritage:

The difference between a wife and a concubine has remained the same from Biblical times down to the present day in the Middle East. A free man could acquire a slave girl for the purpose of sexual gratification, just as he could purchase a male or female slave for the purpose of doing any kind of work in the home. Such a slave girl retained her slave status but her master was not supposed to sell her, and especially if she bore him a child. The children of a concubine had the same status as the children of full wives. They inherited in the same proportion, and if a man had no child by a wife, the child of his concubine inherited his status, position and occupation as well (Patai 1959: 41–42).

The concubine in this case would have to be classified as married to her lover, using Gough's definition of marriage, and the ethnographic literature provides many similar examples. Ritual license, wife-lending, and even the medieval European *jus primus noctis* are examples of relationships in which any resulting children are accorded full birth-status rights, but which are not regarded as marriage either by ethnographers or by the people who practice these customs.

Being obliged to include such diverse relationships in the category of marriage, we suggest that Gough's definition is not adequate as it stands. Could Leach (1955:183) have been correct after all in concluding that no single definition can be found which will apply cross-culturally? To this question, let us reiterate Gough's criticism of Leach:

[2]   As a matter of fact, attempts to apply Gough's definition to the Nayar case also result in some confusion. See, for example, the recent attempt of Gopāla Sarana (1968) to do so.

Instead [of relying on a single definition] he named ten classes of rights which frequently occur in connection with what we loosely term marriage, added that "one might perhaps considerably extend this list," and seemed to conclude that since no single one of these rights is invariably established by marriage in every known society, we ought to feel free to call "marriage" any institution which fulfills any one or more of the selected criteria... [This] would mean in effect that every ethnographer might extend at will Dr. Leach's list of marital rights, and in short define marriage in any way he pleases (Gough 1959:24).

We concur with Gough's criticism of Leach and with her statement that "...for purposes of cross-cultural comparison, we do need a single, parsimonious definition, simply in order to isolate the phenomenon we wish to study" (Gough 1959:23). Furthermore, since all known cultures do have distinctive institutions that "ethnographers commonly refer to as marriage" (Gough 1959:23), it should be possible to arrive at specific criteria that differentiate marriage from other institutions cross-culturally.

Another question occurs at this point: What, precisely, are we examining in order to arrive at a definition of marriage? Early in Gough's article is the statement: "The paper will conclude with a new definition of marriage which will again make the status of CHILDREN BORN IN VARIOUS TYPES OF UNION critical for decision as to which of THESE UNIONS constitute marriage" (Gough 1959:24; emphasis added). It is clear that Gough focuses her attention on sexual relationships ("unions" that may result in "children born") rather than on social relationships. She is in good anthropological company in doing so. Marriage has been defined as: "... a socially recognized union between partners of opposite sex" (Linton 1936:173); "... socially sanctioned mating entered into with the assumption of permanency" (Herskovits 1955:171); "...nothing else than a more or less durable connection between male and female lasting beyond the act of propagation till after the birth of offspring" (Westermarck 1901:19-20); "...everywhere a set of cultural patterns to sanction parenthood" (Beals and Hoijer 1959:473), "...the social institution that regulates the special relations of a mated pair to each other" (Hoebel 1949:187); "... a complex of customs centering upon the relationship between a sexually associating pair of adults within the family" (Murdock 1949:1); "... a relatively permanent bond between permissible mates" (Lowie 1940:231); "... legally founded parenthood" (Malinowski 1960:99); "... the means by which human society regulates the relations between the sexes" (Rivers 1924:37); "... a union between a man and a woman such that children borne by the woman are recognized as the legitimate offspring of both partners" (Comm. of the Royal Anthrop. Inst. 1951:71); "... a transaction and resulting contract in which a person... establishes a continuing claim to the right of sexual access to a woman... and in which the woman involved is eligible to bear children" (Goodenough 1970:12–13); and finally, from *The dictionary of anthropology*, "... the established institution for starting a family. Marriage regulates relations between the sexes" (Winick 1956:344).

At this point, it is important that we recognize a maxim that we all teach but too frequently forget in practice: kinship and marriage are CULTURAL phenomena, NOT biological ones (Gravel and Obermeyer n.d.). What we should explore are the cultural contracts rather than the sexual relationships. Furthermore, in examining marriage contracts cross-culturally we must include ALL of the empirical forms, no matter how bizarre they may appear to us. As a matter of fact, the unusual forms are perhaps the most instructive for our purposes.

African "woman marriage" and "ghost marriage" are well-known to anthropologists. "Man marriage," as reported by Boas, is perhaps less well known.

[Among the Kwakiutl] a man who desires to acquire the use of a crest and the other privileges connected with the name performs a sham [*sic*] marriage with the son of the bearer of the name. The ceremony is performed in the same manner as a real [*sic*] marriage. In case the bearer of the name had no children at all, a sham marriage with a part of his body is performed, with his right or left side, a leg or an arm, and the privileges are conveyed in the same manner as in the case of a real marriage (Boas 1895:359).

Considering such unusual forms together with other forms described in the ethnographic literature, what can we recognize as common characteristics? It is evident from the foregoing that marriage does not necessarily involve partners of opposite sexes.[3] It is also apparent that a sexual relationship need not be involved at all. There are, however, elements which ARE common to marriage in all cultures. And it is just these elements which allow us to recognize marriage as a universal cultural phenomenon.

To begin with, as Dr. Gough has so ably demonstrated, marriages do legitimize children in the sense of according them birth-status rights. A child's position in the social structure is determined, initially at least, by the circumstance of its birth, which is variously defined with respect to marriage, concubinage, or illegitimacy. Marriage, then, everywhere defines a special, legitimate position in the social order for offspring. However, not all marriages result in issue, and in such cases the legitimization criterion obviously cannot apply. Furthermore, there are other ways of legimizing children, notably adoption. Hence, legitimization of children — in

---

[3]  In this vein, we might add to the cases of African woman marriage and the case of Kwakiutl man marriage the contemporary practice in some parts of the United States of marriage between members of the same sex (see Toffler 1971:245–249).

Gough's sense of their being "accorded full birth-status rights common to normal members of [their] society or social stratum" — is a necessary but not a sufficient condition to a definition of marriage.

Examining the ethnographic literature again, it becomes apparent that there is another function that marriage always performs: It establishes several new sets of jural relations — between the marriage partners, between their kinsmen, and between the marriage partners and their own and each other's kinsmen.[4] We commonly refer to these new jural relations as "affinal relationships." Even among the Nayar, as described by Gough in an earlier paper, marriage creates new jural relations of this nature:

At intervals of about twelve years, a festival was held at which all the immature girls of one exogamous lineage were ritually "married" on the same day by men of *enangar* lineages, who represented the remainder of the local sub-caste group to the lineage... Between lineages of the same local sub-caste group there existed a hereditary relationship of ceremonial neighbourliness and ritual co-operation. Each lineage was linked in this way to two or more other lineages of the group, which were called its *enangar*. Each of these lineages was in turn linked to one or more other lineages of the group, so that a chain of *enangar* relations linked all the lineages of one local group... *Enangar* lineages must send representatives of both sexes on important ritual occasions of the linked lineage such as post-natal ceremonies, girls' puberty ceremonies, funerals, and in particular the pre-puberty marriage rite. Social relations between Nayars of the same village and sub-caste were therefore all regulated on the basis of lineage affiliation, affinal kinship relations, or *enangar*-hood (Gough 1952:73).

The significance of affinality as an aspect of marriage has long been recognized in anthropology. Morgan (1871: *in passim*; 1877:404) and Tylor (1889:268), for example, were both quite explicit on this point. More recently, White (1959:97), van Wouden (1968; see especially 9–24), Lévi-Strauss (1969), and Gravel and Obermeyer (n.d.) have stressed the significance of marriage as a means of establishing alliances between kin groups. We wish to caution, however, that one must not interpret too literally such statements as "The role of marriage as a means of ESTABLISH-ING ties of mutual aid... is further indicated by the fact that everywhere in human society MARRIAGE IS AN ALLIANCE BETWEEN GROUPS" (White 1959: 97; emphasis added), unless by "groups" one means merely the respective immediate "families of orientation" (after Murdock 1949:13) of the marriage partners. A look at the ethnographic record reveals that many marriage customs serve to MAINTAIN existing alliances; we have in mind

---

[4] The term "jural relations" denotes a situation in which "one party – be it an individual, a group, or the community — can make a demand upon another party, and there is public agreement that the other is obligated to comply with the demand" (Goodenough 1970:22n; this definition draws on the concepts of Hohfeld 1919).

such well-known customs as the levirate, sororate, and "ghost marriage." Other marriage customs, e.g., cross-cousin marriage in Crow and Omaha kinship systems, serve to STRENGHTHEN existing kinship (consanguineal) ties by adding new jural content (affinality) to them. Still other marital practices, e.g., patrilateral parallel-cousin marriage in the Near East and brother-sister marriage among the ruling families of ancient Egypt, traditional Hawaii, and Inca Peru, would seem to represent explicit mechanisms for PREVENTING the establishment of new alliances through marriage. Especially in these last instances, it is not meaningful to speak of "...marriage as a means of ESTABLISHING TIES of mutual aid..." (White 1959:97; emphasis added), because ties already exist prior to the marriages. What we can say is that these marriages — like all other forms of marriage — establish new jural relations between the marriage partners, between or among their kinsmen, and between them and their kinsmen.

Finally, marriages everywhere are distinguished from other forms of social contracts by a specific public act that proclaims to the society at large the nature of this new relationship. This act may be as simple as the groom's depositing an antelope at the entrance to his father-in-law's hut, as is the case among the Ituri Forest Pygmies (Turnbull 1962:223–224), or as complex as the series of feasts and protracted exchanges among the Bontoc Igorot of the Philippines (Barton 1919:21–25). Nevertheless, every culture has some ritual act that must be performed in order for the tie to be considered marriage. Nowhere, perhaps, is the significance of the proper form of public proclamation stated better than in the words of the Pygmies in contrasting their own marriage ritual with that imposed upon them by the Bantu villagers:

Mulanga, remembering his own wedding, said that he could see no sense in a village wedding anyway. But Masisi pointed out, "If we did not let the villagers think that they arrange our marriages, then how could we expect them to give us such fine feasts and present us with so many gifts?" Moke, picking up his pipe and passing it to his son to be filled, added, "After all, it doesn't really make any difference; you are not married properly until you give your in-laws a forest antelope. If you don't like your village wedding, don't give the antelope."

And so everyone agreed, a village wedding was great fun, but "*bule*"—empty. It was completely empty, completely and absolutely. With that they laughed loudly and slapped one another on the back and forgot all about it (Turnbull 1962:223–224).

We are now in a position to offer a definition of marriage. Marriage is a social contract which (1) provides for the legitimization of any children that might be born to the relationship (in Gough's sense); (2) establishes new jural relations (affinality), and (3) is publicly proclaimed by a customary act as that particular relationship. For a custom to be classified as marriage it must fulfill these three criteria. And, any custom that satisfies these three conditions is marriage. In other words, we now have a definition that sets forth the necessary and sufficient criteria to allow us to recognize marriage cross-culturally, including man-marriage, woman-marriage, ghost-marriage, polygamy, monogamy, or any other variety. Furthermore, it allows us to distinguish marriage from all other social contracts.

It should be noted, perhaps, that this definition has the additional advantage of conforming to our understanding of such related phenomena as the sororate, levirate, bride-wealth, and divorce. It is rather widely recognized that the sororate and levirate are means by which a society insures that the jural relations created by a marriage will not be severed even upon the death of one of the marriage partners. Similarly, bride-wealth, or the exchange of goods which often accompanies the establishment of a marriage, is highlighted as a custom which helps to insure the continuance of these jural relations. As for divorce, it is an act that severs the jural relations between the marriage partners, but which affects neither other sets of jural relations that existed prior to the marriage nor the birth-status rights of children born to the (now dissolved) relationship.

In summary, the usual definitions of marriage, which focus on sexual relations and parenthood, are inadequate to handle the ethnographic data. Therefore, we have proposed a definition that not only encompasses the ethnographic facts of marriage but elucidates allied customs as well.


## REFERENCES

BARTON, R. F.
  1919   Ifugao law. *University of California Publications in American Archaeology and Ethnology* 15:1–186.
BEALS, RALPH, HARRY HOIJER
  1959   *An introduction to anthropology.* New York: Macmillan.
BELL, NORMAN W., EZRA F. VOGEL, *editors*
  1960   *A modern introduction to the family.* New York: The Free Press.
BOAS, FRANZ
  1895   "The social organization and the secret societies of the Kwakiutl, based on personal observations and on notes made by Mr. George Hunt," in *Report of the United States National Museum*, 311–738. Washington, D. C.: Smithsonian Institution.
BOHANNAN, PAUL, JOHN MIDDLETON, *editors*
  1968   *Marriage, family, and residence.* Garden City, New York: Natural History Press.

COMMITTEE OF THE ROYAL ANTHROPOLOGICAL INSTITUTE
1951    *Notes and queries on anthropology* (sixth edition revised). London: Routledge and Kegan Paul.

GOODENOUGH, WARD H.
1970    *Description and comparison in cultural anthropology.* Chicago: Aldine.

GOUGH, E. KATHLEEN
1952    Changing kinship usages in the setting of political and economic change among the Nayars of Malabar. *Journal of the Royal Anthropological Institute of Great Britain and Ireland* 82:71–87.
1959    The Nayars and the definition of marriage. *Journal of the Royal Anthropological Institute of Great Britain and Ireland* 89:23–34.

GRABURN, NELSON, *editor*
1971    *Readings in kinship and social structure.* New York: Harper and Row.

GRAVEL, PIERRE BETTEZ, GERALD OBERMEYER
n.d.    "Corporate groups and marriage: a comparison between Rwanda and Bedouin." Paper read before sixty-seventh Annual Meeting of the American Anthropological Association, Seattle, Washington, 1968. (Abstract in *Bulletins of the American Anthropological Association* 1(3):56.)

HAMMOND, PETER B., *editor*
1964    *Cultural and social anthropology, selected readings.* New York: Macmillan.

HERSKOVITS, MELVILLE J.
1955    *Cultural anthropology.* New York: Alfred Knopf.

HOEBEL, E. ADAMSON
1949    *Man in the primitive world: an introduction to anthropology.* New York: McGraw-Hill.

HOHFELD, WESLEY N.
1919    *Fundamental legal concepts.* New Haven: Yale University Press.

LEACH, E. R.
1955    Polyandry, inheritance, and the definition of marriage. *Man* 55:182-86.

LÉVI-STRAUSS, CLAUDE.
1969    *The elementary structures of kinship.* Translated by James Harle Bell, John Richard von Sturmer, and Rodney Needham. Boston: Beacon Press.

LINTON, RALPH B.
1936    *The study of man.* New York: Appleton-Century-Crofts.

MALINOWSKI, BRONISLAW
1960    *A scientific theory of culture and other essays.* New York: Oxford University Press.

MORGAN, LEWIS HENRY
1871    Systems of consanguinity and affinity of the human family. *Smithsonian Institution Contributions to Knowledge* 17. Washington, D. C.: Smithsonian Institution.
1877    *Ancient society.* Chicago: Charles H. Kerr.

MURDOCK, GEORGE PETER
1949    *Social structure.* New York: Macmillan.

PATAI, RAPHAEL
1959   *Sex and family in the Bible and the Middle East.* Garden City, New York: Doubleday.
RIVERS, W. H. R.
1924   *Social organization.* New York: Alfred A. Knopf.
SARANA, GOPĀLA
1968   Some observations on the definition of marriage. *Ethnos* 33:159–67.
SCHAPERA, ISAAC
1930   *The Khoisan peoples of South Africa.* London: George Routledge and Sons.
SPRADLEY, JAMES P., DAVID W. MC CURDY, *editors*
1971   *Conformity and conflict: readings in cultural anthropology.* Boston: Little, Brown.
TOFFLER, ALVIN
1971   *Future shock.* New York: Random House, Bantam Books.
TURNBULL, COLIN M.
1962   *The forest people: a study of the Pygmies of the Congo.* Garden City, New York: Doubleday.
TYLOR, E. B.
1889   On a method of investigating the development of institutions; applied to laws of marriage and descent. *Journal of the Royal Anthropological Institute of Great Britain and Ireland* 18:245–69.
VAN WOUDEN, F. A. E.
1968   *Types of social structure in eastern Indonesia.* Translated by Rodney Needham, Koninklijk Instituut voor Taal-, Land- en Volkerkunde, Translation Series II. The Hague: Martinus Nijhoff.
WESTERMARCK, EDWARD
1901   *The history of human marriage.* London: Macmillan.
WHITE, LESLIE A.
1959   *The evolution of culture: the development of civilization to the fall of Rome.* New York: McGraw-Hill.
WINICK, CHARLES
1956   *The dictionary of anthropology.* New York: Philosophical Library.

# Matrescence, Becoming a Mother, A "New/Old" Rite de Passage

DANA RAPHAEL

The Tikopia announce the appearance of a new baby, a new group member, by declaring "a woman has given birth." In Western cultures the equivalent announcement would be "a child is born." The shift of emphasis demonstrates a major difference in viewpoint.

For the Tikopia, the child is not the primary, the exclusive, actor in the drama of birth. The real change which attends a birth is the creation of a "house of uncles," a "house of aunts," a new father, a new series of cousins, etc. (Firth 1936). The infant's role is just begun. For her or him, there is no complexity nor change. But, for the mother, the grandfather, the sibling, the birth event initiates major changes. Each kin must assume new or additional roles as a result of the infant's presence. Every set of relationships and the whole focus of interaction within the family group are affected.

Van Gennep's extraordinary insights into the *rite de passage* phenomenon did not ignore pregnancy and childbirth. However, the actors involved in this infant birth were significant for his concept only insofar as they participated in and precipitated rites and rituals. So, we find ourselves sifting through reams of anthropological data which have grandmothers performing rites, chanting oaths and giving haircuts, icy baths or first baptisms. We read of strange birth rites carried out by aunts. We follow compadres as they file in bearing gifts. We wait patiently for the list of persons who share a sacrificed animal.

As for the mother, she is represented as an object who sits up or down for delivery, who is warmed by a fire or covered by ashes, who nurses after saying a prayer or before confessing an indiscretion, and who is house-bound for an exact number of days in cultures without calendars.

Of her activities, we find her getting pregnant, performing a rite, preparing a special site, giving birth, nursing hours or days later, and then weaning — on schedule. Within this routine, she either does or doesn't have sexual intercourse.

When trying to discover where a women gives birth, we find reference to "her friend's" house. Checking further, it appears that she just happened to be there when labor began. As for the birth attendant, we are told that "mother's sister" is the midwife. Checking further, we find she just happened to catch the infant because she was nearest. As for the weaning pattern, we hear the dictum that women stop breastfeeding at "three years." Only in small print do we discover that the informant just delivered another baby and so the first had to stop nursing.

It's not hard to understand these errors and superficialities. Most ethnographers come from cultures where marriage is the more dominant *rite de passage* and motherhood is considered unchanging and dull. Many were trained to look in other directions and do not see where most females are most of their adult lives.

The critical transition period which has been missed is MATRESCENCE, the time of mother-becoming, the period when a woman changes from girl and wife to mother. During this process, this *rite de passage*, changes occur in a woman's physical state, in her status within the group, in her emotional life, in her focus of daily activity, in her own identity, and in her relationships with all those around her.

The matrescent *rite de passage* can be examined as a biological fact, as a cultural event, and as a series of interactions and changed interrelations with other members of the community.

The physiological stage of MATRESCENCE begins at the moment a female delivers a live infant. But, human beings are never limited by biological fact! Van Gennep noted how different cultures interpret and reinterpret the bodily changes of adolescence (1960). In Rome, social puberty preceded physiological puberty, but in Paris it followed it. Adolescence, by Roman standards, occurred when the individual was physically still a child. Parisians delayed giving the individual a mature social role well beyond the time when physical change had occurred. In America, whether or not the lad has as yet developed facial hair or has fathered and assumed responsibility for his children, adolescence ends 18 years from the day of birth, the juvenile delinquent becomes a criminal, and the boy, a soldier.

So it is with MATRESCENCE. Giving birth does not automatically make a mother out of a woman. In some cultures, a woman is transformed into a mother the moment pregnancy is detected. Elsewhere, a female becomes a mother when and only when she delivers an infant of the "right" sex.

Then she is granted full maternal status and everyone begins to treat her as an adult with all the associated restrictions and privileges.

Delaying the assumption of maternal roles until the infant is many months, even years old, is another pattern. Where this happens, maternity is shared by many (mostly women), some of whom breastfeed the new infant along with the mother. The new mother may be treated as if she were an invalid. She and the child are sometimes considered totally dependent and incapable of getting along without enormous help.

High mortality figures, the ever-present danger of losing the neonate from infectious diseases, or an inability of that infant to adjust to his mother's milk (or her personality) may be related to a hesitancy in granting the infant full human status or the mother her maternal role.[1]

The appearance of the human newborn suggests another factor which can contribute to the view that this organism does not yet deserve his humanness. The baby is sometimes viewed as still in the fetal stage, still developing, attached to the mother and nowhere near a separate creature. He is uniquely unhuman, and so fragile it is no surprise that many fear to leave him alone with his "inexperienced" mother. In fact, it often occurs that until the infant is weaned, others will not relinquish their mothering role and allow the "real" mother her motherhood.

In the United States, the infant is separated as soon as the cord is cut. Even before the delivery of the placenta, he can be cared for in a room apart from the mother. An important difference exists between this pattern and one practiced by the majority of people in other cultures. In this American example, two sets of persons take care of two separate individuals, the mother and the infant. In other societies, one set of persons cares for the mother/infant couple.

In America, it is also usual for others to take charge of the infant after birth for several days, permitting the mother to feed the baby, but otherwise preventing her from assuming any caretaking role. But, the moment the mother rises from her wheelchair outside the front door of the hospital, she is handed an infant and motherhood. All of it! A small group of the more affluent members of this culture employ other females and/or professional nurses. Their presence helps delay the mother's full MATRESCENCE for ten days to two weeks. The majority of women, however, must take over the whole role three to five days postpartum.

Many women in the United States would prefer not to ask their mothers

---

[1] Infant mortality figures (from all causes) of one half of all births were documented by the Swidlers for a nomadic group in the North-West Frontier Province, Pakistan (1966, 1972). A guarded attitude or a sharing of caretaking may offer the mother and others a degree of emotional armor in the event the infant should succumb.

to function in the supportive role of *doula*. Unaware of the effort and responsibility involved in this new-mother role, a goodly number of women prefer to call on a friend or stranger when they find they can't manage alone. This, however, is not the most common human pattern. A previous study (Raphael 1966) has shown that there is a worldwide preponderant preference for mother's mother or other members of mother's maternal kin to act as *doula*, as that person who attends the mother during her MATRESCENCE.[2]

When an individual is dealing with such intimate experiences as childbirth and postpartum care, it would seem preferable to share them with those whom one considers close, especially those with whom one has lived during childhood. This is in accord with Homans and Schneider's (1955) concept that the nature of human sentiment is such that it often influences the structure of cultural patterns.

My research confirms that those persons, those *doulas*, who most frequently interact with the new mother at this sensitive time, are also the most influential and supportive in assisting her to accept and acquire her new identity. The presence of brusque, efficient, but not necessarily kin-related persons, or the absence or premature departure of those special *doulas*, could press the mother into a quicker acceptance of her maternity. On the other hand, the constancy of others around her could indicate a reluctance on their part to allow her the full matrescent role. The presence of the mother's mother over a prolonged period would suggest a delay in her daughter's crowning as a full-fledged mother. But this pattern likely evolved and probably persists because it provides support for the daughter and as a result enhances the grandchild's chance to survive.

It is usual to make the most elaborate preparation and fuss over a woman who gives birth to her first infant. And with some justification. Human beings learn how to parent with their first child. Experience is vital. The ceremonies, rites and teachings can be reduced for all subsequent offspring, for they have the benefit of being born to a woman who has learned the major portion of her matrescent role. Multiparous mammals generally have less difficulty with their later offspring than with their first. There is less trauma at all stages from birth to separation. Since even non-

---

[2]   This information might be of importance to those initiating programs relating to problems of population, fertility or maternal behavior. It has been suggested elsewhere (Raphael 1973) that one factor which increases infant mortality is a sequence of events whereby economic stress is followed by population strain, a reduction of supportiveness of the mother from the community, a reduced capacity to succeed at breastfeeding and ultimately the death of the infant.

human primates find it difficult to learn how to mother, we cannot expect it to be automatic for human beings — all the more reason for intensive studies of the way in which mothers of different cultures are taught and gentled into their matrescence.

In addition to spotting the biological and cultural manipulations of the various stages of becoming a mother, other factors which signal the onset of the matrescent role such as caretaking and rituals need careful tracking. The interactional models of Chapple and Arensberg (1940) and Arensberg (1972) can help us determine the steps by which the mother assumes her new role. Foremost are the actors, and their interrelations and repetitious activities in relation to the mother/neonate pair. Quite secondary are the content of the rituals, the particular cultural practice or even the actors' rationale for those actions.

For example, we examine haircutting, bathing, gift-giving primarily to find out who is interacting with whom. And, we look to see if indeed most activity focuses attention towards the mother or directs it elsewhere, and we ask — by whom and how often. Taboos on new mothers are viewed as points and places for discovering who must be there to make sure she abides by them. The roles from which the mother must withdraw can be listed so that we know those persons who must assume them. With such data mapped, we can determine who directs the mother's actions, who assists her to take on her MATRESCENCE — indeed, who is mothering the mother.[3]

And, this must be done at several different stages, such as before her pregnancy, during her pregnancy, at the end of her pregnancy, during labor, after delivery, for the beginning of her lactation, during the days immediately following the birth, for the weeks and months postpartum, etc. It is equally important of course to know who is NOT there, when and why not.

What emerge are changes in the intensity, frequency and direction of these acts. Patterns of interactions directed toward the pregnant woman from father (husband), from other women, other children, other wives are different post-natally toward the mother/neonate. The mother's new sets of interaction with others and the changes in her daily routine begin to reveal how MATRESCENCE proceeds and something about the manner in which it is integrated. What also becomes apparent, if we follow Arensberg's (1972) reasoning, is that "mother," more than a person or status, is an activity, a behavior. Part of "father" is then mother when he

---

[3]  I have also discussed the crucial nature of this mothering for the lactating mother (Raphael 1973). The success of breastfeeding literally depends on such a supportive environment.

mothers. Part of the *doula* role is the active mothering of the mother and mothering of the infant.

The amount of time it takes to become a mother needs study. The parameters to the entire acquisition and incorporation of "the maternal role" can be extended as far back as when the individual girl/child first mothered a pet, a doll, or another baby. By the time women in some cultures give birth, they are well experienced in maternal behavior. In fact, they are so well versed that they may need less mothering themselves than their less exposed sisters in other cultures. This is an important variable in studies of supportive behavior. At the other end of the life cycle, grandmothering in some cultures needs to be included in this lifelong range of matrescent learning because, in some instances, full MATRESCENCE is not reached until one's own children become parents and one learns a new pattern for mothering grandchildren.

Though this paper focuses on female role change, there is a parallel, but not equivalent, male role change. The assumption of fatherhood, father-becoming, or PATRESCENCE — when man and husband become "father" — deserves to be explored.

In summary, the change of role from nullipara to primipara and the whole complex of behavior which it represents is an important *rite de passage* which we call MATRESCENCE. This process can be distinguished in part by using interactional analysis to note changes in behavior of those persons, especially the *doulas*, around the mother/neonate pair during the perinatal period. It can be studied by examining the proscriptions and prescriptions placed on their behavior as well as on the woman/mother. Finally, the father and others who are principals in this drama must be observed performing informal and formalized behaviors which function to support and ease them into their new roles which have been catalyzed by the infant's birth.

## REFERENCES

ARENSBERG, CONRAD M.
   1972   Culture as behavior: structure and emergence. *Annual Review of Anthropology* 1:1–26.
CHAPPLE, ELIOT DISMORE, CONRAD M. ARENSBERG
   1940   Measuring human reactions: an introduction to the study of the interaction of individuals. *Genetic Psychology Monographs* 22(1): 3–147.

FIRTH, RAYMOND
1936   *We the Tikopia: a sociological study of kinship in primitive Polynesia.* London: George Allen and Unwin.
HOMANS, GEORGE C., DAVID M. SCHNEIDER
1955   *Marriage, authority and final causes.* New York: Free Press of Glencoe.
RAPHAEL, DANA L.
1966   "Lactation, its biological and cultural confluence within a matrix of supportive behavior." Unpublished doctoral dissertation, Columbia University.
1973   *The tender gift — breastfeeding.* Englewood Cliffs: Prentice-Hall.
SWIDLER, WARREN
1972   Personal letter, Oct. 16, 1972.
VAN GENNEP, ARNOLD
1960   *The rites of passage.* Translated by Monika B. Vizedom and Gabrielle L. Caffee. London: Routledge and Kegan Paul. (French edition 1909.)

# Matri-Patrilocality and the Birth of the First Child

SUZANNE F. WILSON

A good deal of effort in anthropology has been spent trying to classify residence patterns, to specify their determinants and to characterize the role that they play in relation to other aspects of the social structure. The sheer diversity and complexity of residential groupings has led to questions about the adequacy of classificatory criteria for reflecting or revealing meaningful aspects of residence.

J. A. Barnes (1960) thinks that the main confusion about residence patterns centers around three problems: (1) the descriptive terminology, (2) the class of phenomena being classified, and (3) the social facts that the classification is designed to elucidate. In this paper we deal with the latter two problems. First we will review some of the suggestions that anthropologists have made to improve classifications of residence. We will then examine matri-patrilocality in order to illustrate the importance of considering life cycle events in interpretations of residence patterns.

As Barnes points out, we first must decide if we are interested in describing the current configuration of couples in a household or in deriving rules which govern the change in residence. These are two distinct concerns, and their constant confusion shows that one problem of classification is how to distinguish a rule from the description of current practice.

The decision as to what to classify is but one step. We are still left with the problem of what the classification tells us. For example, are we interested in indicating the relative pull of kin ties in determining residence or in the distance that couples live from their relatives? We must separate the many ways the data can be investigated and decide which interests us most. Barnes (1960) proposes that it would be useful to deal with residence in terms of residential continuity over the generations and to identify the linking relative in each case.

Ward Goodenough (1968) has presented a striking example from his own work of the confusion that can stem from using different classificatory criteria and concepts of residence in analyzing censuses. He and John Fischer differed considerably in their reporting of the incidence of residence patterns on Romanum, a community on Truk, although their data were collected within three years of each other. Goodenough shows that the difference was due to their interpreting similar data in different ways rather than to radical shifts in residence in the interim. He notes that his confusion was probably due to the use of criteria other than the residential census to classify the data and to the use of different concepts of residence. He believes that the residence data become more meaningful when the context in which the concepts were developed is taken into account. Part of the problem is to distinguish between the roles of ethnographer interested in "constructing a theory that will make intelligible what goes on in a particular social universe" and comparative ethnologist concerned with finding "principles common to many different universes "(Goodenough 1968:315).

Fischer (1958) proposed a new classification of residence for use in taking the residential census in any society. He maintained that it was possible to have analytically useful reference points for the classification of residence patterns in any culture. Important points to consider in any typology are the age and physical maturation of the residents, their sex, marital status and the extent of the residential grouping to which the classification refers. In addition, ambiguities in current typologies can be cleared up if marital residence is defined in terms of individuals rather than of couples, if the residence of all individuals in the community is included in a report so that all statuses and stages of life are represented, and if descriptions of current residential composition note when each individual entered the residential group.

Fortes (1962) has emphasized the importance of considering the time factor in studies of domestic organization. The domestic group goes through a cycle of development, a significant feature of which is that it is a process within the domestic field of social relations and one whose movement is governed by a relationship to the politico-jural field. Applied to residence, he thinks that "residence patterns are the crystallization, at a given time, of the developmental process" (1962:3). He distinguishes three main phases within the developmental cycle that can be applied to all social systems. The first phase, EXPANSION, starts with the establishment of marriage and terminates at the end of the period of procreation; the second, that of DISPERSION or FISSION, begins with the marriage of the first child and ends with the marriage of the last; the third,

REPLACEMENT, ends with the death of the parents and the replacement of their family with those of their children.

Murdock (1955) pointed out the dangers inherent in relying on static typologies to inform us about the processes operative in the social structure. He noted that anthropologists were moving away from a classificatory stage to one which emphazised the dynamics of the social structure. This progress from static to dynamic analysis has taken place along at least two continua, the time continuum and the life history stages of the individual. Clearly, a diachronic analysis of residential data may reveal a pattern that a synchronic analysis could not.

Buchler and Selby (1968) have shown that researchers are beginning to take process into account when dealing with residence patterns. A more recent presentation of data on residence (Murdock and Wilson 1972) attempts to indicate the presence of more than one type of residence pattern in a society. One way of doing this is to include variation as part of the definition of a residence category, e.g., ambilocal residence is defined as residence "optionally with or near the parents of either the husband or wife depending upon personal choice or circumstance, where neither alternative exceeds the other in actual frequency by a ratio greater than two to one" (Murdock and Wilson 1972:261). Another way to indicate variation is to combine two categories of residence, setting apart the dominant pattern by one symbol, and using another for the "alternative but less frequent residential pattern or one confined to a particular phase of the developmental cycle" (Murdock and Wilson 1972:261).

In sum, the suggestions for revisions of residence classifications have centered on determining a proper range of material for inclusion in a typology, on designing categories which reflect the range of variation within and between societies and on constructing categories which will facilitate the explanation of the descriptive material. A common thread that runs through these suggestions is the emphasis on analyzing residence as a dynamic process which changes through time and/or according to points in the life cycle of the individual.

## A PROCESSUAL APPROACH

Matri-patrilocality is a unique residence category because it includes the dimensions of time and sequence, i.e. matrilocality is temporary and is followed by permanent patrilocality. Unfortunately, because initial matrilocality is temporary, it is often regarded as of little importance compared to the permanent patrilocality which follows it. Consequently, the significance of the shift in residence and the process underlying this category are often overlooked. The remainder of this paper will focus on matri-patrilocality in an effort to understand the character of the shift from one residence pattern to another and to show the utility of classifying residence in terms of PROCESS rather than only in terms of FREQUENCY.

The cross-cultural method was used in approaching this problem. The sample of 62 societies was drawn from the 186 societies included in the standard cross-cultural sample and is representative of the "world's known and well-described cultures" (Murdock and White 1969:392). The codings were made by this author and based on information ascertained after reading COMPLETE ethnographies and articles, not from selections in the Human Relations Area Files.[1]

In *Social structure*, Murdock (1949) suggests that matri-patrilocality usually arises from one of two specific factors: bride-service as a supplement or partial substitute for wife-purchase, and/or an installment plan for the payment of bride-price. Both of these factors emphasize the way in which exchanges attendant upon the establishment of a marriage can be facilitated. The burden of changing from matrilocality to patrilocality lies with the groom. In both cases, the firm establishment of marriage is contingent upon the groom fulfilling his obligations to the family of his bride. In this interpretation the groom is put in a relatively subservient position *vis-à-vis* his wife's family until he can establish patrilocal residence. If this interpretation is correct, we could expect that matri-patrilocality occurs most often in those societies where bride-price is the most important factor validating the marriage.

To test this hypothesis, we cross-tabulated residence with the factor most important in validating the marriage.[2] The results of this cross-tabulation are presented in Table 1.

As we can see, the results do not confirm Murdock's interpretation. None of the five matri-patrilocal cases was associated with the transfer of bride-price as an important factor in the validation of marriage. Most of the societies (14 of 17 or 82 %) where bride-price is either the most or one of the most important factors in validating marriage are patrilocal. It is of interest to note that of the three other cases where bride-price is important

---

[1]    More specific information on the selection, composition and uses of the sample can be found in Murdock and White's article, "Standard cross-cultural sample" (1969). A list of the 62 societies used for the sample in this study can be found in Wilson (1975).

[2]    Codings of residence were derived from Murdock and Wilson (1972). Codings for "the most important factor validating marriage" and for "the timing of birth ceremonies" are listed for each of the 62 societies in Wilson (1975).

Table 1. Cross-tabulation of residence with the most important factor(s) validating marriage

|  | Children | Children and/or cohabitation | Children and bride-price | Ceremony | Bride-price |
|---|---|---|---|---|---|
| Matrilocality | Nicobarese Toradja Marshallese Huron Hidatsa Miskito | Hadza Garo Siamese |  | Kaska |  |
| Matri-patri-locality | Kenuzi Havasupai Egyptians Yahgan | Yukaghir |  |  |  |
| Ambilocality | Aweikoma |  |  |  |  |
| Avunculocality |  |  | Palua |  | Saramacca |
| Patrilocality | Gheg Japanese | Comanche | Suku Wolof Massa Kurd Manus Lamet Otoro | Balinese Bellacoola | Somali Banen Fon Songhay Gond Tanala Klamath |
| Neolocality | Marquesans Micmac Abipon |  |  | Russians | Ganda |

two are avunculocal, i.e. residence is near the husband's mother's brother, where there is a clustering of the males of the matrilineage. In sum, 16 of the 17 cases where bride-price is important are characterized by residence that clusters related males. In none of the cases where females are clustered either initially in matri-patrilocality or in matrilocality is bride-price of great importance in validating the marriage.

Among the patrilocal cases there are a number which seem to conform to Murdock's interpretation. Among the Klamath, a man may take up residence with his wife's people if he is poor or has no close relatives (Spier 1930). Marriage payment fixes social status, and a failure to pay constitutes a social stigma. A man who must resort to residence with his wife's relatives to obtain a wife is in a contemptible position, for his continued residence with his wife's relatives reflects his low economic status. However, we cannot regard this as a case of matri-patrilocality because the matrilocality is permanent rather than temporary.

Among the Lamet, Izikowitz (1951) says that if a man is poor, he may reside at his father-in-law's house for three years to perform the bride-service necessary to establish his marriage. However, this practice is not prevalent.

W. V. Grigson's description of the Hill Maria Gond (1938) would seem to fit more neatly into Murdock's scheme. They are patrilocal, but Grigson says that it is very common for a man to serve his future father-in-law for his bride instead of paying bride-price. He does not specifically say that there is initial matrilocality in connection with this bride-service, but since villages are exogamous and the service lasts for three to eight years, it would seem that patrilocality would be an unwieldy arrangement involving constant shifts from one village to another. However, the amount of bride-price depends upon the relation of the future spouses and the economic status of the groom's family.

The cash portion of the bride-price is often avoided or reduced by cross-cousin marriage or sister exchange. Of 105 marriages, 57 (54%) were between cross-cousins; this percentage might have been higher but Grigson says it was difficult to check on the remaining 46%. This high proportion of cross-cousin marriage was specifically accounted for by the wish to "obviate the necessity of getting a bride from a new and unrelated family" (Grigson 1938:247), thus being free from paying a high bride-price. The prevalent pattern was cross-cousin marriage and patrilocality. Although matri-patrilocality was common, it was a secondary alternative.

In the above cases, bride-service is a partial substitute for bride-price. However, it seems misleading to characterize the societies in which they are included as matri-patrilocal, because the shift from matrilocality to patrilocality is not a prevalent practice. It is the consequence of a less desirable alternative to a more preferred pattern of obtaining a wife.

In the matri-patrilocal cases, economic labor may be performed while the groom resides with his wife's relatives, but it is not in lieu of or a supplement to bride-price. Smithson (1959) says that among the Havasupai a man shares in the economic endeavors of the bride's family whether or not there is a bridal gift. The bride-price is a token given partly to establish friendly relations (Spier 1928). Gusinde (1937) says that a Yahgan groom gives the wife's father service and gifts because he is anxious to please them though they are not required.

If we examine the cross-tabulation from another point of view we may form a clearer idea of the nature of the shift from matrilocality to patri-locality. All of the cases of matri-patrilocality are associated with THE IMPORTANCE OF CHILDREN IN VALIDATING A MARRIAGE. If we look at the individual cases it is clear that the shift occurs after and because of the birth of the first child. Herzog (1957) says that a Kenuzi woman stays at her parents' house until her first child is born. Ammar (1954) says that an Egyptian woman stays in seclusion in the house until she brings forth a child. Spier (1928) says that a Havasupai husband lives with his wife at her parent's house, usually until she has borne one or two children. Among the Yukaghir a man can take his wife and child and leave her parents' house after the birth of the first child although the change in residence is usually not approved of until the death of the wife's parents (Jochelson 1926). Only the Yahgan do not fit into this scheme. Gusinde (1937) notes that young people who reside matrilocally until the first child is born are exceptional.

Therefore, we can say that the shift in residence is tied to a specific point in the life cycle of the newly married, i.e. to the birth of their first child. Nevertheless, this does not explain why the couple resides matrilocally and shifts to patrilocality rather than residing patrilocally from the beginning.

One way that we might look at this is in terms of the advantages that accrue to one or both of the individuals involved in the marriage as a result of participating in this residence pattern. The advantages to the groom from initial matrilocality might become clearer if we first contrast the matri-patrilocal cases with the patrilocal cases where the birth of children is important in validating the marriage.

In the matri-patrilocal cases, marriage, a move from the natal household, and the birth of a child signify adulthood and greater independence of the groom from his own family. Both Herzog (1957) and Callendar and el Guindi (1971) say that a Kenuzi groom may be present for only a portion of the time that he and his bride reside matrilocally, because of his involvement in migratory labor. The initial matrilocality is a period when he is achieving independence by becoming entirely self-supporting and setting up a household separate from his father's.

Ammar (1954) says of the Egyptians that adulthood comes at marriage and that marriage is declared and acknowledged with the establishment of matrilocal residence. In addition, marriage gives the individual more freedom which increases as he has more children. Jochelson (1926) says that a Yukaghir man gained more authority when he became a father and had the option of leaving his wife's house at this time.

In both of the patrilocal cases where the birth of children is important in validating the marriage, the Gheg and the Japanese, parent-child bonds are stressed to the detriment of husband-wife bonds. The importance of the birth of the child is that it justifies the presence of the new wife in her husband's home; it does not signify the independence of the male from his own family.

Among the Gheg, Coon (1950) says that even after the wife is transferred to her husband and the marriage ceremony is performed, the woman may be sent home if she does not have children within a "reasonable amount of time; she is still on trial" (Coon 1950:24). An intimate husband-wife relationship was discouraged so that the man would remain under the authority of his senior kinsman; everyone in the house was subordinate to the patriarchal head (Hasluck 1954). "Not only did a man seen much in his wife's company lose face, but in a communal household his brother, in addition to railing at him, threatened to make him set up a separate home, which would reduce him and her to a lower level of comfort" (Hasluck 1954:30).

A similar situation exists among the Japanese people of Niike village. A child increased the husband's status and settled his marriage (Beardsley, Hall, and Ward 1959). There is an emphasis on hierarchical relationships in the husband's family rather than on an intimate husband-wife bond (DeVos and Wagatsuma 1961). DeVos (1965) claims that only by bearing a child does a bride gain personal rights in her new family. The birth of the child does not transfer the husband's strong bond with his mother over to his wife (DeVos and Wagatsuma 1961).

Bride-price or bride-price and children are the most important factors validating marriage for most of the remaining patrilocal cases (14 of 17). Since Murdock thought that matri-patrilocality would arise under conditions where bride-service is a supplement or substitute for wife-purchase and/or where there is an installment plan for the payment of bride-price, we will examine these cases to try and find out why matri-patrilocality did not emerge from them.

Although bride-service may be present, it need not entail a change in residence. For example, Nadel (1947) points out that among the Otoro both the prospective groom and his relatives work for the bride's relatives during the engagement, but they do not change residence during this period. Another reason why alternate provisions for the payment of bride-price may not entail a change in residence is that the obligation that the groom incurs is to his own family rather than to his wife's. By the payment of his son's bride-price a father can expect his son to be obliged and dependent upon him. For example, among the Fon a man may work for his father until he has repaid the amount of bride-price that his father gave him (Herskovits 1938). Among the Lamet, the father pays bride-price for his sons and "the latter become dependent to quite a degree on their fathers" (Izikowitz 1951:140).

The most striking case of using bride-price as a basis for control over another male comes from reports on the Manus (Mead 1937). A man's social recognition depends upon the amount of wealth that has passed through his hands. The manipulation of wealth centers on events in the life cycle of a man's wife and his children. Marriage is one of the most elaborate and costly of these events. Since young men are usually unable to amass enough wealth to meet the expenditures required at marriage, they become dependent on their father or another backer and remain under their control until they can repay the debt. Mead says that a "man has power over young men whose marriages he has financed... they are dependents by virtue of continuing expenditures... If he doesn't participate, he loses all standing in the community... A man drives himself hard so that he dies in his early middle age" (Mead 1937:216–218).

In these cases of patrilocal residence not initiated by matrilocality, bride-price provides leverage for senior males to maintain authority over their juniors. It is of interest to note that 12 of the 14 cases of patrilocal residence where bride-price is important in validating marriage are patrilineages. Control over junior males by financing their marriages could be one way of dealing with the problem of ordering authority between co-resident males of different generations, all of whom have a legitimate right to authority in the lineage. While most discussions of bride-price center on its implications of alliance for the group, these cases suggest that it would be profitable to concentrate more attention on the role of bride-price within the lineage.

Thus far our discussion has centered only on the consequences of shifts in residence for the male. This seems to be characteristic of most discussions of residence, i.e. emphasis on residence in terms of the public, political, and economic spheres in which men operate, ignoring altogether the sphere within which women operate. Since residence does entail the movement of A COUPLE, we might ask about the advantages that particular residence arrangements have for the woman.

Since initial matrilocality is generally not replaced by patrilocality until after the woman bears her first child, it seems plausible that the link between the birth of the first child and matri-patrilocality is especially significant. Dana Raphael (1966) postulates that the physical, emotional and social support during the onset of lactation are necessary concomitants for successful breastfeeding and the survival of the infant. Her cross-cultural study confirmed the presence of a supportive figure in some form in most cultures with a predominant preference for maternal kin. Following this line of thought, she has suggested that residence near or with some supportive person at the birth of the first child may be essential for the establishment of lactation.

Lack of information makes it impossible to test this hypothesis by comparing the relative success of lactation under different residential conditions at the birth of the first child. Since matrilocal and matri-patrilocal societies in this sample all share an emphasis on the birth of a child as a major factor in validating marriage, it is possible that the clustering of maternal kin would ensure the support of the woman such that she could lactate and therefore ensure the survival of the child who is important for "cementing" the marriage of the woman and her husband.

We can present some evidence that suggests a woman may receive more attention after the birth of her first child in matrilocal and matri-patrilocal residence than when she is residing patrilocally. We do this by beginning with the assumption that when birth ceremonies occur immediately after the birth of the child, the focus of concern is more likely to be the new mother, than when the ceremony occurs after the mother and child come out of confinement or even later at the baby's naming ceremony. The distribution of times when these ceremonies occur broken down by residence is presented in Table 2.

Table 2.   Cross-tabulation of residence with timing of birth ceremony

|  | Immediately after birth | Other | Total |
|---|---|---|---|
| Matrilocal | 5 | 3 | 8 |
| Matri-patrilocal | 4 | 1 | 5 |
| Avunculocal | 0 | 2 | 2 |
| Patrilocal | 8 | 16 | 24 |
| Neolocal | 1 | 1 | 2 |
| Ambilocal | 2 | 0 | 2 |
|  | 20 | 23 | $N$–43 |

Where the woman is residing with her maternal kin, ceremonies immediately after birth predominate (9 of 13 or 69 %); where she is residing with her husband near his kin, ceremonies after birth do not predominate (8 of 24 or 33 %).

This is not to say that the importance of a woman receiving support from her maternal kin will necessarily entail a change in residence. There are other ways in which this same support could become available. For instance, it is often the practice for mother's mother (or other maternal kin) to come to her newly delivered daughter and remain there for a period of time. In communities where endogamy prevails, the mother of the new mother is likely to be near enough to visit her daughter frequently.

Also, a woman could return to her maternal kin when she is getting close to her delivery time and remain there at least until lactation has been established, in about six weeks. This latter arrangement occurs among the Klamath, Songhay, Manus and Wolof. In these cases it would be important to know not only where the couple reside when they first marry, but how far away the new mother's natal residence is. This information is not included in current classifications of residence which indicate the pull of kin ties rather than the distance from kin entailed by a shift in residence. Since the distance between kin could well affect subsequent residence arrangements, it would be useful to include this information either in the criteria for classifying residence or in the explanation for specific residence patterns.

The above should indicate the importance of considering the establishment of lactation and the survival of the child when we attempt explanations of residence patterns. By considering residence in terms of shifts related to discernable events in the life cycle, we can shed light on the process operative in other residence changes. For example, the Siamese are classified (Murdock and Wilson 1972) as matrilocal with some neolocality. The matrilocality and neolocality are connected in a temporal sequence with the initial residence tending to be matrilocal. The shift in residence occurs when the husband and wife have amassed enough economic goods to become independent, generally AFTER the birth of the first child (Sharp and Hanks n.d.). A temporal sequence is also present in the residence patterns of the Abipon, classified as neolocal with some matrilocality. The couple resides matrilocally initially and can have a separate house AFTER the birth of a child (Dobrizhoffer 1822).

The classification of the Yukaghir as ambilocal is misleading because it obscures the process from which the proportions of matrilocality and patrilocality were derived. The percentage of matrilocality and patrilocality are about equal because each type of residence is associated with different stages of the life cycle. Jochelson (1926) says that the husband stays with his wife's parents until they die or until his wife has their first child. He then returns with his wife and child to reside with his kinsmen. The less frequent initial patrilocality occurs when the husband is the youngest child and remains with his parents, his wife joining him.

The classification of the Palauans as avunculocal with some patrilocality neglects other very important shifts in residence connected with the life cycle of the woman. The pregnancy of the woman and the birth of a child are directly responsible for shifts in residence. Barnett (1960) says that young women insist upon going to their mother's, sister's or mother's sister's home when they are pregnant and must do so for delivery. In addition, the woman's mother's brother expects her to stay with him during some part of her confinement. These shifts in residence are accompanied by monetary transactions attendant upon the pregnancy of the woman and birth of the child. The woman's mother's brother hires a man to hunt and fish for the couple and the woman's maternal kin provide them with food. This is done with the expectation that the husband's group will compensate them for their services at birth and at various points in the pregnancy. With all of this expenditure associated with the change in residence, it is easy to forget that the change in residence may be related to the need for the support and care of the reproducing woman.

A classification such as matri-patrilocality[3] provides more information about the processes involved in changes of residence because it gives us some indication of the sequential progression of residence over time. The usual residence classifications only indicate that one pattern occurs more frequently than another. A classification with a temporal dimension, matri-patrilocality, has led us to consider the importance of life cycle events for both the male and female spouses who shift residence at marriage. It has also led to the conclusion that the advantages of residence patterns for the woman and for the survival of her child have been overlooked. This investigation highlights the paucity of data in the ethnographics necessary for an analysis of residence. Our notions of residence seem to have become overweighted with economic and political criteria to the exclusion of important domestic factors which could significantly affect the choice of one residence over another.

The specification of age at marriage and childbirth as well as death rates is important, for each of these factors can significantly affect the rate of progression from one residence pattern to another. We can then proceed to ask why the shift occurs when it does, why it occurs in one society and not in another, and what are the consequences if no shift occurs? In this way we can combine the events of the life cycle with the more usual economic and political treatments in analyzing residence patterns.

## REFERENCES

AMMAR, H.
  1954   *Growing up in an Egyptian village.* London.
BARNES, J. A.
  1960   Marriage and residential continuity. *American Anthropologist* 62: 850–866.

[3]   This might be more precisely called "matridomiparas patrilocality" as per footnote, page 2. — *Editor.*

BARNETT, H. G.
  1960   *Being a Palauan.* New York.
BEARDSLEY, R. K., J. W. HALL, R. E. WARD
  1959   *Village Japan.* Chicago.
BUCHLER, IRA R., HENRY A. SELBY
  1968   *Kinship and social organization.* New York: Macmillan.
CALLENDER, CHARLES, FADWA EL GUINDI
  1971   *Life-crisis rituals among the Kenuz.* Case Western Reserve University
         Studies in Anthropology 3. Cleveland and London.
COON, C. C.
  1950   The mountain of giants. *Papers of the Peabody Museum Harvard
         University* 23(3):1–150.
DE VOS, G.
  1965   *Social values and personal attitudes in primary human relations in
         Niike.* University of Michigan Center for Japanese Studies, Occa-
         sional Papers.
DE VOS, G., H. WAGATSUMA
  1961   Value attitudes toward role behavior of women in two Japanese
         villages. *American Anthropologist* 63:1204–1230.
DOBRIZHOFFER, M.
  1822   *An account of the Abipones,* third volume. London.
FISCHER, J. L.
  1958   The classification of residence in censuses. *American Anthropologist*
         60:506–517.
FORTES, MEYER
  1962   "Introduction," in *The developmental cycle in domestic groups.* Edited
         by Jack Goody, 1–14. Cambridge.
GOODENOUGH, WARD
  1968   "Residence rules," in *Marriage, family and residence.* Edited by Paul
         Bohannan and John Middleton, 297–316. Garden City, New York.
GRIGSON, W. V.
  1938   *The Maria Gonds of Bastar.* London.
GUSINDE, M.
  1937   *Die Feuerland-Indianer* 2: *Yamana.* Wien.
HASLUCK, M.
  1954   *The unwritten law in Albania.* Cambridge.
HERSKOVITS, M. J.
  1938   *Dahomey,* two volumes. New York.
HERZOG, R.
  1957   *Die Nubier.* Translated by Edith Lauer. Berlin.
IZIKOWITZ, K. G.
  1951   *Lamet.* Ethologiska Studier 17:1–375. Goteberg.
JOCHELSON, W.
  1926   The Yukaghir and Yukaghirized Tungus. *Memoirs of the American
         Museum of Natural History* 13:1–469.
MEAD, MARGARET, *editor*
  1937   "The Manus of the Admiralty Islands," in *Cooperation and competi-
         tion among primitive peoples,* 210–239.

MURDOCK, GEORGE PETER
1949   *Social structure*. New York.
1955   Changing emphases in social strcture. *Southwestern Journal of Anthropology* 11:361–369.
MURDOCK, GEORGE PETER, DOUGLAS R. WHITE
1969   Standard cross-cultural sample. *Ethnology* 8:239–369.
MURDOCK, GEORGE PETER, SUZANNE F. WILSON
1972   Settlement patterns and community organization. *Ethnology* 10: 254–295.
NADEL, S. F.
1947   *The Nuba*. London.
RAPHAEL, DANA
1966   "The lactation-suckling process within a matrix of supportive behavior." Unpublished doctoral dissertation, Columbia University.
SHARP, LAURISTON, L. M. HANKS
n.d.   *The social history of a Thai village*. The Cross-Cultural Cumulative Coding Center, University of Pittsburgh.
SMITHSON, C. L.
1959   The Havasupai woman. *Anthropological Papers* 38:1–170. Department of Anthropology, University of Utah.
SPIER, L.
1928   Havasupai ethnography. *Anthropological Papers of the American Museum of Natural History* 24:81–408.
1930   Klamath ethnography. *University of California Publications in American Archaeology and Ethnology* 30:1–328.
WILSON, SUZANNE F.
1975   "Reproduction in its social context." Unpublished doctoral dissertation, Cornell University.

# Affectivity and Instrumentality in Friendship Patterns among American Women

YING-YING YUAN

In this paper four major characteristics of friendship are selectivity, equivalence, affectivity, and instrumentality. After briefly examining these four concepts, we will investigate the interaction of affectivity and instrumentality in different classes of friendship. It will be seen that while most types of friendship contain both elements, conflict between them exists in certain circumstances.

## THE CHARACTERISTICS OF FRIENDSHIP

It is generally agreed (Firth, et al. 1969: 115; Paine 1969: 507; Pitt-Rivers 1961: 138) that friendship relationships are selected or achieved rather than ascribed. Selectivity implies certain important qualities in the relationship. It allows for the idiosyncratic choice of friends and the formulation of unique arrangements and agreements among friends. Paine (1969) has suggested that the uniqueness of each friendship can result in hidden qualities not observable to an outsider. Persons may be classified as friends even though they do not match a formal description of what friends should do and be. This dissonance between definition and behavior or sentiment makes it necessary to investigate both the formal and the actual behavior of friends toward each other.

Most friendships are thought to develop between equals or at least between those with nearly equivalent status (McGuire 1969; Paine 1969). Equivalency within friendships should not, however, be taken for granted. Two types of exceptions have been of particular note. The first occurs when the absence of mutuality is recognized by the participants as being a dominant characteristic of the relationship, such as in patron-client interaction (Wolf 1966). The second exception is when equivalency is violated in specific circumstances, but such violations are seen as contrary to the norms applicable to friendship (Eisenstadt 1956).

Perhaps the primary characteristic of friendship is that friends LIKE EACH OTHER. Students of friendship from Firth (Firth, et al. 1969) to Schulz (1968) have agreed that "friends" must like each other and enjoy each other's company. Interaction alone is an end in itself among friends (Sutcliffe and Crabbe 1963; Harding, et al. 1968:42). In addition to agreeable companionship, AFFECTIVITY can connote the intimate exchange of confidences (Komarovsky 1967), trust (Cubitt 1971), and frankness (Ervin-Tripp 1964). The degree to which such behavior is practiced has sometimes been used to distinguish best friends from friends (Cubitt 1971; Komarovsky 1967). Dreams, hopes, and disappointments can be shared among friends, and the bond ensures a sympathetic listener. Friends are said to provide emotional security (Marris 1962: 42) whether they criticize or condone behavior (Mayer 1957).

Friends are also associated with INSTRUMENTAL support. This support can take the form of cooperation or helping behavior. (As Mead has distinguished (1961: 17), cooperation is based on shared goals, while helping has the social relationship rather than the immediate task as the major concern). The willingness to help another has been used to measure friendship. For example, Sutcliffe and Crabbe (1963) rated friendships on responses to such questions as the following:

I would loan him an article which I owned if he were in need of it:
— regardless of the inconvenience it would cause me.
— provided it did not inconvenience me very much.
— provided it did not inconvenience me at all.

I would be prepared to support him against the criticism of others:
— no matter what the circumstances.
— provided I know the circumstances.
— in circumstances in which I had no control.

Helping behavior has been closely related to altruism. Leeds (1963) has defined the altruistic act as (1) an end in itself, (2) not directed at gain, (3) voluntary, and (4) doing good. Voluntary helping behavior is altruistic when its cost to the helper is judged to be equal or less than the value of the relationship with the recipient, and when no return is required. Strict reciprocity and paying of debts are usually considered outside the concept of altruism, but "behavior which repays more than it owes, or repays favors that did not generate expectation of return ... seems altruistic" (Krebs 1970: 295).

Within friendship relationships, as the caveat indicates, it may be difficult to identify the altruistic act. Help may be given with an awareness that friends would do the same or would act similarly in another situation. As Pitt-Rivers (1961: 139) has noted, "... while a friend is entitled to expect a return of his feelings and favour, he is not entitled to bestow them in that expectation." In other words, among friends instrumental support should be given without overtly demanding a *quid pro quo*, whatever one's private expectations. Helpers may have also learned that assistance is a norm for the friendship relationship, and therefore they are under an obligation to offer assistance. The helping act may be an expression of friendship and thus contribute to the continuance of the bond. Furthermore, because friends maintain a relationship over time, acts which are only ends in themselves are difficult to isolate. Overtly altruistic acts might indeed be a form of cooperation which postulates future delayed cooperation.

For example, Joan and Liz are friends. Each agrees to take care of her own and the other's child once a week. Because they have the same goal (i.e. sharing the burden of child supervision), they are said to be cooperating. They call it "switching." Occasionally, however, Joan is late in picking up her son, and the son stays for dinner at Liz's house. By helping Joan in this way, Liz is being altruistic. She does not share the goal of feeding the children communally, and she feeds him voluntarily. Feeding the child is not directed at immediate gain, but it does facilitate the continuance of the friendship. Furthermore, without a discussion of rights and obligations, she also expects Joan to do the same for her, if the need should arise. Given that the principles of responsibility (Berkowitz and Daniels 1963) and reciprocity (Gouldner 1960) may underlie altruistic situations, perhaps an important factor is that the act is empathetic, in that the friend knows how to help without being asked.

Knowing how to help requires an understanding not only of the other person but also of the boundaries of the relationship. Givers and recipients need to recognize the limits of acceptable assistance. Three examples from Anglo-American sources are indicative of possible limits. One American woman reported that "No matter how good a friend she is, no friend is good enough to take your kids for several days or weeks" (Yuan 1972: 53). Mayer (1957) found that high-school girls were unwilling to express negative attitudes about their friends' boyfriends even when they thought the relationship was unwise. O'Donnell (1972) voiced the opinion that even good friends cannot give each other money.[1]

---

[1] Assistance in friendship can have several motivating conditions:

## TYPOLOGY OF FRIENDSHIP

Wolf (1966) postulated that there are two types of friendships, expressive and instrumental. He suggested that emotional friendships were to be found in those societies where access to resources was provided by solidary units. Therefore friendship "can at best provide emotional release and catharsis from the strains and pressures of role playing" (1966:11). He also recognized, however, that instrumental friendships must have emotional bonds which provide sanctions in the relationships. Paine (1969) argued that all friendships must be considered as ultimately instrumental, since emotional release is also of instrumental value to the individual.

On the other hand, since the emotional or affective component of friendship is generally recognized, it can be said that all friendships are ultimately affective relationships. However, little can be gained from such distinctions. Friendship should be seen as being composed of both elements. Attention should be given to the cultural definitions and expressions of these components, and the variation in the play between the affective and instrumental components should be studied.

Instrumental behavior in American middle-class culture may not be very costly compared to peasant ritual friendship obligations (Mintz and Wolf 1950), but it may be highly differentiated by the participants. In some cultures affection is expressed through instrumental assistance which is not demanded but is a part of the economic system, while in others, affection is expressed by social visits and communication. Sussman (1953) found that in exchange for being willing to help their grown children with childcare, job-hunting, vacations and gifts of money, American parents expect only affection in the form of telephone calls and "consideration" in return. Such a relationship thus intertwines both affective and instrumental task components.

The relationship between affection and instrumentality will be further examined in cases taken from a study of middle-class American women.[2] The distinctions made in the ethnotypology of friends are reported. It will be seen that the component of instrumentality is relatively weak in

---

1.   X helps his friend Y because he knows that he can be of assistance without being asked (empathy.)
2.   X helps Y because Y has asked him and X likes Y (request and affectivity).
3.   X helps Y because he feels obliged to do so (social norm).
4.   X helps Y because he hopes that Y will help him in the future (future reciprocity).
[2]   Data on twenty-nine women are taken from a study of one neighborhood in Cambridge, Massachusetts (Yuan 1972). The informants had a median age of twenty-eight years, had at least a high-school education, and had been living in the neighborhood a median of two years and three months.

relationships of "acquaintanceship" and "best friendship," and that in "good friendship" the components of instrumentality and affectivity are often in conflict.

## FRIENDLINESS AND FRIENDSHIP

The informants clearly distinguished being friends from being friendly. Friendliness is used to modify the description of a relationship in which the participants are not friends. "I know about six or seven mothers in the neighborhood. They're acquaintances, we rarely get together, but we're friendly enough." Being friendly with acquaintances and neighbors entails going beyond the simple nodding or greeting stage. Encounters with acquaintances are unplanned and of short duration, although of high frequency. Interaction occurs in public places rather than within the private domain. Acquaintances are rarely invited to the house. Although they are occasionally asked for a favor, they are not expected to volunteer help or to recognize a need for assistance. Friendliness may be the product of a general diffuseness of friendship (Parsons 1964: 418) or a front of congeniality (Paine 1969: 515), but it is a relatively untested expression of an attitude which remains unproven and unexamined by either reflection or intensive contact. Being friendly is one step beyond exchanging pleasantries, but several steps behind a commitment to or an interest in a full social relationship.

In discussing hostility in small groups, Balikci (1968: 197) drew the distinction between feeling hostile and overtly expressing hostility. A similar distinction can be made between friendliness and friendship. In certain acquaintanceships and other social relationships, a generalized feeling of friendliness exists without the expression of friendship being made. That is, intimacy is not exchanged, and trust, equivalency, cooperation, and empathy are not in evidence in the interaction between the participants.

## FRIENDS

In addition to having acquaintances in the neighborhood, many women in the study also recognized a need for having at least one close friend. This need was most strongly expressed by non-working women with young children. These informants explained that they made friends with other women whom they liked, but admitted that they grew to know their neighbors to ameliorate their own loneliness.

Having children brings you out into the community. Many people I didn't meet until I had children. You depend on children to find people, but then it's whether you find them congenial or not. It depends on whether the children get along, but really mostly on yourself and the other woman. You have to like each other to be friends.

We decided that getting to know your neighbors is a good policy. It's the best thing for security. You hear about a rapist, for example, and you can protect yourself. I made an effort to get to know and to make friends with the neighbors.

Eisenstadt observes (1956) that the motivation for initiating contact may be the realization of instrumental necessities, although the relationship is one of affective friendship.

The neighborhood friendship relationships among women who also expected assistance and cooperation most clearly showed the conflict which can exist between the affective and instrumental components of friendship. Examples are taken from arrangements which operated primarily on a basis of turn-taking in caring for children.

In one case, three of the four participants thought the fourth mother too lenient in disciplining her son who was consequently disruptive to the group. They wished to discuss the problem with the mother but refrained because they thought that to criticize or comment on her behavior and her son's behavior would be to "hurt her feelings." As friends they wished to avoid doing so. Finally, however, the dissatisfied mothers were compelled to bring the matter up for discussion, and the fourth mother withdrew from the group, but only temporarily. After a few weeks she returned to the group, but without changing her attitude. The three other women said that there was no solution to the problem except to disband the group. The bonds of solidarity could not support further criticism or the use of corrective measures with the unruly child. Striving to maintain an affective relationship, the mothers found the best solution was to reduce the instrumental component. All of the mothers thought that they would continue to be friends after the group was disbanded.

Even among friends it was agreed that credit and debit should be balanced in childcare exchanges. Arrangements were contracts which should not be broken or stretched; anything beyond the contract was a favor which should be returned.

I don't keep track of every hour in our switching arrangement, but I do keep track of how much time I used. I don't want to take advantage of her. I feel strongly about this because she took my son when we went to Canada one time, and I know that it is hard to do. I'll take her son anytime.

If I had to leave my kids for a week, I'd leave them with my friend. I've taken care of her kid before, and she's indebted to me for two days for one child, so I could give her my two for three days at the most, and then I'd owe her some time.

By maintaining a strict balance, the friends accumulated no debts and the relationship could develop or remain at the same level of affectivity without difficulty. When debts were accumulated, ill feeling developed. Because friendship restricted the overt expression of such dissatisfaction, unhappiness over a lack of reciprocity could lead to a severing of the relationship (cf. Wolf 1966:13).

Two other conditions may also result in conflict. First, the instrumental components of the relationship may originally be too diverse or unspecified. When choosing to develop acquaintanceships into friendships, few informants had specific goals in mind. They might feel that in some vague sense they needed to know their neighbors, but failed to discuss attitudes toward dependence among neighbors and friends while getting to know each other. When needs and requests did arise, they might be found to be in dissonance with the relationship which had been established.

Second, the women's friends who were most available to give assistance were often those least strongly bonded by affective ties. Not only were neighborhood friends seen less frequently in situations of enjoyment than were non-neighborhood friends, but most neighborhood friends were not considered to be long-term friends. Informants reported that if they moved away they would like to keep in contact with only a third of their neighborhood friends. Several said that they would not keep in touch with any of their neighborhood friends. Only a very small proportion of neighborhood contacts were viewed as potentially long-term friends.

In summary, acquaintances were rarely called upon for assistance. Friends living in close proximity were depended upon for instrumental task aid, but in cases of continuing cooperation, or long-term assistance, conflicts often occurred. Four conditions contributed to the conflicts: (1) reciprocity of instrumental work-exchange obligations was not maintained, (2) feelings of solidarity conflicted with requirements of instrumental work-exchange activity, (3) potential dependency relationships were unspecified, and (4) neighborhood friendships were often characterized by weak affective bonds.

## BEST FRIENDS

If the theory of bolstering instrumental demands by the unifying quality of affectivity is operative, it would suggest that in neighborhood friendships the bonds of affectivity are not of sufficient strength to provide a leeway for altruistic acts or to remove the burden of strict reciprocity. One might suggest, therefore, that women should turn to those with whom they have stronger feelings in order to lessen such difficulties. For example, they could rely upon their best friends.

The helping attitude of best friends was mentioned by some informants.

Very good friends have proven their friendship without asking. They would think of helping without my having to ask and putting them on the spot. You don't really know people well until you see the good in them. For example, my friend next door and the one across the street, when I was in the hospital, they cleaned the house before I came home. That's an indicator of their friendship for me.

However, the majority of informants stressed qualities which were related to emotional bonds rather than task assistance.

She's a close friend because I have strong feelings towards her, and we have feelings of mutual understanding.

Close friends are people I would talk to if I needed someone to talk to other than my husband or in addition to him.

A best friend is someone who has been supportive in crises in your life. They are listeners who can also lean on you when they need to.

The main theme in discussing the qualities of best friends was that the bond is an affective one based on past experiences rather than current interaction. Best friends were past and potential recipients of intimacies and confidences. They had been known a long time, and the majority of them were living beyond the local area. Even best friends living nearby were rarely called upon to help. Interaction was restricted to socialization for pleasure.

Proximity was an important factor in lessening the instrumental component of best friendship. In daily emergencies or in daily arrangements, women looked to those most convenient to them, even sometimes restricting themselves to other families on the same block. Women who were at home during the day could develop sufficient social contacts to provide the resources for the needs which arose. There were many more acquaintances and friends in the neighborhoods than best friends.[3] It was

---

[3]   The informants had a mean of 10.6 acquaintances, 3.8 friends and 0.7 best friends in the immediate neighborhood.

therefore far easier and far more likely that a friend be used rather than a best friend.

Availability was not, however, the only factor. It was seen that instrumentality was not associated with best friendship. More important was a feeling of being able to exchange intimate confidences. The characteristics which made a best friend were not those which were related to direct assistance or helping behavior, while those which affected the development of acquaintanceships into friendships were. Indeed, the school and college origin of the majority of best friends meant that these friendships had evolved in conditions of commitments and interests different from those which dominated the current daily life. Socializing reinforced these interests and commitments but did not necessarily generate helping behavior in the areas of predominant need. Rather than look to the best friends who could possibly help them, informants preferred to establish non-affective relationships, such as paying arrangements between sitters and families, or to rely on kin. Kin were found to complement the role of friends in both the affective and instrumental spheres of the relationships.

## THE HELPING BEHAVIOR OF KIN

Despite high mobility 17 percent of the informants had parents living within the local area, and 69 percent of the informants had their parents or siblings living on the Eastern seaboard. These informants could maintain close visiting or telephone contact with their relatives. Almost all the informants either saw their parents or spoke with them on the phone once a week or every two weeks.

The proximity of their parents and their husbands' parents enabled the women to depend upon kin for emotional consolation, advice, sharing of news, and assistance in childcare. One woman stated that she could only pity the women who were without nearby kin. Within a reasonable radius, parents and other close kin could be helpful for long-term assistance in cases of illness, childcare or financial need.

The closeness between parent and grown child is specifically related to the differences in age and development. Women with young children could impose upon their parents for assistance, while they could not impose upon their peers who were friends or best friends, even when they had strong affective ties. Parents had the time and the economic ability to undertake such responsibilities. Parents also willingly accepted their children's dependency, often volunteering to visit and care for their grandchildren. Proximity, interest, and affection were influential in promoting contact and instrumental assistance.

Important differences were seen in comparing the role of kin and that of friends. Although distance did reduce the interaction with friends and best friends, distance did little to limit the interaction with close relatives, such as parents or parents-in-law. Women looked to these relatives for counsel and assistance, and they shared many experiences with them. They often said that the grandparents had a right to be informed about their grandchildren. The arrival of the third generation appeared to strengthen the bond between the women and their parents, while it had little effect on the relationship with best friends. The relationship with neighborhood friends also changed with the arrival of children, but although the daily routine was shared, feelings of intimacy and dependency were often still limited to relatives.

## CONCLUSIONS

This paper has focused primarily on the neighborhood friends and the best friends of non-working women with young children. It has been seen that while fulfilling the four major characteristics of friendship, acquaintances, friends and best friends have different roles. These roles are complementary to the role of kinsmen. Neighborhood friends give short-term assistance and provide daily companionship. They are often viewed as temporary necessities, although they may be the most active in giving assistance. Best friends are not relied upon for most instrumental tasks, but share similar interests and provide a reservoir of potential bonds. Parents give counsel and long-term assistance, and the affective and instrumental components are most easily balanced.

It would be of interest to know whether the pattern of frequent imbalance between instrumentality and affectivity in active friendships exists in other contexts. For example, how do men and women maintain friendships arising from their occupations rather than their residential contacts? Do working woman separate the responsibilities and obligations of their work — the instrumental aspect — from their social interaction — the affective aspect — or do they attempt to balance one with the other? Does an environment of competition impede the development of solidarity and affectivity? What instrumental components are evident in friendships of women without children and are they problematic? Preliminary research shows that single women have fewer friends on whom they depend for assistance in daily activities than do married women and they are less likely to base friendship on proximity. A central question therefore is what the changes are in patterns of friendship during different stages in an individual's life.

## REFERENCES

BALIKCI, ASEN
 1968  Bad friends. *Human Organization* 27:191–199.
BERKOWITZ, L., L. DANIELS
 1963  Responsibility and dependency. *Journal of Abnormal and Social Psychology* 66:429–436.
CUBITT, TESSA
 1971  "Friends, neighbors, and kin." Unpublished Ph. D. dissertation, Edinburgh University.
EISENSTADT, S. N.
 1956  Ritualized personal relations. *Man* 56:90–95.
ERVIN-TRIPP, SUSAN M.
 1964  An analysis of the interaction of language, topic and listener. *American Anthropologist* 66:86–102.
FIRTH, RAYMOND, JANE HUBERT, ANTHONY FORGE
 1969  *Families and their relatives*. London: Routledge and Kegan Paul.
GOULDNER, A.
 1960  The norm of reciprocity: a preliminary statement. *American Sociological Review* 25:161–178.
HARDING, JOHN, HAROLD PROSHANSKY, BERNARD KUTNER, ISIDOR CHEIN
 1968  "Prejudice and ethnic relations," in *The handbook of social psychology* (second edition). Edited by G. Lindzey and E. Aronson, V:1–76. Reading: Addison-Wesley.
KOMAROVSKY, MIRRA
 1967  *Blue collar marriage*. New York: Vintage.
KREBS, DENNIS L.
 1970  Altruism: an examination of the concept and a review. *Psychological Bulletin* 73:258–302.
LEEDS, R.
 1963  Altruism and the norm of giving. *Merrill Palmer Quarterly* 9:229–240.
MARRIS, PETER
 1962  *Family and social change in an African city*. Evanston: Northwestern University Press.
MAYER, ADRIAN
 1966  "The significance of quasi-groups in the study of complex societies," in *The social anthropology of complex societies*. Edited by Michael Banton, IV:97–122. London: Tavistock.
MAYER, JOHN
 1957  The self-restraint of friends. *Social Forces* 35:230–238.
MC GUIRE, WILLIAM J.
 1969  "The nature of attitudes and attitude change," in *The handbook of social psychology* (second edition). Edited by G. Lindzey and E. Aronson, III:136–314. Reading: Addison-Wesley.

MEAD, MARGARET, *editor*
1961   *Cooperation and competition among primitive peoples*. Boston: Beacon Press.
MINTZ, S. W., ERIC WOLF
1950   An analysis of ritual co-parenthood. *Southwestern Journal of Anthropology* 6:341–368.
O'DONNELL, PETER
1972   *Pieces of modesty*. London: Pan.
PAINE, ROBERT
1969   In search of friendship: an exploratory analysis in "middle-class" culture. *Man* n.s. 4:505–524.
PARSONS, TALCOTT
1964   *The social system*. New York: Macmillan.
PITT-RIVERS, JULIAN A.
1961   *The people of the Sierra*. Chicago: University of Chicago Press.
SCHULZ, CHARLES M.
1968   *All about friendship*. New York: Hallmark.
SUSSMAN, MARVIN B.
1953   The help-pattern in the middle-class family. *American Sociological Review* 18:22–28.
SUTCLIFFE, J. P., B. D. CRABBE
1963   Incidence and degrees of friendship in urban and rural areas. *Social Forces* 42:60–67.
WOLF, ERIC
1966   "Kinship, friendship and patron-client relations in complex societies," in *The social anthropology of complex societies*. Edited by Michael Banton, IV:1–22. London: Tavistock.
YUAN, YING-YING
1972   "Assimilation and isolation in the neighborhood world of women." Unpublished Ph.D. dissertation, Harvard University.

# An Explanation for Matrilocal Residence

WILLIAM TULIO DIVALE

It has been over a century since the publication of Bachofen's *Das Mutter-recht* where the issue of matrilineal systems was first raised. The early theorists, McLennan, Tylor, Morgan, and Engels, all argued that the matriliny was a stage prior to the patriliny in the evolution of the family. Evidence for their arguments was based, in part, on scattered matrilineal traits, such as the avunculate, found in many patrilineal societies. With the exception of a few scholars in Germany and the U.S.S.R. this perspective is no longer held by many anthropologists. This was partly due to the Boasian reaction against the 19th century evolutionists, and partly to the data gathered on peoples of simple complexity which more often indicated patrilocality and bilateral or patrilineal descent. To date no rival hypothesis has been offered to explain the matrilineal survivals nor have we seen satisfactory explanation for the occurrence of matrilocal residence.

For instance, the most generally accepted explanation for matrilocality is that the sex which contributes most to basic subsistence will determine post-marital residence practices. Thus if females predominate in subsistence activities, residence will be matrilocal. Another theory, postulated by David Aberle and Elman Service, is that tropical rainforest environments are associated with matrilocal-matrilineal peoples. Kathleen Gough has suggested that societies with matrilineal descent are predominantly horticultural rather than agricultural. She argues further that among matrilineal societies, those with matrilocal residence will exhibit low productivity while those with avunculocal residence will exhibit high productivity.

While patrilineal societies are almost always patrilocal, matrilineal societies exhibit a variety of post-marital residence patterns. It seems likely, however, that matrilineal descent could only develop from a matrilocal residence pattern. Logically we might assume that any explanation of why 14 percent of the world's societies have matrilineal descent must ultimately come from an explanantion of the causes of matrilocal residence. The purpose of this paper is to provide such an explanation.

## METHODOLOGY

The theories of matrilocality just described, plus the one to be presented below, were tested cross-culturally on a probability sample of 43 societies (33 patrilocal, 10 matrilocal) and when applicable, on the 1200 societies in the *Ethnographic atlas* (Murdock 1967). The variables used, which were not already in the *Ethnographic atlas*, were coded once by myself and once by an independent analyst who did not know the hypotheses to be tested. There is no significant difference in test results when either coding is used (see Divale 1974a for documentation codings, including page and source references).

## TESTS OF OTHER THEORIES

The hypothesis that residence will be matrilocal when females predominate in subsistence was tested using precoded variables on basic subsistence (gathering, hunting, fishing, herding, and farming) from the *Ethnographic atlas* (Murdock 1967). However, no association was found (see Figure 1). A recent test by Melvin and Carol Ember (1971), as well as another test by Divale (1974b), also failed to find any relationship between female importance in subsistence and matrilocal residence.

The hypothesis that matrilocality is associated with tropical forest climates was also tested using codings on climate for the first 410 societies in the punched card version of the *Atlas* (Barry 1967), but no association was found between rainforests and matrilocality. In fact, matrilocal residence was tested against fifteen types of environments and no association was found. And, as a further check, societies with matrilineal descent were also tested against these environments and only two significant but very small relationships were found — namely that matrilineal descent is negatively correlated with temperate forests and positively correlated with temperate woodlands. Both of these correlations are so low, however, that they afford little predictive power. The results could also be due to chance because when 30 correlations are run, the Poisson distribution indicates that at the 5 percent level, $1^1/_2$ significant correlations would be expected by chance alone when no relationship actually existed. Thus the hypothesis that matrilocal residence is associated with tropical rainforests or any other type of environment was not supported.

Using *Atlas* codings, Gough's hypotheses were tested. No association was found between matrilocality and horticulture. There is a slight correlation between matrilineal descent and horticulture but it is too small to be significant. Further, since the data suggest that matrilineal descent arises AFTER matrilocal residence, a relationship to horticulture cannot be construed as having any causal connection with matrilocality (see Divale 1974a for specific test results on climate and horticulture).

Residence pattern

| Basic subsistence | Predominantly patrilocal | | Predominantly matrilocal | Totals |
|---|---|---|---|---|
| Males predominate | Malays Yakut Koreans Chukchee Lau Yokuts Gros Ventre Yucatec Ma Yahgan Yanomamö Cayua Wolof Mossi | Irish Zazzagawa Tiv Lapps Kurd Rwala Amhara Masai Ngoni Somali Bhil Toda | Trukese Zuñi Cuna Mataco Bororo Mundurucú Khasi | 32 |
| Females predominate | Aranda Kapauku Tikopia Aymara Kanuri Azande Serbs | | Pawnee Iroquois Cagaba | 10 |
| Totals | 32 | | 10 | 42 |

*Phi*=.081     Fisher's exact probability: one tail=.44386

Figure 1.   Female predominance in basic subsistence and matrilocal residence

## SOME CONTRASTS BETWEEN PATRILOCAL AND MATRILOCAL SOCIETIES

Only about 10 percent of the world's societies practice matrilocal residence, while about 75 percent practice patrilocal residence. Thus it would appear that matrilocality is a deviate residence pattern from the norm of patrilocality. Previous cross-cultural tests have uncovered striking differences between patrilocal and matrilocal societies which are relevant to an explanation of matrilocality. Otterbein and Otterbein (1965, 1968) found that patrilocality is significantly associated with extensive polygyny, frequent feuding, and internal warfare (that is, fighting between communities of the same culture). It has also been found that extensive polygyny is an indirect cause of feuding and internal war, because polygyny concentrates adult females among the older males (Divale 1971). This shortage of available women leads to adultery, wife stealing, and fights, with the consequence that many wars stem from fights over women. Elsewhere I have argued that these relationships are adaptive because they have important population control functions (Divale 1973, 1972, 1970, 1971; see also Harris 1972). But these studies and those of Otterbein also suggest that patrilocal societes are characterized by a great deal of internal disharmony, both within the local community through feuding and within the society as a whole through internal warfare.

In sharp contrast to this, Van Velzen and Van Wetering (1960) find that matrilocal societies tend not to have feuding and to be internally much more peaceful than patrilocal societies. Several studies have also found that matrilocal societies tend to make war only with other societies and not amongst themselves (Noberini 1966; Ember and Ember 1971; Divale 1974b). Thus in contrast to patrilocal societies which are characterized by internal disharmony, matrilocal societies are characterized by internal harmony with hostility being directed toward members of other societies. This contrast, established statistically on different samples and by several workers, is central to an explanation of the causes and adaptive function of matrilocal residence.

## THE "CAUSE" OF MATRILOCALITY

When a primitive society (band or tribe) or a large portion of its members migrate into a new region which is already inhabited by other societies of similiar social complexity, matrilocal residence tends to develop. There are many possible factors which cause migration. For instance, over-population in one region causing spill-off into neighboring regions is probably one factor. The introduction of new technology or new methods of subsistence which allow for the exploitation of a previously un-exploitable environment is another factor. European colonial expansion into new areas of the world which tended to crowd the indigenous peoples is another factor.

The movement of large numbers of people into an inhabited region creates a disequilibrium between the indigenous peoples and their environment. Depending on local circumstances, this imbalance could involve land, water, or food resources ratios. Given the limitations of primitive politics, warfare is the major means through which a new equilibrium can be established. Either the newcomers or the indigenous peoples are driven out, or a warfare-induced depopulation of both groups occurs. Under this disequilibrium, the most adaptive response would be for local communities to direct all their hostilities toward the other culture — that is, to have a pattern of external warfare. But most societies are patrilocal and are characterized by feuding and internal warfare. Therefore, it would be adaptive if the society stopped its pattern of internal war and developed a pattern of external war in its place. Otter-bein (1968, 1970) has found that the presence of fraternal interest groups (that is, patrilineages) are conducive to internal warfare. Patrilocality results in groups of related males spending their entire lives in one locale. A man is always near his brothers and uncles on whom he can depend for support in disputes. And since men spend their entire lives in one village, their political focus and concern extends only to their village boundaries — and the people in neighboring villages are usually enemies even though they share a common language and culture.

Matrilocal residence aids in the cessation of internal warfare because it results in the break up of fraternal interest groups. At marriage, males either move to a different village or to another part of their own village and the result is that groups of adult males who live together are related by marriage and not by the closer bonds of blood. This means that a man's agnatic kin are scattered into several villages and are not close by to support him in disputes. In addition, to make war on a neighboring village would be to fight with one's own agnatic kin. Therefore the structural changes brought about by matrilocal residence tend to eradicate the conditions which are conducive to internal warfare. Since related ma es are scattered into several villages, political focus is expanded beyond the village boundaries to include at least the several villages where a man's agnatic kin are located. Political authority and warfare are always in the hands of males regardless of the type of residence or descent pattern. Thus the scattering of adult males under matrilocality has much more political and social significance than does the movement of females under patrilocality. With matrilocal residence, cultural values and rules which promote internal peace, harmony, and group cohesion can develop and be maintained. This internal harmony would be extremely adaptive in the face of external threat and conditions of disequilibrium.

TEST RESULTS

If this theory is correct, it would be expected that compared with patrilocal societies, societies which are predominately matrilocal should have

|  | Residence pattern | | |
|---|---|---|---|
| Society migrated to present locale during past 500 years | Predominantly patrilocal | Predominantly matrilocal | Totals |
| No | Malays Wolof<br>Annamese Irish<br>Yakut Zazzagawa<br>Koreans Kanuri<br>Aranda Serbs<br>Tikopia Lapps<br>Chukchee Kurd<br>Yokuts Amhara<br>Yucatec Ma Masai<br>Yahgan Somali<br>Aymara Bhil<br>Yanomamö | Zuni | 24 |
| Yes | Kapauku<br>Lau<br>Gros Ventre<br>Cayua<br>Mossi<br>Tiv<br>Azande<br>Ngoni<br>Toda | Trukese<br>Pawnee<br>Iroquois<br>Cuna<br>Mataco<br>Bororo<br>Mundurucú<br>Cagaba<br>Khasi | 18 |
| Totals | 32 | 10 | 42 |

Phi=.533    Fisher's exact probability: one tail=.00082

Figure 2.   Recent migration and matrilocal residence

migrated to their present locale in the recent past, and their warfare pattern should be external. This hypothesis was tested on the sample of 43 societies and a significant association was indeed found. Nine of the ten matrilocal societies in the sample had recently migrated to their present area (see Figure 2). The one matrilocal society in the sample which did not recently migrate was the Zuñi, and this discrepancy can be explained by the fact that the Navaho and Apache tribes which surround the Zuni ARE recent migrants to the area. The conditions of disequilibrium which would select for the development of matrilocality would prevail for both the migrating and indigenous societies. Thus it is not insignificant that the Zuni, Navaho, and Apache tribes all practice matrilocal residence.

A second research strategy was used to test for possible bias in my measurement of migration. This second method involved a linguistic

Residence pattern

| Language spoken is dissimilar to immediate neighbors | Predominately patrilocal | | Predominately matrilocal | Totals |
|---|---|---|---|---|
| No | Malays<br>Annamese<br>Yakut<br>Koreans<br>Tikopia<br>Chukchee<br>Yokuts<br>Yucatec Ma<br>Aymara<br>Yanomamö | Wolof<br>Irish<br>Zazzagawa<br>Kanuri<br>Lapps<br>Kurd<br>Amhara<br>Masai<br>Somali<br>Bhil | | 22 |
| Yes | Lau<br>Gros Ventre<br>Yahgan<br>Cayua<br>Mossi<br>Tiv<br>Azande<br>Ngoni<br>Toda | | Trukese<br>Zuñi<br>Pawnee<br>Iroquois<br>Cuna<br>Mataco<br>Bororo<br>Mundurucú<br>Cagaba<br>Khasi | 19 |
| Totals | 31 | | 10 | 42 |

$Phi = .611$     Fisher's exact probability: one tail $= .00008$

Figure 3. Linguistic dissimilarity with neighbor and matrilocal residence

comparison. It was hypothesized that if a society had recently migrated into an area, then it should be linguistically unrelated to its surrounding neighbors. This was indeed the case as all ten matrilocal societies in the sample spoke languages which were unrelated to their neighbors (see Figure 3). The second prediction of the theory, that matrilocal societies should practice only external warfare was also confirmed. Eight of the ten matrilocal societies practice only external warfare (see Figure 4).

Continued research on this problem suggests that due to the long range structural instability of matrilocal-matrilineal social structure, namely the conflict between male authority and female orientated residence, that after external war has established a new equilibrium, matrilocal-matrilineal societies will undergo a series of changes in residence and descent

Warfare pattern

| Residence pattern | Internal or internal AND external | | Only external | Totals |
|---|---|---|---|---|
| Predominantly patrilocal | Malays Annamese Yakut Koreans Aranda Kapauku Lau Yokuts Yahgan Aymara Yanomamö Wolof | Irish Zazzagawa Tiv Azande Serbs Lapps Kurd Rwala Ngoni Somali Bhil | Tikopia Chukchee Gros Ventre Cayua Mossi Kanuri Amhara Toda | 33 |
| Predominantly matrilocal | Trukese Mataco | | Zuñi Pawnee Iroquois Cuna Bororo Mundurucú Cagaba Khasi | 10 |
| Totals | 27 | | 16 | 43 |

*Phi*=.487   Fisher's exact probability: one tail=.00252

Figure 4.   External warfare and matrilocal residence

which will eventually return them back to the norm of patrilocal residence and patrilineal descent (see Figure 5). Preliminary work suggests this may be the case (Divale 1974b and 1974c).

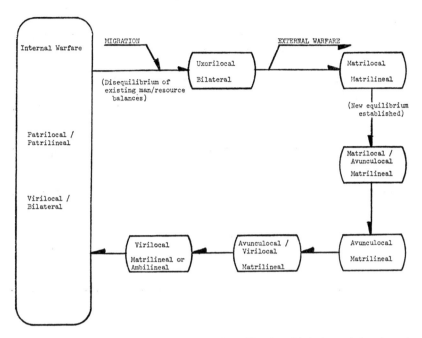

Figure 5. Postulated path of the matrilocal/matrilineal cycle (estimated duration of the process is from one to two thousand years)

## REFERENCES

BARRY, HERBERT, III
1967  Computer punched card version of the *Ethnographic atlas*. Available from *Ethnology*, the University of Pittsburgh.

DIVALE, WILLIAM TULIO
1970  An explanation for primitive warfare: population control and the significance of primitive sex ratios. *New Scholar* 2:172–193.
1971  "A theory of population control in primitive culture." Unpublished master's thesis, California State University at Los Angeles.
1972  Systemic population control in the Middle and Upper Paleolithic: inferences based on contemporary hunter-gatherers. *World Archaeology* 4:222–243.
1973  *Warfare in primitive societies*. Santa Barbara: ABC-Clio Press.
1974a Migration, external warfare, and matrilocal residence. *Behavior Science Research* 9:75–133.
1974b "The causes of matrilocal residence: a cross-ethnohistorical study."

Unpublished doctoral dissertation, State University of New York at Buffalo.
1974c "Toward a theory of residence systems." Educational Resources Information Center System (ERIC), speech communication module microfiche.

EMBER, MELVIN, CAROL EMBER
1971 The conditions favoring matrilocal versus patrilocal residence. *American Anthropologist* 73:571–94.

HARRIS, MARVIN
1972 Warfare old and new. *Natural History* 81(3):18,20.

MURDOCK, GEORGE P.
1967 *Ethnographic atlas: a summary*. Pittsburgh: University of Pittsburgh Press.

NOBERINI, M.
1966 "Ethnocentrism and feuding: a cross cultural study." Unpublished master's thesis, University of Chicago.

OTTERBEIN, KEITH
1968 Internal war: a cross cultural study. *American Anthropologist* 70:277–289.
1970 *The evolution of war*. New Haven: Human Relations Area File Press.

OTTERBEIN, KEITH, CHARLOTTE OTTERBEIN
1965 An eye for an eye: a cross cultural study of feuding. *American Anthropologist* 67:1470–1482.

VAN VELZEN, THODEN, W. VAN WETERING
1960 Residence, power groups and intrasocietal aggression. *International Archives of Ethnography* 49:169–200.

# SECTION TWO

## *Women and Power*

# Women and Power: Introductory Notes

DANA RAPHAEL

A dramatic change in the theoretical and practical consideration of power occurs once women come into the picture. Power is no longer delegated to domestic-female and political-male. The concept that one or the other sex controls these respective domains becomes untenable. A new approach is called for whereby both sexes are incorporated into both spheres of power. The time is ripe to examine how they interconnect and influence the entire decision-making and sanctioning systems within any culture.

When power is seen as limited to the political and economic scenes, "...male activity is accorded preeminence in the public sector" (Friedl 1967:97). When power is defined as the ability to bear, educate, and determine the personality, the values, beliefs, hates and loves of each new human member of a society, in fact, to control decisions of who will or will not survive, then females are certainly dominant. "...If a careful analysis of the life of the community shows that pragmatically the family is the most significant social unit, then the private and not the public sector is the sphere in which the relative attribution of power to males and females is of the greatest real importance" (Friedl 1967:97).

The issue then is not the relative power of females, but the significance and function of the female contribution to any particular segment of society.

We hold that if we had really looked at women, at what they were doing vis-à-vis their children, their male kin, and their female companions, we would have seen long ago that the amount of time and energy and commitment it takes to bear, nurse and rear human beings leaves very little time for much else. The power intrinsic in determining the outcome of each new generation is unparalleled. There is little space and less time left to spend deciding who should be chief, who should distribute a widow's property or who should perform the role of majordomo at a fiesta.

This is equally true for males. The time required for dealing with political and economic concerns of any culture leaves little time for dealing with caretaking functions. If we examine the economic level of most human cultures throughout history, we note, for the most part, that one major role per individual was sufficient for a lifetime and one major category or role per sex was as much as could be taught and learned within any culture.

Recent research has shown that a crucial factor in the restriction of female participation in subsistence activities is women's role in child rearing (Brown 1970). To test this hypothesis, a cross-cultural study of 83 societies was conducted by Nerlove (1974) and it was found that supplementary feeding of infants begins earlier in those culture where participation in the subsistence activities by women are greatest.[1] Clearly, there is only a limited amount of time and energy per day or month or year. Presence in the political arena, in the subsistence scene, in the area of art, etc., is certainly curtailed by the amount of time it takes to bear, feed and tend children.

Nonetheless, women have demonstrated their effectiveness when put into the political/power scene. We have had many examples of Prime Ministers, Queens, and other women who have had very successful and powerful careers. Yet, the data suggest that the "pool" of qualified women who have been trained or exposed to the requirements of political power-roles is far smaller than that of males.

Physiological difference, especially childbirth and lactation, have in the past set limits to female participation in the political scene. Even though a small proportion of the population, as mentioned in the Introduction to this volume, never do reproduce, those individuals are not identified until maturity. Since reproduction is the first order of human survival, it behooves each culture to teach the reproductive roles and to provide people to see that they are learned.

---

[1]   We do need eye witness reports of actual supplementary food input before we can add to this hypothesis. The tendency for ethnographers to use "months" in response to the question of when children are weaned in cultures where no one recognizes this time span, or statements such as "an infant is weaned right from the beginning" or "the infant gets no other food but his mother's milk for the first two years" must be deplored. Not only are they inadequate indicators of the amount of supplementary food offered, the time when it is offered, etc., but in the latter case ("not for two years") it is physiologically impossible. Any infant whose foods are not supplemented with iron and other nutrients after the first six months or so of breastfeeding, would suffer from malnutrition or worse.

Intrinsic in this search for an understanding of the nature of the power of women is this very important statement which defines the interconnection of fertility and politics: "Women cannot hope to participate fully in decision-making until they are able to exercise choice in their childbearing role. And we cannot hope to reduce the rate of population growth until women are able to participate more widely in their societies" (Sipila 1974).

We argue that male/female difference has been influenced by a history of succesfull breeding into each population those members of each sex who were best suited for the assigned sex roles, i.e. females for mothering, males for strength and whatever personality traits make one suited for political activity. Lest we forget, females do become political potentates and males are sometimes excellent as caretakers. Such evidence indicates the persistence of similar behaviorally related genes in both sexes. Ehrhardt demonstrates that masculine traits are available in the behavioral repertory of many females and, conversely, that feminine chacteristics are at one end of the normal male continuum. Her research suggests that the biological as well as social traits necessary for leadership are available to both sexes. Yet we have recently found that human infants (and non-human infants as well, see Poirier this volume) are sexed by their parents as early as a few moments after birth and treated differently even at that early stage — a powerful statement of the pervasiveness of cultural factors in differentiating and determining life-roles.

A time dimension has been added to the expression by women of power in the domestic sphere (Lamphere). The particular stage in the life cycle of those within the domestic group influences WHO has the power and WHEN they have it. Women's strategies are seen as responses to the distribution of power and authority even within the domestic group. Such response would depend on whether authority is in the hands of women or men. For example, a young wife's power would depend on whether her husband held the authority within the family or whether his father (and thus her mother-in-law) was the person who held the authority. In the former case, the younger woman could wield some influence in her early years. In the latter case, the woman would not be influential until her husband gained power and she became mother-in-law. The strategies which females use to manipulate and influence the males who control the power include strong and subtle methods, such as gossip and playing one person off against another. This manipulation of males is a major strategy for women in many cultures.

A qualitative difference in the allotment of power was also noted by Lamphere. Women, in egalitarian societies where domestic and external political spheres are integrated (Navajo, Eskimo, Bushman), are far more equal to men in the decision-making processes. Where public and domestic spheres diverge, as in more developed cultures, so do the authority/ decision patterns between males and females. This is particularly interesting in light of Lomax's correlations of musical style with the developmental stages of subsistence and female participation in the power arena.

Lola Hanson did not submit a paper but her oral report at the Congress showed how she successfully manipulated a traditional pattern into a program of directed change in a situation of sub-dominance. Orphaned Korean girls were taught reading and writing so that they could provide a necessary service function for the male-dominated villagers who were extremely hostile to them. This transformed the status of these children into scribes serving the entire village of illiterates. The orphanage was accepted. In fact, it became the first reading center for peasants in South Korea.

Methods used in three other cultures to temper male authority *vis-à-vis* females are described in this section. In the case of Jerusalem Arabs, the men are highly stratified but the women maintain status equality amongst themselves. This permits them to continue to function on the work/social relationship level essential to a workable society. At the same time, it allows them to chastise loudly those who have wronged them.

Bundu, a rural puberty rite "club" common in West Africa, is the basis by which women who want to enter national politics organize a following (Hoffer). Schlegel attempts to find factors within different types of societies which indicate the relative dominance of males over females.

A review of the women's movement in the United States reminds us that women are considered a minority group. Allen gives us an excellent definition of "minority" as the presence and consciousness of discrimination. In most cultures, women have never been separated from other women as they have been in these last 60 years in the United States. The phenomenon is rare, perhaps unique, in human history. The emergence of a mass identification of female with female is a unique response to the needs of women to get together, question the many male-dominant or discriminatory structures in the society, and to change them. Besides the many social reforms introduced and pressed for by the woman's movement the major contribution may well be GIVING WOMEN BACK TO WOMEN.

The pattern of this movement has been to concentrate first on personal liberation, through consciousness raising programs. Political statements and projects came next. At first, women attempted to use methods that were DIFFERENT from those used by males in their power institutions. An internal structure and party activity based on an idea of non-male patterns was one approach. One needs to ask if there is or could be a different pattern, if the all-female group could develop a feminine-only policy, or, if a democratic, egalitarian political party in a non-egalitarian society is even possible.

For anthropologists, the proper study of power should include both sexes and contain considerations of how their respective roles interrelate within different cultures, on various socioeconomic levels of integration. If we are to begin to understand decision, power and authority, we must investigate them on this multi-dimensional scale. If we choose to see how an all-women institution would differ from the presently developed male-structure types, we still must study not women-and-power but women in relation to men within a matrix of a cultural setting.

## REFERENCES

BROWN, JUDITH
    1970    A note on the division of labor. *American Anthropologist* 77:1073–1978.
FRIEDL, ERNESTINE
    1967    "The position of women: appearance and reality," in *Appearance and reality: status and roles of women in Mediterranean societies*. Special issue of the *Anthropological Quarterly* 40(3).
NERLOVE, SARA B.
    1974    Women's workload and infant feeding practices: a relationship with demographic implications. *Ethnology* 13.
SIPILA, HELVI L.
    1974    United Nations Assistant Secretary General for Social Development and Humanitarian Affairs, as reported in *OAS Weekly Newsletter* 12(12). Washington, D. C.

# Women and Domestic Power: Political and Economic Strategies in Domestic Groups

LOUISE LAMPHERE

In most societies women are primarily associated with their domestic and familial roles of wife and mother, while the social and political spheres are dominated by men. But even within the domestic domain, decision-making can be the prerogative of women, of men, or shared between adults of both sexes. WHO exercises domestic power and HOW others respond to it varies from society to society. In discussing the determinants of domestic power, it is important to examine women's roles, attitudes, and relationships as well as those of men.

Most studies of the family and domestic groups focus on the rights and duties of family members, the ways in which rights are transferred at marriage, and the continuity in rights to land, movable property, or group membership (e.g. Radcliffe-Brown 1950; Leach 1955; Gluckman 1950). Those who have taken a more dynamic view of the domestic group have emphasized a "developmental cycle" which characterizes the formation, development and fission of groups within a particular society (Fortes 1949; Goody 1958). Both of these approaches — whether focused on the normative or cyclical aspects of the family — ignore the female point of view. For instance, in their papers on domestic groups among the Ashanti (Fortes 1949) and the LoDagaba (Goody 1958), the authors emphasize the long-term continuity of domestic groups and the transmission of property and authority within the "developmental cycle." Since both of these societies focus power in the hands of males, the authors tend to ignore women, slight their views of the male domestic power structure and do not even touch on the methods and strategies women use in dealing with male-defined situations.

## AN ALTERNATIVE PERSPECTIVE

This paper presents an approach which emphasizes the woman's perspective and alters traditional analyses in three ways. First, rather than describing rights and duties within family groups, the focus is on the political aspects of domestic life. I outline the distribution of power and authority[1] within the family and specify which aspects are in the hands of men and which are allocated to women. Second, I will retain the concept of the developmental cycle of domestic groups. I specify the way in which the structure of the domestic group changes, authority roles shift, and property is transferred over a period of time. I not only discuss male positions of authority and inheritance within domestic groups, but stress that women's roles also have a developmental cycle, so that a particular woman's relationship to the allocation of power and authority changes as she grows older and as her children mature.

Finally, I analyze the strategies women employ in attaining their own ends, whether this entails making decisions themselves, exercising influence over those who make decisions, or circumventing the domestic power structure. It is suggested that women's strategies are a response to the distribution of power and authority in the domestic group and that they differ depending on whether decisions are in the hands of women or men.

As Rosaldo (1973) suggests with her structural model of the status of women, one dimension which affects family authority structure is the relative integration or separation of political and domestic spheres. As the following data will show, societies where domestic and political spheres are integrated, authority within the domestic group is shared by both men

---

[1]  Following Weber, I define power as "the probability that one actor within a social relationship will be in a position to carry out his own will despite resistance, regardless of the basis on which this probability rests" (Weber 1947:152). Authority, in turn, is the exercise of POWER within a hierarchy of roles which rests on legitimacy, i.e. the notion that an individual has a "right" to impose his will on others (Parsons 1963a). If an individual does not hold a position of authority, she or he may seek to influence the decisions of others, i.e. attempt to bring about a decision on another's part, through an appeal that such a decision would be a "good thing" in itself (Parsons 1963b) or in accordance with a particular norm.

and women. Women's strategies focus on cooperation for everyday activities and are "economic" in nature. Furthermore, even though there is a division of labor between the sexes so that kinsmen (mother, sister, father, cross-cousin, etc.) are recruited depending on the sex of the individual and the type of task, strategies for that recruitment do not differ between men and women. In contrast, in many societies where domestic and political spheres are separated, and where extended family structures predominate, power and authority is built around a hierarchy of males. Women's strategies are centered on "political" goals, that is, on influencing the men who hold authority.

In order to contrast strategies used to recruit aid with those used to gain influence or power, it is necessary to first examine domestic groups in societies where domestic and political spheres are integrated and then compare these cases with more stratified societies where political and domestic context are distinct. Examples in the latter case will be drawn from peasant communities in state societies, and African tribal societies. Within these two types of society, I will also look at the relative effect of economic factors, specifically a woman's contribution to household resources and how this shapes her strategies within the domestic group.

## WOMEN, STRATEGIES, AND COOPERATION AMONG THE NAVAJO

The first example comes from data collected on domestic groups and patterns of cooperation among the Navajo Indians of New Mexico and Arizona (Lamphere 1973). The Navajo, a loosely-organized American Indian population, migrated to the Southwest as hunter-gatherers and through contact with Pueblo and Spanish peoples adopted agriculture and began to raise livestock. Under present-day reservation conditions they are increasingly involved in a wage and welfare economy.

The pre-conquest political organization consisted of leadership by a "headman" who had very little authority, but who settled disputes and gave advice. These leaders were male as were most other public officials such as raid leaders and medicine men. Even today, with a fullfledged modern tribal government, though women are not excluded most political offices are held by men.

The reservation system has imposed a political superstructure on Navajo life, but most important decisions are still made within the domestic group or by individuals. Property is individually owned and there is an emphasis on autonomy. Requests for help are made indirectly, and Navajos expect generosity from others in response to any indication of need (Lamphere 1971). These qualities suggest that there is relative equality between men and women, particularly in the family, and indicate that political and domestic spheres are not basically differentiated.

Navajo domestic groups often take the form of "matrilocal grandfamilies" which are structured around female bonds and backed up by a positive cultural valuation of the role of the mother (Witherspoon 1970). These scattered extended families follow a common developmental cycle. When a couple marries, they may live with either the wife's mother or the husband's mother. However, uxorilocal rather than virilocal residence is preferred since the mother-daughter bond is stronger. After marriage a young couple sets up a dwelling of their own within the camp.

In these extended families, the parents or the widowed mother hold positions of authority. They decide on matters which concern sheep herding, shearing, dipping, or agricultural work, although each new household also has a great deal of autonomy. Navajo concepts of authority are egalitarian, not hierarchical. An individual's decision is not binding on another person or on a group. Instead, a Navajo makes a decision and requests a similar one from another Navajo. If the latter's decision is congruent with that of the former, it obligates both to participate in joint activities (Lamphere 1971:97).

Navajo parents or a widowed mother do not IMPOSE their decisions on other households, but serve as a focus of communication and of organizing cooperation. Requests for aid are made directly between parents and children, though a father may use the mother as an intermediary with his daughters. In-married affines are in a peripheral position, especially a son-in-law living uxorilocally. In the early years of marriage, a man and his wife do not form a team. Rather the wife is a buffer between her husband and her parents. Navajo marriages are brittle. This is especially true in the early years because of the strains created by the wife's loyalty to her kin and the husband's obligation to his own parents and siblings, all of whom usually reside in another camp. If a marriage endures, the couple become more and more of a unit. Eventually they establish a new camp in the same neighborhood as the wife's or the husband's parents. A son-in-law gains by moving off because he becomes a decision-maker in a wider range of situations and is no longer at the daily "beck and call" of his in-laws.

Another beneficial effect of the move is that as the parental couple get older and especially after the death of the mother (who is more of a focus of communication and dispute settlement than the father), tensions between married children in the same camp increase. Brothers and sisters quarrel over livestock, for instance one sibling may accuse the other of not contributing enough goods towards a ceremony. By moving, tensions are decreased, and daily cooperation is changed to more occasional requests.

During the final phase of the developmental cycle of a residence group, the couple become head of their own camp, which eventually contains married children and grandchildren. Ties with the husband's and wife's siblings are maintained for help in curing ceremonies, the girls' puberty ritual and funerals.

Cooperation beyond the residence group is recruited on an ego centered set of kin. In obtaining help for ceremonies, both men and women use what I have termed a "proximity strategy." For the organizer, residence group members are the "closest" and most easily recruited participants. Next to be activated are ties to primary and secondary kin[2] outside the residence group, with those in the same neighborhood being the most likely to participate. Then, neighbors with whom an individual has clan ties are recruited. Finally, distant clan relatives are likely to participate only in funerals or very large ceremonies. Usually two individuals (such as a husband and wife) organize a ceremony. More members of one person's set of kin may be activated if the other person has few kin, or one individual's kin are residentially distant from the camp where the ceremony is held (Lamphere 1973).

Thus, among the Navajo, domestic and political spheres are relatively undifferentiated and most crucial decisions are taken within the domestic group rather than in a wider political arena. Authority within domestic groups is egalitarian with the emphasis on individual autonomy. Under these conditions, Navajo women have a great deal of control over their own lives. They do not need to wrest power from others who hold positions of authority, or attempt to influence decisions which are not theirs to make. The strategies women use in recruiting aid are not substantially different from those of men. Women rarely "work through" men, but are themselves mediators between men, as, for instance, between a young husband and his father-in-law.

## HUNTER-GATHERER GROUPS

Among hunter-gatherer groups where the band is the largest social unit, political and domestic spheres are even more integrated than among the

---

[2] Primary kin are those separated from ego by one genealogical link (i.e., parents, siblings, and children) while secondary kin are two genealogical links apart (parents siblings, siblings' children, and grandchildren).

Navajo. Material from the Bushman (Marshall 1959, 1960; Lee 1972) and
Eskimo (Briggs 1970; Damas 1968; Spencer and Jennings 1965; Hoebel
1954) confirms the relationship between the distribution of power and
authority and the strategies women employ. Authority is egalitarian,
decisions are by consensus, and individual autonomy is maximized.[3]

In contrast with the Navajo, the nuclear family is the major domestic
unit for both the Bushman and the Eskimo, and the husband-wife dyad is
stable throughout life. The developmental cycle of the nuclear family does
not bring about changes in women's interests or cooperative relationships. Rather than a gradual shift in emphasis from cooperation with natal
kin (mainly females) to that with a husband and grown children, Eskimo
and Bushman women work independently or with their husbands throughout their adult lives. At the same time, they have a continuing network of
occasional cooperators among other women in the band, the closest of
whom are sisters, mothers, cousins, and possibly sisters-in-law.[4]

Bushman and Eskimo women see their goals as primarily coinciding
with those of their husbands. The husband-wife relationship among the
Eskimo (Briggs 1970) is definitely a dominant/subordinate one, in marked
contrast to the Bushman situation, perhaps due to the Bushman women's
contribution of 2/3 of the diet (Lee 1968). Despite the differences between
family structure and the extent of husband dominance, a comparison of
the Eskimo, Bushman and Navajo still show that women's strategies revolve around recruiting help in primarily economic tasks. Although men
and women may work separately, and are likely to cooperate with kin of
the same sex, women's strategies of recruitment do not differ from those
of men. Women have positive ties with female kin and other women in the
two band societies where the nuclear family is important, while Navajo
women have very close ties with female kin in a system where uxorilocal
extended families are important.

## THE PATRI-CENTERED PEASANT FAMILY

What happens to relationships between women of the same family in
which domestic and political spheres are highly differentiated and where

[3]   Leadership positions are held by men, but at least in the Bushman case (Lee 1972:
129) leaders do not control rights to resources; these instead reside with the whole
group. Furthermore, unlike Radcliffe-Brown's model of the patrilocal horde, Bushman
band membership is flexible and based on ties between siblings of either sex.
[4]   The data presented by Briggs, Lee and Marshall are not detailed enough to draw
definitive conclusions, but I suspect that recruitment for aid follows a "proximity
strategy" based on ties within a bilateral kindred. In contrast, Navajo strategies seem
more skewed toward matrilateral kin, because of the importance of uxorilocal residence.

authority is hierarchical and in the hands of male members of the group? The question is complicated by the variety of political systems found cross-culturally (ranging from acephalous tribal societies and pre-industrial states, on one hand, to modern industrial societies and third-world nations on the other). The authority structure of the domestic group itself is affected by economic and power relations within the larger society. Strategies available to women are in turn related to rules of descent and inheritance, marriage, and access to economic resources. The interaction of these factors can be seen by examining examples of domestic group structure and women's strategies in two different kinds of societies where political and domestic spheres are differentiated: (1) peasant communities in state societies and (2) tribal societies in Africa.

In analyzing family structure and sex roles in forty-six peasant[5] communities, Michaelson and Goldschmidt (1971) find that in both patrilineal and bilateral household types, economic control is in the hands of men. Margery Wolf's material on Taiwanese family life (1968) gives a detailed view of women's responses to the patrilineal extended family patterns which are more generally outlined by Michaelson and Goldschmidt (1971:330). In Taiwan, as in many other peasant societies, women enter patrilocal households as strangers, legitimize their place through the birth of male offspring, and spend their lives involved in domestic chores and the socialization of children. Wolf's hypothesis is that a woman builds a uterine family (i.e. a family based on ties with children and excluding the husband) as a means of counteracting her isolation and as a way of establishing security for her old age. But, of course, this process interferes with the uterine family already established by the young wife's mother-in-law. While raising her children, the older woman has already invested a great deal of effort in securing the loyalty of her son. Thus, a young bride is seen as a threat, someone who can undermine that loyalty. The son, of course, is "in the middle" in the conflicts which arise over each woman's attempt to build her uterine family (Wolf 1972:33–36).

The young wife creates relationships in the women's community outside the family (Wolf 1972:28). She meets other brides who become her allies. In these extra-domestic neighborhood groups, women exercise a good deal of influence over men's decisions through subtle manipulation of opinion and by creating rumors which will damage reputations or cause the menfolk to "lose face."

[5]  Goldschmidt and Kunkel (1971:1058) define peasants as those populations which consist mainly of agricultural producers who have rights in their land, produce primarily for their own subsistence, though also for exchange, and are part of a state-organized political system.

The Taiwanese material in combination with the cross-cultural data presented by Michaelson and Goldschmidt gives the following generalized picture of women's roles and strategies in patrilocal, patrilineal extended families. A father has authority over his sons, and a husband over his wife, which in turn brings about conflict rather than cooperation between women in these groups. The developmental cycle of these peasant extended families (in contrast to the Navajo and hunter-gatherer examples) brings sharp changes in the status of women. As a young bride, a woman enters the group at the lowest status, but as her own children grow she gains influence with her husband and builds loyalty in her sons. As a mother-in-law, she has authority over her daughters-in-law but also sees them as competing for what little influence she has been able to achieve. Women's strategies revolve around "working through men," either through their husbands or through their sons. Within the extended family women's interests never coincide; competition and conflict are to be expected. Cooperation and alliance with other women is usually limited to the less intense relationships outside the domestic group. These informal women's groups, through gossip, exert another kind of informal pressure on men.

Strategies women use, especially in attempting to influence men, differ in bilateral households in peasant societies where the nuclear family, rather than the extended family, is important. A good example comes from Ernestine Friedl's study of a Greek village (1967). Men hold power and authority in the public sphere and are also the official decision-makers in the home. But women have an effective voice in many domestic decisions due to the dowries which they bring to their marriages. In other words, nuclear family structure means that there is no male hierarchy within the domestic group, and the wife, through her control of economic resources, is able to counteract her husband's dominance. She exercises influence over him, but in doing so she is not brought into competition with other women.

## EXTENDED FAMILIES IN AFRICAN SOCIETIES

Tribal societies contrast with peasant societies and allow us to examine additional factors which affect the structure of domestic groups, the distribution of power and authority, and women's strategies. In tribal societies corporate kin groups are the "building blocks" of the political structure. The importance of these extra-domestic kin groups in turn suggests that wives might retain ties with their own groups after marriage and that divorce might be frequent. These ties would give women more leverage against men in the domestic group into which they married, while matrilineal rather than patrilineal descent could also enhance the power of women. Further, polygyny will affect the structure of domestic groups, reduce the unassigned power of each wife, and alter the strategies of women. In order to examine these factors, as well as the importance of a woman's control over economic resources, I will discuss examples from several African societies.

Polygyny itself tends to be associated with societies where women do the bulk of the agricultural work and where husbands can obtain sufficient land to support a number of wives (Goldschmidt and Kunkel 1971:1061). Political or socially stratified divisions within a society also favor the emergence of polygyny, since economic rights to women's labor can be acquired and since marriages can be used to create political alliances between unequal groups (Clignet 1970:21). Further, polygyny is associated with the predominance of male orientations, as indicated by the fact that 84% of African peoples who practice polygyny are also patrilocal (Clignet 1970: 23). Thus in polygynous African societies a common form of the extended family at its most fully developed stage is that of a male head of household with two or more wives (each with her own hut) and their children. Since these domestic groups are most often two generational and not three generational units, the dominance of the husband over the wife is structurally more important and the competition of co-wives is more critical than conflict between mother-in-law and daughter-in-law.

These tensions are clearly illustrated in Cohen's study of marriage and divorce among the Muslim Kanuri of Borny (1971). The typical Kanuri compound is composed of a patrilocal, polygynous family. Women are married very young, often to middle-aged men. A women's ability to control a husband's dominance depends on her ability to withdraw food and sexual services. A second wife can be a considerable threat since the first wife receives less attention, acquires fewer material goods for her children, and loses some of her ability to gain compliance from her husband.

Within the polygynous extended family, then, conflict between co-wives is likely since women compete for goods and services from the husband and since each wife attempts to build a uterine family at the expense of her co-wives and their children. The high divorce rate indicates that divorce itself is a strategy for achieving independence for Kanuri women. Where influence over the husband fails, a woman may force a divorce through insubordination and return to her father's or brother's compound until remarriage. If subsequent marriages are equally unbearable she has the option of living with her son or other male kinsmen over whom she will have a measure of influence and whose respect she commands. There are examples of polygynous extended families where co-wife conflict is minimized, often by a set of rules which carefully govern how often a husband sleeps with each wife and how often she is obligated to cook for him (Leis 1973).

As in peasant societies, a woman's control over economic resources (a factor absent in the Kanuri case) may give her more control over decisions within the domestic group. Furthermore, in many African polygynous societies women gain economic autonomy through trading. Trading not only gives *de facto* independence from the husband's authority (and may ease tensions between co-wives), but it also brings women together in extra-domestic cooperative groups such as trading associations (G. Marshall 1964: Leis 1973).

Another factor which influences female independence of male authority in any given society is the rule of descent and inheritance. For instance, among the Ashanti, matrilineal descent and inheritance, the ability of women to acquire land, and the absence of polygyny appear to maximize the common interests of women and minimize a husband's dominance. Either a man or a woman can become head of an extended family. Marriage ties are brittle and women often live with their mothers or maternal uncles instead of with their husbands (Fortes 1949). Women have equal rights to matrilineage land and occasionally become wealthy, owning more property than their menfolk. Although Ashanti women are often subordinate to their husbands in early married life, they are always able to acquire the beginnings of an independent livelihood from their own matrilineal kin. In other words, an Ashanti woman as she grows older has two possible strategies: either she can build a uterine family which, since it is also the core of a matrilineage, can become a viable household with her at the head, or, she can live with a brother with whom she has considerable influence.

The preceding examples from African societies support the conclusions reached with patri-centered peasant families. As in peasant societies, political and domestic spheres are differentiated (though tribal political systems are very different from peasant ones). Domestic power and authority are in the hands of men, so that women are in a position to influence or "work through men," either sons or husbands. Women's interests do not coincide, and the co-wife relationship is particularly full of conflict. As in the case of bilateral peasant families, where a woman has access to economic resources, her ability to influence those in authority is increased.

Three patterns emerge which contrast the tribal examples with the peasant ones and highlight the effects on women's strategies of ties to a natal kin group, access to economic resources, and rules of descent and inheritance. First, since a woman usually retains ties with her own kin, she may use the support of her male relatives against her husband or sever the marriage tie altogether. Second, women's access to land or cash may make possible the formation of extra-domestic women's groups which have economic functions and which yield considerable political power, in contrast to the Taiwanese neighborhood groups where women seek influence through gossip.[6] Third, a woman's position in a system of matrilineal descent and inhertitance is such that she is likely to have more access to economic resources and domestic authority, making it possible for her to achieve economic independence and the headship of a household in her own right.

Women's strategies and domestic power among working class English and Black lower class families (Lamphere 1974), are two examples from western urban industrialized societies where domestic and political spheres are separated. Superficially, many elements of women's authority and strategies may resemble those found among the Navajo and hunter-gatherer groups. Women make important decisions within the domestic sphere, women's interests often coincide, there is high cooperation between female kin, and strategies of recruitment are similar for both men and women. Women's strategies also focus on "economic" activities (e.g. on the exchange of goods and services among a network of kin). But unlike Navajo, Eskimo, and Bushman women, who have decision-making ability in societies where authority is shared and where politics becomes domestic, authority of working-class and Black women comes by default, for the men are away from the home due to long work hours or they cannot always fill the role of husband-provider because of low positions in unskilled, low-paying jobs. More important, neither women nor men from these groups have access to the centers of power in the larger society nor an equal place in the labor force. These Black women and their white working class counterparts operate autonomously only in the domestic, not in the political or social sphere.

---

[6]   Jane Collier (personal communication) suggests that a necessary condition for the formation of women's groups is a dense rather than scattered settlement pattern (e.g. villages or towns). If domestic power and authority are in the hands of men, women's interests within the domestic group are in conflict and they are unlikely to form groups. Extra-domestic groups would be likely only where women with common interests are living fairly close together. This implies that economic and social factors more accurately account for the absence of female bonding and the paucity of female groups, rather than biological propensities as Tiger (1969) suggests (see Leis 1973, for a more complete analysis).

## CONCLUSIONS

In examining family relationships in a variety of cultures I have taken a female perspective, treating women as political actors who employ strategies to achieve ends. Women's strategies are directly related to the structure of power and authority in the domestic group, and to a woman's position with relation to the developmental cycle. In societies like the Navajo, Eskimo, and Bushman, where domestic and political spheres are integrated, women's strategies focus on cooperation for everyday activities. They are "economic" in the sense that they center on the exchange of goods and services.

In contrast, many societies where domestic and political spheres are separated are also those where the extended family structure is built around a hierarchy of males. Women's strategies here are centered on "political" goals, that is, on influencing the men who hold authority. Thus, wives have subtle methods of changing the minds of husbands, mothers build loyalty in their sons, neighborhood groups of women use gossip to affect the decisions of males within the community, and wives play male kinsmen against their husbands in settling their grievances. Access to economic resources, the ability to withdraw goods and services, or even sheer defiance, give women unassigned power or increase their influence over husbands, sons, and brothers.

An adequate analysis of domestic power not only involves an account of male authority roles, but also an examination of women as strategists, both in terms of making their own decisions and in terms of influencing those of men. Women's strategies are best understood through an analysis of the differences in family power structures, the varying position of women in each type of structure, and the factors which shape the relationship between the domestic sphere and the larger society.

## REFERENCES

BRIGGS, JEAN
   1970   *Never in anger.* Cambridge, Massachusetts: Harvard University Press.
CLIGNET, REMI
   1970   *Many wives, many powers.* Evanston, Illinois: Northwestern University Press.
COHEN, RONALD
   1971   *Dominance and defiance, a study of marital instability in an Islamic society.* Anthropological Studies 6. Washington: American Anthropological Association.

DAMAS, D.
1968 "The diversity of Eskimo societies," in *Man, the hunter.* Edited by Richard Lee and Irving DeVore. Chicago: Aldine.

FORTES, MEYER, *editor*
1949 *Social structure: studies presented to A. R. Radcliffe-Brown.* New York: Russell and Russell.

FRIEDL, ERNESTINE
1967 The position of women: appearance and reality. *Anthropological Quarterly* 40:97–108.

GLUCKMAN, MAX
1950 "Kinship and marriage among the Lozi of Northern Rhodesia and the Zulu of Natal," in *African systems of kinship and marriage.* Edited by A. R. Radcliffe-Brown and Daryll Forde. Oxford: Oxford University Press.

GOLDSCHMIDT, WALTER, EVELYN JACOBSON KUNKEL
1971 The structure of the peasant family. *American Anthropologist* 73: 1058–76.

GOODY, J., *editor*
1958 *The developmental cycle of groups.* Cambridge Papers in Social Anthropology 1. Cambridge: Cambridge University Press.

HOEBEL, E. A.
1954 *The law of primitive man.* New York: Atheneum.

LAMPHERE, LOUISE
1971 "The Navajo cultural system: an analysis of concepts of cooperation and autonomy and their relation to gossip and witchcraft," in *Apachean culture history and ethnology.* Edited by Keith Basso and Morris Opler. University of Arizona Press.
1973 *To run after them: cultural and social bases of cooperation in a Navajo community.* University of Arizona Press.
1974 "Love and hate begin at home: women's strategies, cooperation, and conflict in domestic groups," in *Woman, culture, and society.* Edited by Michelle Rosaldo and Louise Lamphere. Stanford: Stanford University Press.

LEACH, EDMUND
1955 Polyandry, inheritance, and definition of marriage. *Man* 55:182–86.

LEE, RICHARD
1968 "What hunters do for a living or how to make out on scarce resources," in *Man, the hunter.* Edited by Richard Lee and Irving DeVore. Chicago: Aldine.
1972 !Kung spatial organization: an ecological and historical perspective. *Human Ecology* 1(2):125–147.

LEIS, NANCY
1973 "Women in groups: Ijaw women's association," in *Women, culture, and society.* Edited by Michelle Rosaldo and Louise Lamphere. Stanford: Stanford University Press.

MARSHALL, GLORIA
1964 "Women, trade, and the Yoruba family." Unpublished doctoral dissertation. Columbia University, New York.

130   LOUISE LAMPHERE

MARSHALL, LORNA
1959   Marriage among the !Kung Bushman. *Africa* 29(4):335–65.
1960   !Kung Bushman bands. *Africa* 30(4)325–54. (Reprinted in *Comparative political systems*. Edited by J. Cohen and J. Middleton. New York: Natural History Press.)

MICHAELSON, EVELYN JACOBSON, WALTER GOLDSCHMIDT
1971   Female roles and male dominance among peasants. *Southwestern Journal of Anthropology* 27(4):330–353.

PARSONS, TALCOTT
1963a  On the concept of power. *Proceedings of the American Philosophical Society* 107:232–62.
1963b  On the concept of influence. *Public Opinion Quarterly* 27:37–62.

RADCLIFFE-BROWN, A. R.
1950   "Introduction," in *African systems of kinship and marriage*. Edited by A. R. Radcliffe-Brown and Daryll Forde. Oxford: Oxford University Press.

ROSALDO, MICHELLE
1973   "Women in cross-cultural perspective," in *Woman, culture, and society*. Edited by Michelle Rosaldo and Louise Lamphere. Stanford: Stanford University Press.

SPENCER, ROBERT F., JESSE JENNINGS, *et al.*
1965   *The native Americans*. New York: Harper and Row.

TIGER, LIONEL
1969   *Men in groups*. New York: Random House.

WEBER, MAX
1947   *The theory of social and economic organization*. Translated by Q. M. Henderson and Talcott Parsons. Oxford University Press. (Free Press paperback, 1964.)

WITHERSPOON, GARY
1970   A new look at Navajo social organization. *American Anthropologist* 70:55–65.

WOLF, MARGERY
1968   *The house of Lim*. New York: Appleton-Century-Crofts.
1972   *Women and the family in rural Taiwan*. Stanford: Stanford University Press.

YOUNG, MICHAEL, PETER WILLMOTT
1957   *Family and kinship in East London*. London: Routledge and Kegan Paul.

# A Note on a Feminine Factor in Cultural History

ALAN LOMAX

Perhaps a comparativist like me can contribute to the contemporary debate on the woman's questions by pointing out that patterns of male-female relationship, including those that gall this generation, have important social value for some societies and are therefore adhered to by most of its members, as a very keystone of existence. In each of these patterns, each sex has a specialized role which includes a division of labor, structured by and for a particular ecological niche, along with a division of the social attributes of authority, love, credibility, power and creativity that reward each sex in proportion to the duties and risks each must take. This variability in sexual specialization, based on biological differences, has been an important factor in the success of the species, enabling the human race to raise children in every corner and climate of the planet and use as nourishment whatever a society's technology could procure in all these environments.

Nine months of pregnancy, childbirth, carrying and feeding infants for at least a year — these functions with all their burdens and satisfactions have led in most societies to feminine dominance of the nurturant re-

The work for this article was made possible by research grants in aid from the National Institute of Mental Health, The National Science Foundation, the National Endowment for Humanities, the Ford Foundation and the Rockefeller Foundation. The cantometrics and choreometrics projects mentioned are sponsored by the Anthropology Department of Columbia University and are located at 215 West 98 Street, New York, New York 10025.
The cantometric system is a joint invention of the writer and Victor Grauer; codings were done by Lomax, Grauer and Roswell Rudd. The choreometric system is a joint invention of the author, Forrestine Paulay and Irmgard Bartinieff; codings were done by Forrestine Paulay, Irmgard Bartinieff and Lomax.

sponsibilities in the preparation of food and maintenance of the family center. Cross-cultural child-rearing studies show that females are trained for these specialized tasks and more emphasis is put upon nurturance training in raising girls than boys. There is also evidence that the sex that nurtures is rewarded with more than love (Barry, et al. 1957). De Havenon's analysis of family patterns in the Bronx demonstrates that the authority of a family member varies directly with the amount of calories in the food she (or he) habitually ladles out (De Havenon 1971). This is one small indication of the special respect (as well as love) that women derive from their nurturant role.

The sexual division of labor in food production seems to be a crucial factor in determining many other aspects of the relationship between the sexes (Lomax and the Cantometric Staff 1968). This hypothesis and those presented below were tested for correlations using a sizable and well-balanced sample of world cultures. The cultural data was obtained from the *Ethnographic atlas* (Murdock 1967) and from my own cross-cultural studies of performance style. Several hundred cultures have been characterized on the basis of types of food production — gatherers, hunters, gardeners, etc. and then rated according to the contribution of each sex to the central and principal food-getting activity on a scale of relative complementarity of the two sexes (Lomax and the Cantometric Staff 1968).

The division of labor between males and females appears to be a function of climate-linked activity. In the high, cold latitudes, men as hunters and fishers brought in most of the food, whereas women as gatherers and gardeners were responsible for producing more of the food in cultures found at lower, warmer latitudes.[1] In the North, where game and fish often abound, the "wives" of hunters and fishers must stay in some sheltered place in severe weather to protect themselves and keep their small children alive. In the tropics, however, the women who worked as collectors and gardeners could more safely and conveniently take their babies and children with them to their work. Thus, warmer climate has usually favored the complementary productive role of women without reducing their valued nurturant role or putting their babies in danger.

John Marshall captured a glimpse of this prehistory in footage (unpublished) of a young !Kung Bushman mother at work berrying. She is

[1]  The association of hunting and fishing with locations north of 30 degrees latitude and of gardening with locations between 30 degrees north and south has a chi square of p greater than 0.01 level. The association of male dominance of food producing to 30 degrees north and of a complementary role for women in food producing to locations of lower than 30 degrees latitude is at the same level.

singing and dancing as she picks, eats and feeds the tot clinging to her knee and the babe slung to her shoulder, and funnels the rest into her leather bag. Close by in the berry patch, other women, with their children, answer her in sung counterpoint. This same open-voiced choralizing links the bands of gathering women and becomes the basic of the tightly textured vocal polyrhythms to which their hunter/male consorts dance. This performance situation, where women "call the tune," is frequent for the Bushman, but rarely occurs elsewhere.

This "gatherer" style, which makes a tightly woven texture of independent and equal parts (in essence counterpoint), I take to be symbolic, first of a feminine preference for egalitarian interaction and, second, of African gatherer inter-sex complementarity. The feminine contribution to the economy is more than equal and thus may be represented in public communications, such as in music performances. Indeed, every type of multi-leveled, integrated vocalizing is strongly associated with both warmer climates and complementarity in food producing.[2] One notable exception seems to be those societies, such as aboriginal Australia, where women's roles appear to be slave and drone-like.

The contrastive set is found in societies with non-complementary socioeconomic patterns — notably: (1) among the northern hunters and fishers, where women often form passive and eager AUDIENCES for stories of male adventures in food-getting, and (2) among pastoralists, with large animals, and plough and irrigation agriculturalists. All these tasks require great strength or preclude the presence of small children. The main song performance model in all these cases is solo[3] (symbolic of the lone, risk-taking male) or rough unison, the form of coordination frequently employed by male groups from diffusely organized societies in heavy or dangerous tasks.

The historical fluctuation of these two models offers another dimension to the process of cultural evolution. There is general agreement that man's stock of tools, techniques and organizational structures have steadily piled up. My study of performance style in song, dance and speech indicates that modes of articulation and differentiation in communication also increase as aids and reinforcements to man's increasingly complex control of his habitat (Barry, et al. 1957; Lomax and Berkowitz 1972).

---

[2] The association of low latitude (less than 30 degrees) is at the $p < 0.001$ level for polyphony and choral overlap, while the association of productive complementarity with overlapped singing, integrated choral groups and polyphony are at the $p < 0.01$ level as well.

[3] Repetitive solo songs have $p < 0.01$ relative to hunting and fishing and text-laden solo songs have a $p < 0.01$ association to plough and irrigation agriculture.

Now, with the discovery of what I choose to call "the feminine factor" in interaction, it is clear that another climate-and-sex dependent variable has been at work, alongside that of economic development (see Figure 1).

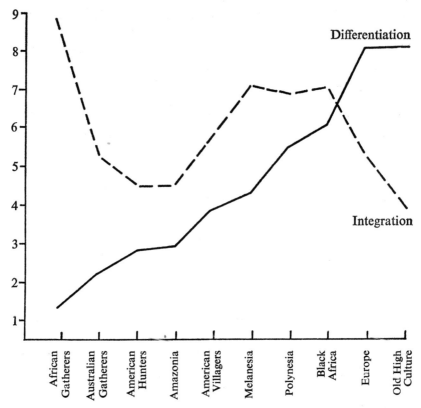

Figure 1.   The weighted means of a differentiative factor (solid line) and an integrative composite factor (broken line) are plotted along a range of culture zones ranged in increasing order of economic complexity. These are two of the main 14 factors derived from factor analysis of 71 scalar measures factored over the sample of 148 world cultures. Half of the measures deal with aspects of social organization, the other half with aspects of song performance. In this analysis song stands for public communication in general. The combined set of variables is useful since it represents the communicative and interactional, as well as the societal and economic.

As my collaborator Conrad Arensberg might put it, the sexual composition of the teams in relation to the economic activity is crucial to the texture of interaction and performance that a culture adopts as its norms. Figure 1 charts this co-variation. The feminine, integrated, polyparted performance factor is high at the beginning of productive history, among tropical gatherers. It is replaced by solo and rough unison among hunters and fishers in the north. It rises again with the advance into full agriculture and peaks in the Amazon, Africa, the Insular Pacific and Central Europe where teams of women tend the fields and reap the harvest. It is replaced by the wailing solos of the "grand pastoralists," and those using the plough and irrigation techniques. Now, as women move into industrial jobs, it begins to emerge again in a general preference for large, cohesive performances in collectives, like ballet, and in mass dramas, such as marching bands. This final trend is perhaps clearest in the socialist world, where children are cared for by the community while their mothers are away at work (see Note 3).

Another though brief look at the cross-cultural evidence about performance differential features of the male and female styles in song and dance indicates that the two sexes bring a different approach to public interaction. The data are derived from the Cantometric analysis of 4000+ field recorded songs from 400+ cultures and from the Choreometric analysis of 400+ dances from 300+ cultures. Both samples include widely distributed cultures. Though most of the differentials are at the level of 10% or less, the general tendencies are very clear.[4] Males perform more frequently in public than females in singing, dancing and especially in playing instruments, and they display more aggression and strength, employing harsher voices and slashing arm movements, loud and accented voices, and large, heavy, straight, swift movements. Males sing more frequently in solos that are wordier, more ornamented and with longer melodic forms than women. Male dances seem to have more movement variation, more spiral movement and more elaborate stepping than do the dances of women. This more aggressive, more forceful and somewhat more articulated model, found in performance, seems to be task linked in the ways already suggested. In this dance/song model the most apparent traits are the animal-like, wind-harshened voice and a wide-legged stance, essential to strong efforts or balance in the snow. This performance profile is prominent in the traditions of the northern latitudes and among peoples of Central Asia, Northern Europe, Amerindia, Malaysia and Australia.

[4] This material is to be published in detail elsewhere. Each of the relationships mentioned is based on the following calculation: first the relative frequency of each trait in the performance of the two sexes is calculated separately, then these relative frequencies are compared. For example, males use harsh singing voices 30% more frequently, sing in public 35% more frequently and play musical instruments in public 69% more frequently at a $p < 0.01$ level of association. On most of the other differentials mentioned the ratios are less than 10%, but significant nonetheless. They indicate that area by area men and women strongly resemble each other in behavior, but do occupy sufficient though closely adjoining segments of the ranges on the behavioral scales cited.

The feminine performance differentials lean in another direction, toward rapport and cooperation. The most outstanding feminine world model employs: (1) a more narrow stance, (2) higher frequency of small range movement. Noisy harsh voice qualities are less frequent. Instead we find vocal openness, high, bell-like notes, soft volume and gentle accents. Feminine dance movements seem to be distinctively more flowing, more rounded, lighter and smaller than those of men. The tenderness of this performance profile suits the role of mother, of nurturer; the slower, softer refrain-filled, rhythmically regular, relatively unembellished and melodically repetitious style of women presents the profile of the lulling song and thus may be its source. This gentle, flowing, regular and simply structured song style makes it easier for the child or others to join in, while the presentation of open palm and the erotic movement of the central body appear to be an active invitation to dance. Indeed, feminine performance symbolizes and reinforces a choral, integrated style; women sing in better vocal blend than do men and their dances are marked by more cohesiveness, especially in the rhythmic sense. It must be noted that these feminine traits mark the performances of the majority of cultures in the warm latitudes and therefore may represent an overall feminine influence upon culture.

These somewhat contrastive male/female profiles are central tendencies from which there is considerable deviation. The largest deviations occur, so far as the present sample can inform us, in two different situations: (1) in Australia and Melanesia, where women have low status, men adopt many of the traits of the feminine dance profile, (2) among African gatherers and Malays, where women might be said to exploit their social advantages over men, women often dance in a more "masculine" way than men do. Thus a basic, though variable, pattern of male/female behavioral differentials seems to be an ancient and functional aspect of the equipment of the human species. The highest peaks of this contrast occur in the Arctic and the Tropic Zones. The balance of the two roles varies somewhat with the balance of economic and political power between the sexes. Thus these male/female differentials have continued to have adaptive usefulness, not only because they are flexible and can be relearned, but because they have met essential biological and cultural needs. The feminine factor, that emerges from these comparative studies, is clearly rooted in the nurturance training of girls and somewhat biases women toward an integrative nurturizing and integrative role in culture. It may be a basic force in shaping some aspects of human culture.

# REFERENCES

BARRY, H., III, M. K. BACON, I. L. CHILD
 1957   A cross-cultural survey of some sex differences in socialization. *Journal of Abnormal Psychology* 55:327–332.

DE HAVENON, ANNA LOU
 1971   "Patterns of superordination in low income urban domiciles." Unpublished paper presented to the American Anthropological Association, New York City.

LOMAX, ALAN, NORMAN BERKOWITZ
 1972   The evolutionary taxonomy of culture. *Science* 177 (July 21):228–239.

LOMAX, ALAN, THE CANTOMETRIC STAFF
 1968   *Folk song style and culture.* American Association for the Advancement of Science.

MURDOCK, GEORGE P.
 1967   *Ethnographic atlas: a summary.* Pittsburgh: University of Pittsburgh Press.

# Non-Hierarchical, Hierarchical, and Masked Reciprocity in the Arab Village

HENRY ROSENFELD

Reciprocal behavior still pervades most areas of daily life in Arab peasant society in Palestine. This is less so today in Israel where most Arab men have become wage laborers outside the village. With the change in the routine and economy of peasant agriculture many customs and occasions for reciprocity lose their point of reference. Nevertheless, "generalized," "balanced" and "negative" reciprocity (Sahlins 1965; Gouldner 1960: 172), what Mauss emphasizes as the triple significance of the obligation to give, to receive, and to repay (Firth 1967:8) still hold true for Arab villagers.

Our concern in this paper is the way in which the expressions and behavior of the men and women engaged in reciprocity reflect their status and condition.[1] We also emphasize the differential meaning for women and for men in the Arab village of reciprocal and economic relations.

The way in which women understand the give and take of reciprocity emphasizes the basic equality that exists among them. That is, there is no status hierarchy between peasant women in the village other than that which may exist within an extended family. Men, on the other hand, who have removed women from the definitive statuses connected with property ownership and power, have the ability to control others, and have established an ideology which rationalizes their superiority, are involved in a ceaseless struggle for positions in a village-wide status hierarchy, and translate the demands of reciprocity into distinctions between themselves. Women, declassed since their mobility is restricted by males, are

---

[1] Perhaps this is close to one of the facets mentioned by Firth in regard to Malinowski's concept of reciprocity: '...throughout his analysis is the demonstration of how such gift exchanges symbolize and maintain status relations' (Firth 1957:218).

the dependents of males (closest male partilineal kin), and protected by them. They cannot engage in reciprocity with men. Nevertheless, kin, especially brothers and sisters, do practice a form of concealed or unconscious gift compensation, what may be called "masked reciprocity," that points up the ongoing structural distinctions which separate them on the one hand and join them on the other.

It is important to understand the position of males in this culture. The backward agrarian economy and repressive tax system has made significant differences in wealth between individuals within a village very unusual. Therefore, status is measured by the property and labor power differences present, and the ability of any single element, family, lineage segment or faction to maintain an advantage. New forces such as growth or decline in the number of lineage members, changes in productive means, changes in factional alignments, etc. impinge on this struggle (Rosenfeld 1964, 1968a). Favoritism, privileges and minor authority given by overlords intensify struggles within and between units, and set the conditions under which social-political relations became structured. The dynamics of politics and of property ownership structure attitudes of prestige, honor and good name, which underlie male hierarchical reciprocity. Male control of village politics and property fixes their dominance over women, influences the non-hierarchical level of reciprocity that prevails between females as well as the ambivalence of reciprocity that exists between the sexes.


## "GENERALIZED" AND "BALANCED" RECIPROCITY IN THE ARAB VILLAGE

The Arab village described in this study is situated in the lower Galilee of Israel (formerly Palestine). There are approximately 3,300 inhabitants, three-fourths Muslim, one-fourth Christian. The economy, until recently, was based on subsistence agriculture in grain crops, vegetables, olive trees, and flocks of goats. Today, wage labor outside the village is fundamental to the livelihood of almost all families.

In this culture there are numerous formal occasions for the expression of "generalized" and "balanced" reciprocity. In many aspects of the daily informal routine, the measuring of what is and what must be given and what is and what must be returned is clearly defined.[2] This includes words

[2]  See Sweet (1960:143) for equivalence in reciprocity: "Between unrelated families, *qurda* 'debt', the custom of reciprocity in kind holds. Bread given one day was promptly returned on the next baking day. The same equivalence held for other items: money for money, tobacco for tobacco, flour for flour; money could never be substituted for the item originally borrowed."

of greeting, visits, feasts, cups of coffee, house building, lending a hand in the fields, giving expression to joy and sorrow, etc. When people give they expect a return.[3] This holds for material and non-material things. Thus recompense is involved when time, interest, even good will are given or shown. For example, the bearer of good news is always presented with a gift. The word for good tidings, *bshara*, also includes the idea of reward.

When one of the women present at the birth is told (by the midwife) that a son has been born, she runs to tell the father. 'O————you have good news. A son comes to you. I want the reward (*bshāra*)'. Then he will give a dress or money. Who will long for it will give. (Granqvist 1947:43–4, 76, 81.)

The person who receives the reward has a duty to return something, albeit a token. There is a clear distinction between the feeling of duty (*wajib*) and strict debt (*dēn*).

If one gives me 2 Pounds *nqūt* (a wedding gift) at my wedding, I must return 2 Pounds. If they give me *bshāra* for announcing Ibrāhīm's return from America, I will return some sweets to them for 10 Pounds, maybe for 10 grush. I told you good news (*bshāra*) and you gave me the reward of sweets (*hilwit bshāra*). I made the duty (*wājib*) which is upon me (by returning something). In *nqūt* I honored you (by my coming) and lend you money, and you will honor me (at some future occasion) and (also) pay back the debt (*den*).

Everyday acts are under the closest scrutiny and the feeling of obligation is intense. A poor, "unloved" co-wife who rarely saw her husband, and had no male children, reported her relations with her husband's elder brother:

Even when I return some coffee, he will let me know that he eased my condition. I am indebted to him (literally, carrying the nice, *haml jmili*). He will not let me rest. Even by speaking they place me in their debt. When we quarrel and then do not talk to each other he is happy. Then he knows I will not come to his house to ask for anything. If they do not speak to me I do not care. If they (her husband's brother's family) visit me then they let me know I am free to borrow from them.

[3] Other examples of reciprocity are from my field notes. Mhammad A. invited the new groom Mahmud R. to dinner because ten years ago Mahmud's father had invited him to dinner after his wedding. When 'Ali M.'s wife gave birth to a son, Salih T. sent a baby goat as a gift; but he had received a lamb at the circumcision of his own son. When Ahmad A. died ten years ago the entire lineage was fed by the S. lineage. Now when 'Abdallah S. returned from a year in prison, the head of A. lineage sent word to the S. people that he was slaughtering for them. Hasan S. prepared supper and invited those who had invited him as a new neighbour when he moved into the house he had bought. Ibrāhīm M. went, some half-hour after his wife who was already working there, to lend a hand in the roofing at Slemān A.'s new house. When he arrived Slemān told him there was no need for him, but Ibrāhīm reminded him that eight years ago he, Slemān, had helped in the building of Ibrāhīm's house.

Reciprocation does not always function smoothly. Individual differences in personality, as well as factors of social structure militate against it. The well-off can afford to be more generous. Face-saving arguments over whose right is greater, which debt has priority, can be settled by giving away property. Here are a few examples:

When the brothers Salem and Salīm S. had their sons circumcised, they invited those of their relatives who had given gifts. They had 4 or 5 pigeons for twenty people. The men were angry and clearly insulted. "If they are poor then better to do nothing. This is not the full duty."

When 'Abdallah D.'s paternal aunt received only a kerchief from him at the circumcision of his son, she refused to attend the festival and gave nothing in return. She was insulted and told her brother to teach his son the custom of the people.

And,

Mhammad A. and 'Ali R. argued bitterly as to who had the right of preparing the meal at the circumcision of 'Abed M.'s son. Mhammad declared the right his, since 'Abed's father had invited him to food when his father died, while 'Ali said he had the right because 'Abed had made the festive meal at his son's circumcision. The people decided the right to be with Mhammad and he gave the feast. A woman said, "His debt was older. And he prepared the feast first. If both are ready then the one with the greatest debt has the right. Mhammad's debt came also from sorrow (the obligation stemming from his father's death)."

Numerous occasions for formalized gift-giving and recompense connected with marriage have been dealt with by Granqvist (1931:124, 127–131, 1935:146; 1947:185). For example, Arab villagers stress the overwhelming FEELING OF INDEBTEDNESS. The need for recompense involves not only material, economic factors, but values, levels of generosity (karem), the threats of magic, etc., what Mauss called the "total social phenomena" (1954:76).

There is also the idea of EQUALIZATION involved in meeting obligations. The two are interrelated. They are the "norm of reciprocity" (Gouldner 1960). Equalization is at the heart of reciprocity: givers and receivers, men and women demand their dignity, good name, face, respect, honor; and seek equality. "'They never come with empty hands... And all must be repaid, or else a man is not a man'" (Granqvist 1965:168).

## RECIPROCITY BETWEEN WOMEN: EQUALITY IS ABSOLUTE

Granqvist discusses the intense feeling of indebtedness and the strict rule of recompense which prevails in women's lives:

Every celebration signifies an increased debt account and new duties; in this way the *fellahin* are burdened with permanent debts. An expression of the strict rule of recompense which prevails in their lives is the proverb: "All is debt even the tear in the eye...." This means that the customary exhibitions of sympathy with another in his sorrow create a debt; if a woman weeps at the death of anyone, the latter's relatives must go and weep with her when one of her relatives dies. Nothing is to be had for nothing; sorrow as well as joy, both are debts (Granqvist 1931:130–31).

And,

...to all the women who now dance for the festival of her sons she must in her turn later on go and dance when they have some celebration. The more she herself dances the less do the other women of the village need to dance at this festival. It is in order not to owe so much dancing to the others that she now dances so much at her sons' circumcision festival (Granqvist 1935: 69–70; also 1947:191).

Women can be active at festivals which are prime occasions for reciprocal behavior. Unlike men they are permitted to personalize and overtly express their feelings about debts and recompense. That is, women can be seen weeping, dancing, carrying gifts, and saying what they think about the failure of other women (and sometimes of men) to do so. Men, who must be extremely careful about loss of face, tend to mask their feelings and, at least, when it comes to the status hierarchy, to mask their reciprocal behavior.

Life for village women is more circumscribed than it is for men. Traditionally, women were restricted to their village of birth or marriage. Occasionally they could visit local markets and participate in festivities of kinspeople living in neighboring villages. Women moved about only with other women or a male family member. Old women however were free of the threat of stain to their family's honor. The restrictions placed on females meant that male contact with females was limited to their kinswomen. However, males could move about alone. The political and economic conditions made for extra-village relationships and enlarged their extra-kin contacts.

The reciprocal relations that obtain among women are demonstrated by the condolence gifts of food given to the family of the deceased by relatives, friends, neighbors. "...Meals are given also in honor of the deceased and his family. But at the same time they are considered debts and loans which the family of the deceased have to repay." The condolence feast is little different from the feast given for those who bring money or other gifts during times of joy at a wedding or circumcision.

Sometimes the family requests the villagers not to bring any food when paying condolences, for they are afraid of the waste and some are afraid of the debt they will incur. From my notes:

When E. S. (a Christian) died, his son, A. E. S., called out before the gathered village women: "O village women, God rewards you for your presence and God willing we will return it to you in marriage (e.g. on a happy occasion). Do me a favor and do not bring any food."
But the woman H. S. A. (from the most prominent family) told him, "No. I am going to bring. Because when my husband died your mother came and the jar of coffee was with her. My husband IS NOT BETTER THAN YOUR FATHER AND I AM NOT BETTER THAN YOUR MOTHER."

As one woman related the event:

"So she brought food. The tray was on her head and the pot (of food) was on the tray and the jar of coffee and the cups were in her hands. And she came with other women from the A. (the prominent Muslim lineage) area. When the Christian women saw them all coming with trays on their heads, they went and brought food also. They were afraid of censure. This is a debt. If the Christian women didn't bring food the deceased's family will be very angry. If the Muslim women bring food and they are not of the same religion how can you appear with your hands empty? They will say, 'As I made your duty big (respected you) so you must make me big.'"

The women pay condolences by weeping at the graveside and during visits to the house of the bereaved. They are either repaying old obligations or creating new ones.

When the neighbors decided to visit H. F. on the death of her son, Umm E. refused to accompany them. "SHE IS NOT BETTER THAN ME AND HER SON IS NOT BETTER THAN MY SON. When my son died, where was she? And I came (previously) and wept for her father." She was adamant in her refusal.

In the following example the women behave (and talk) differently than do the men:

When one of the wealthy notables from a neighboring village died some years ago, his sons sent invitations to all the surrounding villages to attend his burial. All the big men from the A. *hamūla* in the village went. A daughter, R., of the *hamūla* is married to one of the dead man's sons. The women went, as is the custom, the first Thursday after his death. When R.'s mother started off she asked two women (both over fifty years old) of one of the families of the A. *hamūla* to accompany her. They went to get dressed for the visit. Here their mother-in-law intervened:
"No you will not go. They did not come when your uncle (her husband, their father-in-law) died, and last year when your husband (her son and husband of one of her two daughters-in-law preparing to go) died. Why didn't they come? THEY ARE NOT BETTER THAN US. It is forbidden. If you go I will put myself in

front of the wheels (of the bus)." Although many women from the *hamūla* went, the above two did not; two of the mother-in-law's sons, including the husband of one of the above women, attended the burial.

Although the men in this family were offended at the time of their bereavement because this particular family did not pay their respects, the dead man was from such an important family, they still wanted to put in an appearance. The woman just quoted made her accounts with all the women involved. The men were expedient. It is not that men cannot arrive at simple and direct acts of equalization in their reciprocity; they do, but even then, it is in spite of the distinctions they feel exist. Women, meanwhile, are direct and personalizing in their acts and words. They do not allow status distinctions between them. One woman is as good as the next. Two phrases, used between all village women from all families without distinction as to wealth or status, give expression to their feeling of equality: "You are not greater than me and your father is not greater than mine" and "You are a nine month daughter and I am a nine month daughter."

The sphere for active reciprocity open to women is almost totally limited to expressions of joy and sorrow connected with the *rites de passage*, at birth, marriage and death. The quality of reciprocity between women is more clearly personal and equal, and certainly more immediate and direct than it is among men. Women see their common condition, and will not tolerate distinctions within their ranks of assumptions of superiority on anyone's part. No woman is allowed to assume a status position which gives her the ability to control or to have authority, though within their daily work routines or on occasions when reciprocation is in question, the bickering can be far sharper than among men. Men struggle either to humble one another or to preserve the existing hierarchy by manipulating social, political and economic forces; they require little bickering to establish the existence of an hierarchy. "They do not waste their words, the men" (Granqvist 1945:156). Women have long been humbled and their struggle has been to not allow a status hierarchy to form among them. They do not allow a woman to assume the status of a man.[4] It is therefore the women who are more sensitive to what they consider to be discrimination. They measure everything, every act and every woman. They demand

---

[4] There are the rare exceptions that serve to emphasize the rule: the loved and perhaps pampered daughter of a sheikh who speaks her mind, sometimes sits with the men, etc. or the wealthy widow with grown sons and a strong personality who may have economic concerns in common with men. These moments of structural freedom rarely last, e.g. the sheikh's daughter eventually marries and must contend with her husband's status demands and the widow's sons marry and they and her daughters-in-law demand their right in the household.

·   equality, which they personalize, and the smallest distinction among them
does not go unnoticed.

All positions of authority are in the hands of males. They are the household heads and control the household economy. They own or control
productive means. Village women rarely own real property other than
their personal clothing and part of their bride price. The patriarchs operate
the lineage-factional power struggle within the village and, at times, in
regard to other villages. Women, through their marriages, connect families
and lineages into power factions. But, they have little say in these or any
other matters. All women in the village toil; there are no female servants.
Even though there are differences in family status, the bride price for all
the village women is relatively the same. Endogamous marriage costs the
most in the largest and most powerful lineages, and women of these lineages enjoy a prestigious name. But because of the factional conditions
existing in the village, and the struggle within and between lineages for
position, this endogamy is never complete. In order to extend alliances,
every family or lineage takes wives from outside its group as well; and in
order not to alienate allies, and to make sure that the latter will not use
their women for their own political purposes, they must also give women
to others[5] (Rosenfeld 1968a:257–259).

Women enjoy a husband's status, or that of their patrilineal kin line.
Their sense of pride and person is inseparable from their family-lineage
tie, but they are not allowed to exploit it. Women are dependents. They

---

[5]   In this study I discuss peasant women [*fellāhāt*]. In most villages in Israel (and in the
past in Palestine), they represent the ONLY village women. In some villages, however,
there are women who enjoy higher status. This can be seen for example, in the seating
arrangement at weddings or other festivals when these women are seated on chairs
(in a more or less ranked order from the center out), and not on mats as are the
*fellāhāt*. This is so in villages where some of the men are truly 'big' men, big landowners
with many hired workers. Their wives and daughters may benefit by both the economic
condition and status privilege that marriage or birth has given. They are commonly
women who are married within and between important families. They do not do physical labor outside the household. They often have the wives and daughters of the
husband's share-croppers and helpers to haul and fetch water for them. They often
take on the urban created veil; they are 'CITIFIED' women. In these situations where a
village dwelling family assumed a power and economic position not so different from
that of non-village dwelling landlords and merchants, the status of their women, old
and young, was higher than that of the peasant women. In some instances, such women
received small property grants from their fathers. This however remains rare. It is an
ascribed status, not an independent status where the woman enjoys her father's and/or
her husband's status. The man loses nothing in the process, rather he gains for she
reflects his higher status. However, the high status a woman gains can only be enjoyed
in regard to women, it never allows her power. The conditions which create the higher
status of these women, highlight the operation of the structural conditions which make
a male status hierarchy.

enjoy kin-family protection as long as they forfeit their claim to the property of their father's house to their men (Rosenfeld 1960). It appears that living in a world of kinship, and being restricted to kin relations, makes for the highly direct and personal usages of women in regard to their acts of formal reciprocation.


## RECIPROCITY BETWEEN MEN: EQUALITY IN OVERT BEHAVIOR WHILE UNDERLYING STATUS DIFFERENTIALS EXIST

Men have been instrumental in keeping the status of equality among women. They cannot change their status. There are concrete material differences between the propertied patriarch and the son who owns nothing; or between the better-off landholders and the poor craftsmen, tenant farmers, servants, watchmen and shepherds with whom they deal. However, control over the affairs of a large descent group, representing a faction or an entire village or becoming the civil representative of the external government, shape distinctions between males. Altering statuses and material conditions make their worlds one of constant struggle. An extreme example of "negative" reciprocity where men exploit the accepted patterns of generosity, honor, and face-saving by a simple "visit" was described.

My companion O. tells me that his friends are out to ruin I. (a notable from a village seven miles away). On one pretext or another, they have come to visit I. six or seven times over the last couple of months.O.'s friends bring notables and their followers to I.'s house and I. must slaughter each time in honor of their visit or lose face. O. tells me they have finished I.'s flock and intend "to destroy his house down to its foundations."

The above, is an extreme instance of men "working" the visiting system. Generally speaking, the existing distinctions between men in terms of material means and power dictate a pattern of formalized ranking in their reciprocal acts. For example, at the end of the Great Feast of *Ramadan*, families visit and bless one another. While respect may be given first to the aged, it is the key personages in the key families of a lineage who are actually given precedence. The greater does not visit the lesser first, rather he honors those who acknowledge his superiority by a return visit.

At this time of formal reciprocal visiting, the village internal status-power system is writ large. The guest room of the lineage's head, of the common guest house of the lineage or area which this man controls, is his seat. His kinsmen and members of the families and lineages joined to him in a factional alliance come to pay respect and reassert their formal allegiance.

Often a person who has been reduced by government intervention or by changing factional fortune will see a close relative of a member or another lineage elevated by the rapid transfer of political recognition to another. For a year or two, his close kinsmen may pay him their first visits at the Great Feast, but it is their own dependence on an alliance with THE POWER and with government allocated authority that is finally definitive. Allies cannot remain indecisive too long. They become former allies to the old power and new allies to the new power. They pay first respects at the mutual visits after the Great Feast. They set a new direction for the old pattern in reciprocal visiting.

Reciprocity functions according to status differences. When a "big" man comes to visit a "lesser" man, the entire household of the latter is honored. For example when friends and neighbours were invited for the circumcision feast of A.'s son, it was the household head who did the inviting. Many of the guests, especially those from other villages, came because of him and regarded it as his celebration. Some gave presents directly to him. In these terms one man is not as good as another nor are their fathers. There are men in similar circumstances, both relatives and friends, who act simply and directly with one another, who minimize or disregard the etiquette of perfect (of "generalized" or of "balanced") reciprocity. But, in general, the format of reciprocity provided one of the means of expressing inequality as well as equality.

RECIPROCITY BETWEEN MEN AND WOMEN: THERE IS LITTLE MEETING GROUND FOR RECIPROCITY BETWEEN THE SEXES; BUT, COVERTLY, MEN SENSE THAT THEY ARE INDEBTED TO WOMEN

Although women are declassed by men, and the life spheres of male and female are distinct and often separate, there are situations when acts of "masked reciprocity" link them together. Here men give gifts to women. The gifts are in fact a way of discharging indebtedness. Male gift-givers do not say that they are reciprocating for what the women have previously given them. In fact they do not consciously recognize that they owe these females anything. The term "masked reciprocity" refers to the fact that men hide the true reasons for the gifts they give, refuse to or cannot understand why they give them, or offer only superficial reasons for doing so. Further, there it is not an immediate give and return, but rather an unconscious and long term, and perhaps never-ending, process, which is an expression of the ongoing structural-ideological relationship existing between male and female kinsmen. There are three such institutionalized expressions of compensatory, but masked, gift-giving.

1. *'Īdiyye*, a gift. It is the duty of the brother or father to send his sister or daughter a gift *'īdiyye*, of money, food or clothing on the occasion of the Great Feast. While giving *'īdiyye* is formalized and done on a specific occasion, the brother may also send his married sister meat when he has a surplus of it, extra food from feasts, etc. Her mother may also send her *'īdiyye*. Behind these gifts is the commitment that the sister-daughter remain part of the extended family of origin.

As the villagers say, "The women is a short rib. She cannot take her right alone. She is always under the rule of her father, brother, or uncle. This is *'īdiyye*, for her sake." Failure of the brother to give a gift is a great blow to the sister, for it weakens her position in her own eyes, as well as those of her husband and neighbors.

The sister gives her property rights to her father's house over to her brother. But she keeps her kin protected status. The gift of *'īdiyye* is called a duty but it is in reality a debt payment. It is a COUNTER-GIFT in compensation for her forefeiting her rights to property. If she does not yield her rights in property, then there are no gifts, no rights of kin protection and the house is closed to her. In other words there is no reciprocity, overt or covert.

2. *Sdaq raqbatha*, the bride price. The villagers separate the words for the whole bride price and that share of it that goes to the woman. Most of the bride price paid in the last two hundred years had gone to the father, brother or guardian. The remaining share was not an additional payment but the total portion the bride received, approximately 30–50% including clothes, bracelets, other ornaments and often a necklace of gold coins.

Today a larger portion is sometimes given to the bride among the Muslims in the village we are discussing. The Christian Arabs tend to give most (and often all) of the bride price to the girl. In addition, her father often adds to it. Moreover, the present-day demands placed on the groom to build a house or a room as part of the terms of the marriage agreement, often reduces, or absorbs the bride price, and lessens the investment in the bride's share.

Thus, among the village Arabs the father or brother uses the bride price. The daughter gets her wedding outfit and perhaps other objects, and is given a compensatory gift, which means that she is protected, watched over and still a family member. But it also means that there are limits to a father's or brother's ability to underwrite their daughter's/sister's future, since they have declassed her by not allowing her full rights, they have restricted her freedom of movement, her possibilities of employment, her independence, etc.[6]

There are many social contradictions that harass women. A young widow will be remarried, but if she has children they must remain behind in her husband's house. In the rare instance when she is allowed to remain with her children without remarrying, she may be forced to compensate her brother or father by giving half a bride price (a widow's bride price). She not only does not take her property rights in her father's house, she does not take them in her husband's house either. Her property will go to the sons and, while a mother is not put aside, she is a dependent and moves about from son's house to son's house (Rosenfeld 1957; 1960).

3. *The man's gift of clothing to his sister at his son's wedding.* It is customary for the father to buy his sister some clothes or a dress on the occasion of his son's wedding. Often other female relatives, members of his immediate paternal line or in-laws, sometimes wives of close friends, are also given dresses. This customary duty is often overlooked if the sisters are numerous, or the father is short of money. The women are sensitive about their brother's failure to appear with a gift. Her husband's family and her neighbors measure the strength of the relationship between brother and sister according to the degree of attention he shows her and the gifts he gives.

The long history of the numerous gifts at weddings and especially of clothing and mantles (Granqvist 1931:126–130) often makes it difficult to establish a simple function for each particular one for they have multiple significance (Mauss 1954:36–37). When a man gives a gift to a friend's wife at his own son's wedding it can have the very general meaning of a show of respect and happiness, or it can mean he regards her as his own female relative. It can also be given to reimburse his friend for the wedding gift he anticipates receiving. There appears to be a definite and enduring structural meaning behind the duty to give a gift to one's sister and other female relatives at one's wedding and on the occasion of a son's

---

[6]   Granqvist emphasizes that there is a feeling of guilt, perhaps because the bride herself ought to have the bride price. These guilts are linked to the presents a brother gives to his sister.

"The consciousness of guilt may be partly due to the feeling the woman herself ought to have the bride price when really one of her male relatives – usually a brother – benefits at her expense. Closely connected with this is probably the feeling of guilt towards a sister which a brother always has, especially the brother who gets his bride by means of her marriage, and which is expressed in the obligation to protect her and give her presents as long as she lives" (Granqvist 1931:138–139).

wedding. Men are saying to their women that they are valued, protected, not forgotten and that their natal house is always open to them in time of need. What is not made explicit is that he does his duty because he is indebted to women who have paved his way to being a household head and that he owes and continues to owe a debt to his sister.

There is also a difference in degree of obligation when a groom gives a gift to his own sister or when the father of the groom is giving the gift. In the former instance, a gift must be given. But in the latter, the feeling of obligation remains. There is less sense of immediacy. That is, with the passage of time there is less need to express the protective element towards a sister who by then probably has grown children of her own. The gift of clothing now means little more than the habit of concern of a brother for a sister.

A counter-gift is also given. If the sister gets such a gift from her brother on his son's wedding, she and her husband return a wedding gift (today usually in the form of money) equal to or of more value than the garment she received. The root of the habit is in the ongoing indebtedness of the men to their sisters. Males take females' property which they use to marry. The son inherits the father's debt and his gift (a dress, cloth) is a symbolic repayment.

A sister should but does not necessarily give a counter-gift at her brother's son's wedding. Moreover, of course, her husband also has to some degree become involved in the force of indebtedness and the multiple demands of in-lawship. Men (in those instances where their sisters and females are involved) do not necessarily expect a gift and are not insulted when one isn't given.

The gifts of brother to sister at his son's wedding are counter-gifts by men to women whom they have declassed and who have or are going to forfeit their right to property.


## THE MEANING OF RECIPROCITY TODAY: FOR MEN THE STATUS HIERARCHY IS NOW MINIMAL; FOR WOMEN, SOME STATUS DIFFERENTIALS HAVE BEGUN TO APPEAR

Though these patterns of reciprocity are present in the Arab village today, economic and social transformations are altering their form. For example, although farming is important, most village income is from wage labor outside it. Tractors and rented harvesters now appear in the village. The owners are not interested in reciprocal harvesting but rather in the profits obtained with the machines, and since most young men work outside the village, it is in any case very difficult to get reciprocating hand-harvesting work gangs together. Formerly an entire village quarter of kin and neighbors was active in the roofing of a new house. Today, the cement mixer reduces by half the number of people required to do the job. Technological and occupational changes have reduced the opportunity for routine reciprocity. And, the effects are strong. In one case, workers from the most prestigious families and lineages in the village, stopped young men from less prestigious lineages and demanded to know why the latter hadn't returned a gift on their brother's wedding. In each case they said, among other things, "Don't think we need your money. AND YOUR FATHER IS NOT GREATER THAN MY FATHER."

Thus, while many men try to preserve the fictions of the past status hierarchy, the effect of the economic and occupational transformation of the village has been to have men regard themselves as equals. They state their equality, and on occasion demand it.

On the other hand, piped water and electricity are changing the nature of household labor and the equality of female relationships is also changing. Some women are new "housewives," that is, they do not deal with the round of tasks of the *fellahat,* so they no longer consider themselves peasants. They are a small but distinct group who (like their non-manual working husbands) tend to separate themselves from other women in the village. Their spheres of interest are different and their reciprocal concerns are becoming more limited. They become less expressive, less personal, and more reserved in their reciprocal behavior. As educational and occupational distinctions between women appear, the equality between them becomes less. At the same time, though gifts for condolence, marriage, circumcision still have some prominence, they more and more tend to be combined wife-husband gifts given in the name of the individual household. That part of a woman's sense of individuality and self-importance formerly derived from her family-lineage is decreasing.

## REFERENCES

CHATILA, KHALED
    1934    *Le marriage chez les musulmans en Syrie.* Paris: Paul Geuthner.
FIRTH, RAYMOND, *editor*
    1957    "The place of Malinowski in the history of economic anthropology," in *Man and culture: an evaluation of the work of Bronislaw Malinowski.* Edited by Raymond Firth. New York and Evanston: Harper and Row.

1967 "Themes in economic anthropology: a general comment," in *Themes in economic anthropology* Edited by Raymond Firth. A. S. A. Monographs 6. London: Tavistock Publications.

GOULDNER, ALVIN W.

1960 The norm of reciprocity: a preliminary statement. *American Sociological Review* 25:161–178.

GRANQVIST, HILMA

1931 *Marriage conditions in a Palestinian village*, volume one. *Commentationes Humanarum Litterarum*. Helsingfors: Societas Scientarium Fennica.

1935 *Marriage conditions in a Palestinian village*, volume two. *Commentationes Humanarum Litterarum*. Helsingfors: Societas Scientarium Fennica.

1947 *Birth and childhood among the Arabs*. Helsingfors: Soderstrom.

1965 *Muslim death and burial. Commentationes Humanarum Litterarum* 34:1. Helsingfors: Societas Scientarium Fennica.

MALINOWSKI, BRONISLAW

1940 *Crime and custom in savage society*. London: Kegan Paul, Trench, Trubner.

MAUSS, MARCEL

1954 *The gift*. Glencoe: The Free Press.

ROSENFELD, HENRY

1957 An analysis of marriage and marriage statistics for a Moslem and Christian Arab village. *International Archives of Ethnography* 68:32-62.

1958 Processes of structural change within the Arab village family. *American Anthropologist* 60:1127–1139.

1960 On determinants of the status of Arab village women. *Man* 40:66–70.

1964 "From peasantry to wage labor and residual peasantry: the transformation of an Arab village," in *Process and pattern in culture, essays in honour of Julian H. Steward*. Edited by Robert A. Manners. Chicago: Aldine.

1968a "The contradictions between property, kinship and power, as reflected in the marriage system of an Arab village," in *Contributions to Mediterranean sociology*. Edited by J. G. Peristiany. Publications of the Social Science Centre Athens, 4. The Hague: Mouton.

1968b Change, barriers to change and contradictions in the Arab village family. *American Anthropologist* 70 (4).

1972 "An overview and critique of the literature on rural politics and social change," in *Rural politics and social change in the Middle East*. Edited by Richard Antoun and Iliya Harik. Bloomington: Indiana University Press.

SAHLINS, MARSHALL D.

1965 "On the sociology of primitive exchange," in *The relevance of models for social anthropology*. A. S. A. Monographs 1. London: Tavistock Publications; New York: Frederick A. Praeger.

SWEET, LOUISE E.

1960 *Tell Toqaan: a Syrian village*. Anthropological Papers 14, Museum of Anthropology, University of Michigan. Ann Arbor: University of Michigan.

# Bundu: Political Implications of Female Solidarity in a Secret Society

CAROL P. HOFFER

In societies where women bond together through initiation ceremonies and life-long membership in a secret society, their political status appears to be enhanced. The Bundu[1] society pervades Sierra Leone where an estimated 95% of all women in the provinces are initiates (Margai 1948:228), and spills across the border into Liberia.[2] It has existed in this area at least since 1668 when it was accurately described by Olfert Dapper (Fyfe 1964:39-40). Women are assured of respect as wives, procreators and rearers of children through the traditional laws of Bundu, these laws being binding upon all adults, both male and female, initiate and non-initiate.

Bundu women have the right to impose fines upon men or women who break their secret society's laws, and to treat offenders for any illness that might result from their transgressions. Disrespect toward women not only offends the living, but also the ancestors, who are the ultimate source of all secret society law and all blessings.

Bundu women learn herbal and psychic medicine and have the recognized right to use them negatively if their special interests are threatened, or positively for the welfare of the larger society. This socially patterned and recognized control of women's "medicine" constitutes a kind of political authority and power. Officials in local chapters of Bundu acquire

This paper is based upon a year's field work in the Moyamba District of Sierra Leone in 1969–1970 and a follow-up study in 1971–1972, generously financed by the National Science Foundation and Franklin and Marshall College.
[1] *Bundu* is the Temme term commonly used in anthropological literature. *Bondo* is the Sherbro term and *Sande* the Mende and Kpelle terms for the same sodality.
[2] Fulton's statement that "men dominate all aspects of Kpelle life," including the secret societies (1972:1231), might be reassessed in the light of this paper.

leadership experience that comes with holding responsible office, and because of their ability and influence are often chosen for secular offices such as headman or chief (Hoffer 1971, 1972, 1974).

Although childbearing and rearing is the essential core of a woman's role in the domestic domain, through Bundu and their economic activities women's influence extends easily into the juro-political domain as well. Women who are at the same time mothers and political figures occupy 10 of the 81 paramount chieftaincies in the Mende/Sherbro ethnic area of Sierra Leone today. Women also have served in the Sierra Leone civil service, parliament, and, in international organizations, women have enjoyed high office for centuries (Hoffer 1972:151).


BUNDU AND POLITICAL BONDING

There are anthropologists who take a speculative evolutionary view of the human condition and conclude that women in high office constitute an aberration of human nature. Emphasizing hunting over gathering, they suggest that because women do not share in the risks of the hunt they are not able to bond into political groups and do not have experience in decision-making. Therefoie, since women have no experience in political decision-making, according to Tiger, "even a partly female dominated polity may go beyond the parameters of 'healthy possibility'" (1969:259).

Recent work by Goodale (1971:169) and Lee (1968:259) indicate that in tropical environments women hunt medium and small game with trained dogs, as in the Tiwi case, and may provide 2 to 3 times as much food, including protein. This is true for the Bushman case. One might even speculate that the decisions women make in the food quest are superior to those made by men who expend great effort for lesser returns. Among the agricultural people of Sierra Leone, women take major responsibility for growing, storing and marketing food.

In regard to risk-taking and social bonding, females in the hominid line have been experiencing the hazards of childbirth for at least as long as males have been experiencing the risk of hunting large animals. Childbirth is no less a social act than hunting, usually involving at a minimum the woman in labor and the midwife. In some societies the kind of social group focused upon childbirth, child care, and the acquisition of other womanly skills and graces has become highly institutionalized. The Bundu society enhances female solidarity based upon mutual assistance, and its leaders do enjoy a great deal of political experience in their decision-making and executive roles.

## INITIATION

At puberty, girls are ritually separated from the larger society for weeks or months. They go into the Bundu bush, a cleared place in the forest, where men and other uninitiated persons must not go. There they are intensely trained to womanly responsibilities by mature Bundu women. They are made vividly aware of their incipient womanhood and their value to the larger society, especially as the bearers of children.

Shortly after entering the Bundu bush, girls experience the surgery distinctive of a Bundu woman in which the clitoris and part of the labia are excised. It is a woman, the *Majo* (Mende), or head of a localized Bundu chapter, who usually performs this surgery. Bundu woman told me that excision helps women to become prolific bearers of children. A *Majo* reputed "to have a good hand" will attract many initiates to her Bundu bush, increasing her social influence in the process. Informants also said the surgery made women clean. One might speculate along the lines Douglas has developed that by excising the clitoris, a rudiment of male-ness, all sexual ambiguity is removed from the incipient woman. She then fits purely and "safely" into the social structure, free from the impurity and "danger" of categorical ambiguity (Douglas 1966).

In most societies with initiation surgery, the resultant visible scar or body modification is a sign that the initiated adult has been brought within a moral sphere. For a member of Poro, the men's initiation society in this Mende/Sherbro ethnic area, the pattern of scars on a man's back signify that he is one of "those who may procreate." In the Poro bush he was in-structed in the social responsibilities that go with sexual intercourse, and has sworn an oath to behave responsibly or suffer the consequences which an affront to the living and the ancestors would engender.

For a Bundu woman, her scars and body modifications can only be known through intimate contact, by the partner with whom she is sharing a sexual relationship. He, upon knowing she is a Bundu woman, can be confident that she is also trained in the moral and social responsibilities of a potential procreator.

In the initiation grove girls bathe often and are inactive during the healing stage. Later they become more active in the pursuit of farming and household skills, especially by giving service on their leader's farm, in-creasing that leader's wealth. Since these girls have been assisting their mothers for years, the emphasis is not on learning new skills so much as on learning new attitudes toward their work. Instead of doing this work in the role of a daughter, they begin to anticipate the role of wife who must work cooperatively with her co-wives and her husband's female kin. Although new attitudes are learned, there is marked continuity in the daily activities a female performs throughout childhood and adulthood. There is no imagery of death and rebirth in Bundu initiation ceremonies, as there is in Poro where boys give up a more carefree childhood in taking on adult tasks.

There is pain and risk of death from infection in the initial ordeal in the Bundu grove. This shared experience helps to bond the initiates together into a cohesive social group. They swear an oath in the Bundu bush never to reveal any fault of another Bundu woman. There are pleasures to be enjoyed as well as ordeals, and the girls go gladly into the initiation grove. Food is plentiful since the initiation season occurs in the post-harvest dry season and each girl's family is obliged to send large quantities of rather special food into the initiation grove on her behalf. There are also special Bundu songs, dances and stories to be enjoyed around the fire in the evening. The stories usually end with an instructive moral linked to Bundu laws given to the living by ancestresses of the secret society. Girls also learn a great deal about the medical and magical properties of plants, feminine hygiene, and childbirth, which commonly takes place in the Bundu bush in rural areas.

After the initiation ceremonies have been completed and the girls reincorporated into society in the status of women, they are eligible for marriage and childbearing. Bundu has a monopoly on certifying women as eligible wives, and women as a social group have a monopoly on production of a scarce resource: offspring for their husband's patrilineages. To withhold that "good" is to have great power. A woman can justifiably withhold herself from her husband if his behavior contravenes Bundu law. Rarely, however, would she do so since it is in her own self-interest to bear children. Children give her an honored status and rewarding roles to play during her fertile years. Children also give her emotional and economic security in old age. After death, her children will remember her, giving her immortality.


BUNDU ORGANIZATION

Bundu is not centrally organized but exists in autonomous localized chapters, whenever a prominent woman who herself has been initiated and knows the secrets of the society, can attract a following. In some villages, Lungi in Moyamba District for example, all Bundu women were buried in an area within the village, the great mound being a daily reminder of their on-going blessings and the authority of their laws.

Although Bundu lack an over-all hierarchical organization, the local chapters do have a leader, a council of advising elder women, and women in other offices with specialized functions. The leaders of discrete chapters communicate with each other and travel to other chapters to assist in initiation ceremonies, thus achieving an informal integration of the society through a wide area. Each leader has a tangible symbol of her office, and can also make her position known through speech and gesture. She will be received with respect among other Bundu women, even in foreign ethnic and linguistic areas.

Poro is the equivalent men's initiation society, and leaders of autonomous chapters of Poro in Sierra Leone dramatically coordinated their activities in planning and executing the Hut Tax War, a sudden rebellion against British colonial domination in 1898 (Fyfe 1962:556ff; 1964:247; Mannah-Kpaka 1953:36). There has been no Women's War in Sierra Leone as there has been for Igbo women of Nigeria, but if their special interests are grievously threatened, it is possible that the women of Sierra Leone, through the Bundu society, could cooperate widely in rebellious behavior.

Poro and Bundu do not exist in opposition to each other, but each has its particular domain of social control which complements the other. Poro officials, for example, see that wells are kept clean and scarce resources are conserved while Bundu officials act as midwives or treat certain illnesses. The particular restrictions imposed or services rendered emanate from only one sodality without any overlap of authority and the risk of a contest of power. The restrictions and services pertain as much to those within a secret society as to those without, the sodalities existing to serve the welfare of the larger society.

Poro and Bundu, both guarding their respective secret knowledge and powers, are connected through a few extraordinary women who are members of Poro. An important official of the Poro society must be a woman. Other women who inadvertantly discover Poro secrets are initiated into the secret society in order to be brought directly within its moral sphere of control. The female co-leader of the (Mende) Njaye society (Yasse in Sherbro), by virtue of her office, is also a Poro member in some areas. Bundu, on the other hand, has no male members.

## THE EXERCISE OF POWER BY WOMEN THROUGH BUNDU

Paramount chiefs in the Mende and Sherbro ethnic areas are secular leaders. They are the descendants of pioneers or warriors who first settled or conquered an area. Their ancestors give guidance and blessings to the people and the land. The chief, as a descendant of the founder, is the "owner of the land" and is concerned with such matters as the proper behavior of immigrants within a patron-client context, the adjudication of land boundary disputes, or the collection of taxes for the national government.

Bundu, Poro, and other secret societies act as a religious counterbalance to the secular power of chiefs. Traditional laws of correct behavior come from the time of the ancestors. Certain classes of traditional law are upheld by the secret societies in the name of the ancestors, the ancestral spirits being made manifest during special occasions as masked figures. Should a chief transgress against those laws, he would be especially advised by secret society elders, and in case of extreme intransigence, might be carried away to the appropriate secret society grove for further instruction and even physical punishment.

The incumbent Paramount Chief of Kagboro Chiefdom has chosen the local head of the Bundu society as her top-ranked sub-chief, and the head of the Poro society as her speaker, indicating the importance of secret society support and cooperation if one is to rule successfully. Two of the wards in her domestic household, as well, are children of heads of secret societies. Twice in recent years she has been involved in contests of power with the secret societies in this dynamic political system of checks and balances (Hoffer 1971:294ff., 312ff.).

In 1957 in Tane Chiefdom in the Temne area, a commission of enquiry recommended that the paramount chief, a man, be deposed for having "offended against native law and custom" (Sierra Leone 1957:19). One of his offences, as reported by the leader of Bundu in his area, was to enter the house where Bundu women and initiates sleep during the initiation season, strike a match, and see them. Another Bundu woman testified that he looked on at a ceremony and saw the "medicine" of the society: "It is not allowed for him to see our medicine; but, as he has done so, he has destroyed my life" (Sierra Leone 1957:19).

In this case in which a paramount chief was deposed, women of the Bundu society gave testimony as representatives of a political interest group, and their interests are clearly protected by native law. Had not justice, from their point of view, been done, the offending chief or his kin risked retributive sickness, impotence or death from the ancestresses of the Bundu society. Had the paramount chief lied and tried to deny his offences, he would have been asked to swear an oath on the "medicine" of the Bundu society. Most likely he would tell the truth rather than risk the consequences, for the "medicine" directly links the defendant to the power of the ancestors.

Turning again to Kagboro Chiefdom, Paramount Chief Samuel Africanus Caulker, who ruled from 1919 to 1932, became an imperious old fellow, and used abusive language in talking to his wives. As the story is told, after an especially colorful outburst, an abused wife said: "Excuse me sir. Did you say...?" and she repeated the offending phrase. "You are... right," he replied. The wife went away, but returned with the Bundu women of the town. They physically carried the paramount chief away to the Bundu bush. When he came back, a (male) informant narrated, "he was soooo mild."

Within neighborhoods of larger provincial towns, Bundu women tend to stick together, giving each other advice and assistance. During holidays and the initiation season, groups of Bundu women go out through the streets of the town, singing their songs and dancing. To see a close-packed contingent of Bundu women dancing through the street, singing their exclusive songs, shaking their gourd rattles in time with their swaying, is to see a display of female solidarity. Even in Freetown, the only truly urban area in Sierra Leone, Bundu offers companionship, mutual help and assistance in life crisis events which most women experience (Banton 1957:185).

Bundu domestic and social functions have survived urbanization and the Western institutions of parliamentary democracy which could have made Bundu's political functions obsolete. Members of the Sierra Leone House of Representatives are elected by direct vote, both men and women being enfranchised. A Mende paramount chief in Moyamba District is most prominent in the Bundu society. With her sister as leader of a chapter she has in the past requested that all initiates in her chiefdom come to the Bundu bush outside her residential compound for initiation. Both male and female informants have told me that she uses the Bundu society to attract a personal following just as her father who preceded her in office used Wunde, a secret society of warriors, to obtain oaths of loyalty. This kind of support can be translated into votes in the ballot box, and members of the House of Representatives, standing for election, actively court the support of chiefs and secret society leaders.

In the mid-1960's the above-mentioned paramount chief was also a cabinet minister in the Sierra Leone government. When she stood for election to one of the chief's seats in the House of Representatives, she was accused of "swearing them in the bushes." This is a commonly-heard charge in Sierra Leone elections, meaning that the candidate was insuring votes by administering an oath of loyalty sworn upon the "medicine" of a secret society in that society's grove or "bush." In this case,[3] the voters'

---

[3]  Cartwright (1970:247-8) gives 3 other cases. In one, an official of Bundu in the

oaths were allegedly being sworn on medicine of the Bundu society and other societies in which she had influence.

This particular election is instructive since the chief described above had another woman paramount chief as her opponent in the election. The latter chief is something of an anomaly, not being a member of Bundu. Whenever she rose to speak at political rallies a contingent of Bundu women would also rise, drowning her words in their singing.

At least one woman chief has used Bundu to augment her political alliance-making capacity. She was Paramount Chief of Kaiyamba Chiefdom (Mende) at the turn of the century, renowned for her womanly grace as well as her political power. Families sought to have their girls trained and initiated in the Bundu chapter she sponsored. She selected girls from powerful descent groups, initiated them into Bundu, and at their parents' urging, kept them in her household as wards. Later, acting as their marriage guardian, she gave them out in marriage to men of prominence, thus making alliances in two directions with each girl (Hoffer 1974).

## CONCLUSION OF THE GENERAL STATUS OF BUNDU WOMEN

Bundu provides a highly institutionalized social group through which some women rise to great prominence in political decision-making and executive roles. But in looking at politically elite women we must not lose sight of the general status of ordinary women. Bundu law enhances the status of all women by protecting them, for example, from degrading acts such as male voyeurism. Should a man fail to make a warning noise as he approaches the place where women bathe, he will be charged for his offence. Should he make sexual advances to an uninitiated girl, he risks illness and death unless he goes to the Bundu leader, confesses, pays a fine, and submits to ritual cleansing. Husbands are wary of offending their wives in marital disputes. There is always a chance that the abused wife, or her mother, will use "medicine" known to Bundu women to harm him, especially to render him impotent.

There is a very deep social solidarity among Bundu women stemming from their shared ordeals and good times in the Bundu bush, continuing throughout life in the spirit of cooperative assistance. They enjoy rights and duties which enhance their social status, and they represent a formidible block of votes in national elections.

---

Kenema area (Mende) allegedly called all Bundu women into the initiation bush and told them to vote for the Sierra Leone Peoples' Party candidate.

# REFERENCES

BANTON, MICHAEL
1957 *West African city: a study of tribal life in Freetown.* London: Oxford University Press.
CARTWRIGHT, JOHN R.
1970 *Politics in Sierra Leone 1947–1967.* Toronto: University of Toronto Press.
DOUGLAS, MARY
1966 *Purity and danger.* London: Routledge and Kegan Paul.
FULTON, RICHARD M.
1972 The political structures and functions of Poro in Kpelle society. *American Anthropologist* 74:1218–1233.
FYFE, CHRISTOPHER
1962 *A history of Sierra Leone.* London: Oxford University Press.
1964 *Sierra Leone inheritance.* London: Oxford University Press.
GOODALE, JANE C.
1971 *Tiwi wives.* Seattle: University of Washington Press.
HOFFER, CAROL P.
1971 "Acquisition and exercise of political power by a women paramount chief of the Sherbro people." Unpublished doctoral dissertation, Bryn Mawr College. Ann Arbor: University Microfilms.
1972 Mende and Sherbro women in high office. *Canadian Journal of African Studies* 6:151–164.
1974 "Madam Yoko: ruler of the Kpa Mende confederacy," in *Women, culture and society.* Edited by Michelle Z. Rosaldo and Louise Lamphere. Stanford: Stanford University Press.
LEE, RICHARD B.
1968 "What hunters do for a living," in *Man the hunter.* Edited by Richard B. Lee and Irving DeVore. Chicago: Aldine.
MANNAH-KPAKA, J. K.
1953 Memoirs of the 1898 rising. *Sierra Leone Studies* n.s. 1:28–39.
MARGAI, MILTON A. S.
1948 Welfare work in a secret society. *African Affairs* 47:227–230.
SIERRA LEONE
1957 *Report of the commission of enquiry into the conduct of certain chiefs and the government statement thereon.* London: Her Majesty's Stationery Office.
TIGER, LIONEL
1970 *Men in groups.* New York: Vintage.

# Three Styles of Domestic Authority: A Cross-Cultural Study

ALICE SCHLEGEL

In his paper "Structural analysis in linguistics and in anthropology," Lévi-Strauss took note of the sentimental opposition between husband and brother of the woman who links the brothers-in-law. Where she has "free and familiar relations" with the one, her relations with the other are characterized by "hostility, antagonism, or reserve" (Lévi-Strauss 1963: 44). This opposition seems to characterize not only the structure of sentiment, but also the structure of authority within the domestic group. With this model in mind, I have defined three domestic authority patterns, which I call Husband Dominant, Brother Dominant, and Neither Dominant. The Husband Dominant domestic group is one in which the husband has authority, to a greater or lesser degree, over his wife within the sphere of her domestic activities. In the Brother Dominant domestic group, the woman's brother or mother's brother has ultimate authority over her, even though she may be living apart from him with her husband. The Neither Dominant pattern is that in which neither the husband nor the brother has greater control over the linking woman's person, property, and activities. The focus of this study, then, is upon the woman, the linking figure in the marital exchange network.

In order to generalize about these authority patterns, I designed a cross-cultural study utilizing a sample of matrilineal societies coded for domestic authority pattern and various other traits. The study was limited to this universe for two reasons. First, by restricting it to one descent pattern, variations which might be due to descent differences are controlled for (cf. Homans and Schneider 1955). Second, by selecting matrilineal societies, one is assured of finding enough Brother Dominant societies to make statistical testing feasible. Interestingly, Husband Dominance seems to characterize matrilineal societies more than any other authority pattern: out of 64 societies, 29 were coded Husband Dominant, 21 Brother Dominant, and 14 Neither Dominant.

The sample was drawn from all matrilineal societies reported in the *Ethnographic atlas* (Murdock 1967). It was stratified geographically, with one society drawn from each of the culture clusters that contained one or more matrilineal societies. There are 79 of these societies, but adequate information was available for only 64 societies. The breakdown by world area is: Africa – 19; Asia – 8; Oceania – 16; North America – 13; and South America – 8.

The societies were coded as to type of domestic authority pattern, where the coder was requested to look for any statement by the ethnographer, based upon his observations or upon native statements, or for any statement by a native, regarding the presence or absence of male authority over adult married women. Authority is defined as the legitimate control over the woman's person and/or activities and/or any domestic property in whose production, distribution, or consumption she is involved. Other variables were selected according to the light they might shed upon the nature and origin of domestic authority patterns. Included were those customs which symbolize authority or subordination, such as deference behavior, bride-capture and the presence of menstrual restrictions. Also studied were those social features which might lead to the development of domestic authority patterns, such as control over domestic group property, type of subsistence pattern, and intensity of craft specialization. Finally, there were cultural features which appear on theoretical or empirical grounds to result from domestic authority patterns. The two most important of these were the type of preferred unilateral cross-cousin marriage, and the relative sanctions of the incest taboo, that is, whether father-daughter incest or brother-sister incest were considered to be worse.

This paper will be confined to a discussion of those tests in which the domestic authority pattern was the dependent variable. The tests used were the chi square and Fisher's Exact tests. Where no bivariate testing was possible, univariate descriptive statistics were the basis for generalization. The variables in different combinations were also tested by factor analysis.

The section that follows presents brief ethnographic sketches of three societies exhibiting the three domestic authority patterns.

THREE STYLES, THREE CASES

*The Husband Dominant Tuareg*[1]

The Ahaggar are a northern Tuareg group of about 300,000, divided into eight main political units. Goats are important for subsistence and for providing the raw materials of trade objects, but camels are the mark of wealth. The subsistence system is based upon herding, and the exchange system involves long-distance trading, by means of camel caravans with agricultural peoples. A Tuareg custom which has captured popular imagination is the fact that it is the men among them who wear the veil, whereas women, like slaves, go unveiled.

The Tuareg have been romanticized as a society in which women have high status. Indeed, the freedom with which men and women interact, particularly before marriage, contrasts with other Islamic peoples of the Sahara. In the evenings, the young people join together to sing, and this may be followed by pairing off for lovemaking. Lovers have a tender joking relationship with one another.

This relationship changes upon marriage, when the wife shows great respect toward her husband and uses respect terms instead of his name. Bridewealth is substantial and is paid in camels according to the status of the families, whether noble or vassal, and their wealth.

Residence is virilocal after an initial year spent in the bride's camp. The couple reside with the husband's father until his death, when they move to the camp of the husband's maternal male kin. Divorce is common, and the wife and her children return to her father's camp.

Although chastity is not required before marriage, adultery by the wife can be severely punished by the husband, who may kill both parties with impunity. The same restrictions are not put upon the husband, who may have sexual relations with slaves (Lhote 1944:154). However, it is likely that most husbands do not take such drastic measures, as there are established fines in camels to be paid to the chief by both the adulterous woman and her partner (Nicolaisen 1963:102).

As among other Muslim peoples, women inherit from their parents, receiving only half of the portion, usually livestock given to the sons. They have the right to dispose of this property at will; but as with the property of males, the meat, milk, or sale price should be used to benefit the entire household. They do not participate in the long-distance trade, and, in most cases, it is unlikely that they control very much property.

---

[1]  The data on the Ahaggar Tuareg come from Nicolaisen (1963) and Lhote (1944).

The deference the wife shows the husband extends beyong his death, when she goes into a period of isolation. Husbands do not practice this for wives. Women occupy a subordinate position outside the home as well. The generally lower value placed upon women is indicated by the difference in blood price. The set fee is 100 camels for men and 50 for women.

While Tuareg women do have considerable personal freedom when compared with other Saharan peoples, they are clearly under control of and subordinate to their husbands. Frequency of divorce should not be taken as a measure of women's personal freedom, even though they seem to instigate it more than men (Lhote 1944:586). What actually occurs is an exchange of one dominant figure, the husband, for another, the father or another husband. When she marries, the Tuareg woman's sexuality and most of the property she is involved with comes under the control of her husband. Publicly and in the home she defers to him and shows him unilateral formalized respect.

## *The Brother Dominant Yao*[2]

The Yao, of Nyasaland (now Malawi), were once a congeries of chiefdoms who were active in the slave and ivory trade until they were brought under control of the British in the 1890's. Formerly, chiefs controlled territory and granted land within it to village headmen. Today, since pacification destroyed the power of the chiefs and obviated the need for large villages, villages have split up into small, almost autonomous units, and chiefs are part of the administrative structure.

In many African societies, men show their status by gathering around them a number of wives. Among the Yao, it is a mark of a man's success to have his sisters clustered around him and to act as their warden. In order to found a homestead or a village, a man must persuade some of his sisters to go along with him. Brothers compete for the loyalty of the sororal group, and there is considerable evidence of fraternal hostility. The warden and the village headman bring their wives in to live virilocally, but most couples reside uxorilocally, the man coming into his wife's and wife's brother's homestead. Patrilateral cross-cousin marriage is preferred. Most marriages occur within the same or neighboring villages but even so, the husband spends much of his time at his natal homestead. While the warden cannot force a sister to marry someone not of her choosing, he can refuse to allow a marriage or send away a husband who displeases him. Further-

[2]   The data on the Yao come from Mitchell (1956 and 1959).

more, even a woman living virilocally in another village can be recalled by her brothers, and a husband knows that his wife can always run away and find a welcome at home.

The prestige of being a warden is accompanied by the drain on his time and energy that managing the sororal group entails. Women are believed to be as helpless as children, and it is the duty of the warden to look after them in time of trouble or illness and represent them in any court case. According to one warden: "To live with a sorority-group needs courage" (Mitchell 1956:151).

The relationship between husband and wife is of secondary importance to the sibling relationship. The wedding does not provide the groom with any symbolic payment for his bride. Rather, there is an equivalent exchange of food between the sororal groups of the marrying pair. Sisters should take precedence over wives, and at his installation the headman is exhorted not to listen to the tales of his wives against his sisters. Adultery on the part of the wife may be fairly common, as it is the most frequent cause of marital discord. Evidently, the woman is not held culpable, for there is no mention of her being punished. Her seducer, however, may be fined.

In the important events in her life, and in her domestic relations, the Yao woman finds her brother an intervening figure of authority. If she lives uxorilocally, she is under his management in her daily life. If she lives virilocally, she is subject to recall at any time. Her very nature, perceived as childlike and helpless, puts her into a position where she must be protected and controlled.

## *The Neither Dominant Hopi*[3]

The Hopi are a Pueblo people of northern Arizona, who have adapted to a dry and uncertain climate with horticulture, hunting, and herding of sheep and cattle.

The term "Neither Dominant" can have two connotations, the first that neither the husband nor the brother has greater authority (which is the way it was defined for this study), the second that neither has very much authority over the woman at all. It is the second that most aptly describes the Hopi, for in the domestic sphere the women rule. There is a native saying that "the man's place is outside the house;" and men do spend

---

[3]    The data on the Hopi come from my own field notes and Eggan (1950), Simmons (1942), and Titiev (1944).

much of the time not devoted to economic activities, with other men in the kiva (the ceremonial chamber that doubles as an informal men's house).

Women propose marriage by offering the chosen man a special corn cake, and the marriage ceremony formally begins when the bride goes to the groom's house to grind corn for his female relatives. After this short period of groom service, the bride remains in the groom's house until his male relatives have woven her wedding robes. The two families exchange food, and the groom accompanies the bride back to her mother's house, where he will work under the direction of his father-in-law. Although there is village endogamy, which means that the groom keeps up close ties with his matrilineage, the feeling is that "he goes over to her side" and should be a hard worker for his wife and her family.

Houses are owned by women, even though their husbands build them, and they are inherited by ultimogeniture. While the men do almost all of the work in the fields, when the produce is brought into the house and the wife has formally thanked her husband, it belongs to her. Men work the fields their wives receive through the clan, and it is the Clan Mother who has the final say in any dispute over allocation. Livestock, however, is owned by men and passed down to their sons.

The strongest ties are between mother, daughter, and sister, who form a triad of solidarity to the point that one may act or speak for all. Although the Hopi claim to want children of both sexes, women admit that "you raise up a daughter for yourself, but you raise up a son for somebody else." Men wish for sons as companions, but they also need a daughter to provide a home for them in their old age, should they outlive their wives. A daughter is insurance against an old age spent as a burden in the home of a more distant relative.

There is no formal divorce, but divorce, if used in the sense of breaking a partnership, is common. Women can order their husbands out at any time, and men can leave and return to their natal home or move in with another woman. A brother or adult son will farm for a husbandless woman if need be.

The principle of noninterference in the activities of another pervades Hopi social and family life. A husband or wife may go out for hours at a time without informing the spouse. Adultery is frowned upon, but if it does occur, the offended spouse is expected to ignore it or talk reasonably to the adulterous partner about it if it becomes flagrant. Husbands are not allowed by custom to beat their wives or aggress against them in any way, nor can brothers do so toward sisters. The attitude, expressed in many ways, is that men should respect women and be grateful to them because of their life-giving role as mothers and feeders.

As in many societies, the Hopi divide their activities into the public and the domestic spheres, the men participating most in the former and the women controlling the latter. Each sex, however, plays necessary and honored roles in the other sex's sphere of action. Men are essential to the home if women are to fulfill their life-giving role, and women hold important positions in the politico-ceremonial system dominated by men. Hopi society can be characterized as one in which the sexes are separate but equal.

The foregoing discussion has presented examples of the three domestic authority patterns. In the following section, we shall look at generalizations that can be made about the three patterns on the basis of the cross-cultural sample.

## DOMESTIC AUTHORITY PATTERN PROFILES

The evidence from both the bivariate tests and the factor analyses shows clearly that there are three distinct patterns, or syndromes of traits, of domestic authority. In this section, we shall look at the three domestic authority patterns plus the combined pattern of general male dominance. We shall consider those traits strongly or significantly associated with each of the authority patterns. The number of cases are those for which there are data.

### Husband Dominance

A wedding symbolizes the transfer of authority over the woman to her husband. We find bride capture (7 cases) an obvious symbol of possession exclusively associated with this authority pattern. Substantial bridewealth is also characteristic of this form, indicating that many rights over the woman are being paid for. Woman exchange, in which an exact equivalent is given, is exclusive to this authority pattern.

Virilocality is the most frequent residence pattern for this authority type, and when divorce occurs, the woman bears the brunt of disruption by having to leave. Husband control of property is strongly associated with this type. In sexual matters, the wife is under control of the husband. All seven of the cases in which the husband can offer his wife as a sexual partner without her consent fall into this category. The right to punish a wife for her adultery is also significantly associated with this type (20 out of 24 cases).

A woman is likely to be a member of a polygynous household, and she is likely to be jealous of those of her co-wives who are not her sisters. In fourteen out of twenty Husband Dominant societies this was the cultural expectation. Even where sisters are expected to live amicably as co-wives, as among the Crow, non-sororal co-wife jealousy is believed to be characteristic. The husband is likely to have ultimate control over children, as is also the case in Neither Dominant domestic groups. The woman is likely to defer to her husband, and aggression against her on the part of her husband — short of killing or maiming is allowed (in 21 out of 24 cases).

### Brother Dominance

The two cases of groom capture, Garo and Minangkabau, belong with this type. This act symbolizes the bringing in of a man into a household under the authority of another man. Once the marriage takes place, it is liable to be disrupted by the wife's brother (14 out of 16 cases). In a little less than half the cases (10 out of 21), marital residence is wife-centered, either matrilocal (eight) or avunculocal with preference for matrilateral cross-cousin marriage (two). In over half of the cases (10 out of 19), the brother controls the domestic group property of his sister and her husband.

An adult sister is liable to aggression, i.e., punishment, on the part of her brother (in all nine cases for which there were data). He is also likely to have ultimate authority over her children (16 out of 20 cases). Four Brother Dominant societies leave the punishment of an adulterous wife to her brother, but the majority of these (11), like most other societies, leave such punishment, where punishment is allowed and expected, to the husband.

The woman in 12 out of 13 Brother Dominant societies defers to her brother. However, she is likely to defer to her husband as well (11 out of 16 cases). She is liable to aggression from her brother; but also from her husband (10 out of 12 cases). This suggests that the woman in the Brother Dominant society is likely to be under pressures toward subordination from both sides. Hobhouse (1924:160) remarks that "The woman is not necessarily any better off because she is ruled by a brother in place of a husband."

### Male Dominant

We have already looked at some of the traits shared by Husband Dominant and Brother Dominant societies: wife's deference to her husband; tolerance of husband aggression; male control of property; and punishment of wife's adultery. Both types are significantly polygynous (although expected co-wife jealousy is not a characteristic of Brother Dominant societies).

One feature of the economic system emerged as significantly associated with both forms of male dominance and absent from the Neither Dominant type: that is, craft specialization. In the majority of these societies, the domestic group is the productive unit for both subsistence and production used for exchange purposes. In other words, the domestic unit is the manufacturing unit. Where production exists only for subsistence and the minimal, casual sort of exchange that characterizes simple societies and those at the lower end of the middle range of the societies so classified in the *Ethnographic atlas* (Murdock 1967), there is a less pressing need to organize productive activities, for only a given amount can or needs to be produced with the limited resources at hand. However, when craft specialization is developed and the productive unit becomes a manufacturing one as well, skilled labor becomes a valuable asset. The quantity the manufacturing unit can produce depends in part upon the raw materials it has available; but it also depends upon how hard the manager can coerce or persuade the laborers into working. A strong managerial figure becomes an asset, or even a necessity, to such a domestic group. One would expect his economic authority to spill out into other domestic matters, and that seems to happen. We can hypothesize, then, that any domestic economy requiring a strong managerial figure might lead to male dominance.

The Male Dominant societies differed from the Neither Dominant type in the kind of unilateral cross-cousin marriage preferred and in the direction of the incest taboo.

I had hypothesized, on logical grounds, that Husband Dominant societies would prefer matrilateral cross-cousin marriage, as this would enable the dominant male figure to bring into the domestic group over which he had control (his wife's) a man in whom he had an interest (his sister's son.) On the other hand, Brother Dominant societies should prefer patrilateral cross-cousin marriage, as this permits the dominant male to bring into his sister's or sister's daughter's domestic group, over which he has control, a man in whom he has an interest (his son). This was confirmed and stands in contrast to the Neither Dominant societies, for which there was only one society out of 14 where preference for unilateral (matrilateral) cross-cousin marriage occurred. This indicates that the domestic authority pattern has some consequences for the larger patterns of social organization.

On empirical grounds, based upon a pilot study sample, it appeared that Husband Dominant societies are more likely to be concerned with father-daughter incest than with brother-sister. The reverse holds true for Brother Dominant societies, whereas no such distribution characterized Neither Dominant societies. This was supported by the test results and illustrates one area in which the domestic authority pattern may affect the system of beliefs and values (Schlegel 1972). It also leads to speculations about the relationship between power and sexuality.

*Neither Dominant*

Neither Dominant societies are characterized by the absence of the traits associated with one or both of the male dominant types. This indicates that there is not only a lack of direction of authority, but a general lack of authority altogether. In other words, as power disperses it declines. Interestingly, half of the Neither Dominant cases (7 out of 14) are from North America, and over half of the North American cases are Neither Dominant (7 out of 13). Neither Dominance appears to be the mode in North America, a world area that underplays interpersonal dominance in general.

CONCLUSION

We have examined three patterns of domestic authority. The two male dominant ones stand in clear contrast to the Neither Dominant one, in which women have a high degree of autonomy, or control over their own person, property, and activities. To what degree autonomy in the domestic sphere carries over into autonomy, or even areas of control, in the public sphere cannot be determined from this study. So far only one variable has emerged as significant, namely, that Neither Dominant societies allow women to hold exclusively female public positions to a significantly greater degree than do the two male dominant types.

We have examined the relationship of domestic authority to features of the broader sociocultural system. Craft specialization, and possibly any domestic economy requiring a strong managerial figure seems to lead to male dominance. Control over domestic property is also related to male dominance; in fact, of all of the variables tested, it is the one most strongly associated with domestic group authority. However, the data of this study give no support to any causal theory, which must depend upon structural and historical investigations of representative cases. The domestic authority system is also seen to have an effect upon cultural factors — preference for one or the other type of unilateral cross-cousin marriage, and the direction of the incest taboo.

The most important questions regarding male dominance and female autonomy have yet to be answered. We need to know what features in the adaptive system, and the environment to which it is adaptive, depress or elevate female autonomy. We need to know what types of societies — by socioeconomic levels, political organizations, and subsistence and economic types — foster autonomy of women. We need to know the relationship between autonomy in the home and autonomy, and positions of power, in the public sphere for we cannot assume that high domestic autonomy necessarily entails high public status. We need good case studies to understand the dynamics of those situations which foster or suppress female autonomy, and cross-cultural studies to make generalizations.

## REFERENCES

EGGAN, FRED
   1950   *Social organization of the Western Pueblos.* Chicago: University of Chicago Press.
HOBHOUSE, LEONARD T.
   1924   *Morals in evolution: a study in comparative ethics* (fourth edition). New York: Henry Holt.
HOMANS, GEORGE C., DAVID M. SCHNEIDER
   1955   *Marriage, authority, and final cause.* Glencoe: Free Press.
LÉVI-STRAUSS, CLAUDE
   1963   *Structural anthropology.* New York: Basic Books.
LHOTE, HENRI
   1944   *Les touaregs du Hoggar.* Paris: Payot.
MITCHELL, JAMES CLYDE
   1956   *The Yao village: a study in the social structure of a Nyasaland tribe.* Manchester: Manchester University Press.
   1959   "The Yao of Southern Nyasaland," in *Seven tribes of British Central Africa.* Edited by Elizabeth Colson and Max Gluckman. Manchester: Manchester University Press.
MURDOCK, GEORGE PETER
   1967   *Ethnographic atlas.* Pittsburgh: University of Pittsburgh Press.
NICOLAISEN, JOHANNES
   1963   *Ecology and culture of the pastoral Tuareg.* Copenhagen, Nationalmuseets Skrifter, Etnografisk Raekke 9.
SCHLEGEL, ALICE
   1972   *Male dominance and female autonomy.* New Haven: Human Relations Area Files Press.

SIMMONS, LEO
  1942    *Sun chief.* New Haven: Yale University Press.
TITIEV, MISCHA
  1944    *Old Oraibi: a study of the Hopi Indians of Third Mesa.* Papers of the
          Peabody Museum of American Archaeology and Ethnology 22(1).
          Harvard University.

# A Review of the Women's Movement
# in the United States

BETTIE SCOTT ALLEN

## A MINORITY GROUP: WOMEN

Regarding women as a minority group was a new insight. It was also a
surprise to many that an identifying factor in the definition of a minority
group is the presence of discrimination. A "minority group" is not a
statistical concept, nor does it necessarily denote an alien group. It is
"any group of people who, because of their physical or culture characteristics, are singled out from the others in the society in which they live
for differential and unequal treatment, and who therefore regard themselves as objects of collective discrimination" (Hacker 1951:61). Members
who are denied full participation in the opportunities which the value
system of a culture extends to other members of the society, fulfill the objective criterion:

As citizens, women are often barred from jury service and public office. Even
when they are admitted to the apparatus of political parties, they are subor-
dinated to men (Hacker 1951: 63).

This definition implies not only discrimination, but an awareness of this
discrimination and the emotional reactions to that awareness. On the other
hand, many women may know that because of their group affiliation
they receive differential treatment, but accept this response, and feel this
treatment is warranted because of the distinctive characteristics of this
group. They believe that they have special interests to follow or unique
contributions to make via women's clubs, women's auxiliaries of men's
organizations, women's professional and educational associations. Most
women in the Movement, however, believe themselves to be members of

a minority group and are filled with resentment at the discriminations directed against their sex. Their reactions have made the Women's Liberation Movement one of the most controversial in America today.

I here analyze the Womens' Liberation Movement and suggest that it has passed through two phases and in 1972 moved into a third phase.


PHASE 1: GENESIS IMPETUS

Many events, societal changes, and social movements were responsible for the genesis of the Women's Liberation Movement. During World War II, women went outside the home and held down jobs formerly assumed by men. When the war was over, these women gave up their jobs to veterans and stayed home. For fifteen years they raised children and centered their lives on the role of house/mother. By 1960, women began to doubt that this role was fulfilling their needs. These doubts were confirmed by governmental recognition of discrimination against women and by changes in attitudes about reproduction. The easing of government restrictions on the dissemination of birth control information and contraceptives gave women the option of either limiting their families or not having children. The massive Civil Rights Movement, now gaining momentum, also had a reinforcing influence. The Women's Liberation Movement then developed from three major sources. The first was discontent among white, middleclass women in the wife/mother role. The second was anger over job and educational discrimination by career oriented women, and the third, the indignation by women activists in Civil Rights when they were not treated as equals by male leaders.

The life force of the Movement came from women who had the opportunity to articulate their distress and could afford to demand changes. It did not stem from the poor white, black, or other minority groups who had actually suffered the most severe discrimination.

Various communication events gave impetus to the Movement. One was Betty Friedan's *The feminine mystique* (1963). In this initial "bible" Ms. Friedan was cautious, yet expressed the confusion and indecision felt by so many housewives:

The problem lay buried, unspoken for many years in the minds of American women. It was a strange stirring, a sense of dissatisfaction, a yearning... each suburban housewife struggled with... alone (1963:11).

Intrinsic in this early rhetoric was the feeling of guilt by potential members for having accepted their traditional roles.

Gradually... I came to realize that something is very wrong with the way American women are trying to live their lives today. I sensed it first as a question mark in my own life, as a wife and mother... half-guiltily... using my abilities and education in work that took me out of the home (Friedan 1963:7).

Friedan's theme in the first quote implies that each woman had to come to terms with herself as a person. This is the essence of what is now called "consciousness-raising." Lucy Komisar of the National Organization for Women (NOW) explains consciousness-raising as the "exhilarating experience of women's discovery that their anger and frustration is shared," and this discovery leads to "new strength" and "self-respect," a focus not on men but on fellow women, and the strength to challenge "the legitimacy of the sex role system upon which our civilization is based" (1970: 77).

Consciousness-raising sessions began to occur in neighborhood homes. In small groups, women slowly began to express how they felt about themselves, their thoughts about other women, and their feelings about a childhood which focused their life on being a wife and mother rather than a professional. These sessions were attended by women who spent most of their time in the home raising children and attempting to fulfill the cultural expectations of "wife" and "mother," and surprisingly, also by career women who were responding to the impact of the national Movement.

President Kennedy created the first Commission on the Status of Women. Congress passed the 1963 Equal Pay Act. President Johnson added the word "sex" to a 1967 Executive Order which prohibited discrimination in government employment. Congressional hearings were held to determine the wisdom of passing an equal rights amendment for women. The report of the 1970 House Committee on Education and Labor Hearings on the Equal Rights Amendment was one of the most useful for legislative action.

In an address delivered at the Conference on Women's Employment which was also included as testimony before the Special Subcommittee on Education and Labor, Congresswoman Shirley Chisholm (1970) said that being black and being a woman was a "good vantage point from which to view at least two elements of what is becoming a social revolution: the American black revolution and the Women's Liberation Movement." However, she also stressed that it was a "disadvantage because America as a nation is both racist and anti-feminist." She asserted that "of course women dare" to fight discrimination, and told her audience that "all discrimination is eventually the same thing — anti-humanism" and then admonished them to go home and "work for, fight for, the integration of male and female — human and human." Stressing the extent of discrimination, Ms. Chisholm said:

In 1966, the median earnings of women who worked full time for the whole year were less than the median income for males who worked full time for the whole year. In fact, white women workers made less than black male workers, and... black women made the least of all. Whether it is intentional or not, women are paid less than men for the same work... employment for women is regulated more in terms of the jobs that are available to them... when it becomes time for a high school girl to think about preparing for her career, her counselors... will think first of her so-called natural career — housewife and mother — and begin to program her for a field which children and marriage will not unduly interfere (1970:41).

Another essential part of the first phase of the Women's Liberation Movement was the formation of two organizations which have also been the mainstay of the Movement — NOW (National Organization for Women) and WEAL (Women's Equity Action League).

In 1966, at the Washington Conference of State Commissions on the Status of Women, Betty Friedan and other women activists created the National Organization for Women for the purpose of "taking action to bring women into full participation in the mainstream of American society." It was dedicated to the proposition that "women... are human beings who, like other people in our society, must have a chance to develop their fullest human potential." The main thrusts of NOW are for the legalization of abortions, equality of opportunity in employment, education, and civic and political responsibilities for women, and the raising of the consciousness level of both women and men.

WEAL was formed in the same year and has specialized in court action on equal pay. This group has brought suits against several major universities concerning hiring and salary practices for their women employees (Cudlipp 1971:138).

Although the rhetoric of the first phase was demanding, it was at the same time cautious. It contained more "revelation" and petition than promulgation and confrontation. The early leaders had to be cautious as they were still in the organization stage and needed favorable publicity. It might have damaged and delayed the Movement if career women, already frustrated by trying to play all the roles which society demanded of them, had also been alienated by the Movement.

PHASE 2: ACTION/REACTION

The Movement became more aggressive and strategies turned on promulgation and polarization as members moved into the second phase. It grew in strength and in diversity. New organizations were formed under the label "feminist." The members of these new groups felt that NOW and WEAL were too conservative — reformist rather than revolutionary.

In her book *Born female: the high cost of keeping women down*, Caroline Bird challenged women when she wrote:

Women make no noisome ghettos, join few unions, rarely organize demonstrations, come when called and go quietly when bidden (1968:45).

As if in answer to her challenge, these new militant organizations were formed and women began to demonstrate. They demonstrated against the Miss America Pageant by throwing stink bombs, and carrying banners which read "Miss America Sells It," and "Miss America Is a Big Falsie." The press was extremely critical of this demonstration, and failed to make clear the meaning of the demonstration, namely, that all women are forced to play Miss America, and that the Movement should seek to awaken women to the extent and nature of their oppression. It was after this failure that the feminists developed some sophistication in their communications.

The feminists believe that action must derive from theory. One of their main revolutionary tenets is that economic discrimination is related to marriage.

Marriage is an institution which employs women for the essential, though usually debasing, work of society without the payment of wages. What this means is that society exists on the backs of women. The conclusion: women must eliminate both marriage and our service function in society (Kearon 1969).

Ti-Grace Atkinson, one of the founders of the Feminist organization, has written a document on "Radical feminism and love" (1969). In this article she states that women are an "oppressed class" and must confront the powerlessness they experience under the phenomenon of love. In a speech given at a Catholic University two years later, Atkinson charged the Roman Catholic Church of being an institution guilty of prostitution and rape, and charged that women who enter into marriage lend themselves to this oppression.

Another militant Movement group is the Women's International Terrorist Conspiracy from Hell (WITCH). Its leader, Robin Morgan, explained this organization development as a splintering off of the female sector of male dominated SDS and other New Left organizations. "Women are the real New Left," she said (Cudlipp 1971:161). The manifesto of Lilith, the operating paper of this group, concludes :"This revolution has got to go for broke; power to no one, and to everyone; to each the power over his/her own life, and no other" (Tanner 1970:115–116). Following their belief, the members of WITCH joined with the Black Panther Party and the Welfare Rights Organization of New Haven, Connecticut, and demonstrated on behalf of six Black Panther women in prison in Niantic, Connecticut.

Another offshoot of the New Left organizations was a group called Redstockings, a play on "bluestockings," with the blue replaced by the color of revolution. Organizers of this group were Shuli Firestone, a rock-music columnist for the *New Yorker*, and Ellen Willis, a serious student of Engels' "Origins of the family." Their Manifesto asserts that "Women are an oppressed class," and "exploited as sex objects, breeders, domestic servants and cheap labor." They call for unity among "all sisters" and ask men to "give up their male privileges and support women's liberation in the interest of... humanity" (Tanner 1970:109–111).

In February, 1969, the Redstockings organized a hearing on abortion utilizing the consciousness-raising technique. Twelve women testified about their own abortions to an audience of 300 men and women. They had been thrown out of a government hearing on abortion for trying to do this. As the Redstockings were staging their "speak-out," NOW was lobbying for repeal of restrictive abortion legislation. These different approaches to the same problem illustrate the difference in methods used by the two wings of the Movement (Brownmiller 1970).

There are of course some less revolutionary groups within the Movement. One such group is the Older Women's Liberation group (OWL). This group is concerned with establishing divorce referral services and job training for women. There is also the Southern Female Rights Union (SFRU) which deals with such issues as public child-care and a guaranteed annual income (Tanner 1970:112–118).

The Annual Congress to Unite Women (ANCUW) is one of the less revolutionary groups with a long list of demands such as: 24-hour day care centers which would be staffed by both women and men, the rewriting of history texts and literary anthologies so that the achievements of women be equally represented with those of men, the guaranteed right of all women — regardless of marital status or pregnancy — to attend school, the establishment of women's studies programs at universities, and a request to the academic community to restructure language so as to reflect a society in which women have equal status with men (Tanner 1970:123–126).

By late 1969 the media had discovered the feminist movement, and it was common to find feature stories or sometimes an entire issue of a major news magazine devoted to an analysis of the Movement. Soon, as many predicted, a counter-movement developed.

The strategy of the "establishment" (government, press, and other traditionally-oriented opinion leaders) up to 1972 was one of avoidance, through there have been examples of ridicule and insensitivity from influential people. Such prominent people as novelist-journalist Norman Mailer and anthropologist Margaret Mead have voiced reservations about some aspects of the Movement. Margaret Mead (1970) rejects the more militant aspects and humorously expresses skepticism:

The members of the Women's Lib Movement in its extreme form, walk around saying how well they get on without men. There are too many women, and if some of them would get on without men it would relieve the pressure.

Richard Nixon's invitation to the wives of Cabinet officers to attend a Cabinet meeting and sit around drinking coffee while the men made policy was deplored by members of the Movement. Although the Nixon administration would not blatantly "lead" a counter-movement, some of the members have demonstrated insensitivity. Secretary Rogers is quoted as referring to a Women's Lib demonstration as a "burlesque." Health, Education, and Welfare Assistant Secretary Pat Hitt told reporters she could not offer the name of a single woman who would be qualified to fill a cabinet post (Anderson 1971:6).

By far the most damaging attacks, surprisingly enough, came from career women and housewives. Many career women seem to take the position that since they "made it," all other women could have too. Some outspoken housewives on the other hand seem to express the idea that women in the Movement are all militant, unpleasant, and unfeminine. Data indicate that they tend to make very few decisions and to follow their husband's choices of political candidates, and, if they vote at all, to copy their husbands.

This second phase of the movement saw the development of more diverse organizations, the continued petitioning to the "establishment," an increase in public recognition, and the development of a counter-movement.

## PHASE 3: CHANGE, 1972–

The criteria for the Movement's entrance into the third phase include such things as increased membership in existing organizations, extension of those organizations into other sectors of society, increased influence, favorable attitude change toward goals, confrontations with members of the counter-movement, and most importantly, the accomplishment of some of the early objectives.

In regard to the latter, let us look at employment. On March 6, 1973, we read about the promotion of a woman to Commander (the highest military rank) of an all male division. The highest academic positions and civil service classifications occasionally go to women, often due to continued pressure from the women's rights organizations. Women are being appointed to administrative positions in colleges and universities, to editorial positions on newspapers and magazines, and to executive positions in business offices. However, it is understood by all that these are minimal in proportion to what is yet to be achieved in pay, kinds of jobs, hiring practices, and rates of promotions. The Movement currently has two challenges to meet in this third phase: (1) to keep their supporters from lapsing into apathy and complacency and (2) to continue their persuasion campaigns in such a way that they have less chance of being labeled "harpies."

Another point of change is found in our language usage. A female person is signified now as "Ms." instead of "Miss" or "Mrs." by women themselves, many newspapers, and some organizations and companies. The word "person" often now replaces "man" or "woman" as in such words as "chairperson."

Attitude change from an initial unfavorable predisposition towards the Movement to one of support for many of its goals seems significant. Carol Tavris (1972), senior editor of *Psychology Today*, surveyed 20,000 readers and found that the great majority of men and women agree that women are discriminated against, and prefer that groups include both women and men to help overcome discrimination. In response to questions, over 50% of the men, non-group women (not active members of the Movement), and group women supported public day-care, abortion on demand, and equality in child rearing. Almost 50% supported the Equal Rights Amendment as well.

By far the most significant accomplishment has been the formation of the National Women's Political Caucus (NWPC). This group has attempted to increase women's participation in politics. It is supported by women both in and out of the Movement. By using the strategy of working with both parties to support women, or any other candidate who is willing to strike out against "sexism, racism and poverty," the Caucus works for proportionate representation of women and other minority groups at the political conventions. In the summer conventions of 1972 the National Women's Political Caucus did not achieve equal representation, though its goals and influence were acknowledged by nearly all the presidential candidates. Even though such members of the Movement as Gloria Steinem and Congresswoman Bella Abzug could not get abortion included in the platform, a strong women's rights provision and the candidacy of women for both the presidency and vice presidency was a major innovation. This is particularly true if one agrees with Betty Friedan that the Movement had to go political or it would die (U.S. News 1971:67–68).

As of 1974, the reformist branch of the Movement had accomplished some of its goals but it still has much work to complete. The revolutionary branch has even further to go.

## IMPLICATIONS FOR THE FUTURE

The Movement could very well remain in this third phase for several years. Kate Millet has said of revolutions:

Changes as drastic and fundamental as those of the sexual revolution are not easily arrived at. Nor should it be surprising that such changes might take place by stages that are capable of interruption and temporary regression (1970:64).

One way the Movement could progress is to have the two branches unite around a common commitment to the ultimate goal of equality for all people. Another is to show more concern for the needs of other minority groups, recognizing that women are but one of the minority groups. Another important step would be an increased effort to extend the membership core beyond the white middle class. If such unity within the Movement were achieved, membership would probably increase dramatically, and the Movement could organize more on a national basis and experience more success as a political bloc. With the unity of the reformists and revolutionary women, and an identification with other minority groups, both male and female, the Movement could emphasize the relationship between real political power and freedom from discrimination. Then the messages of the Movement could become less abstract, and could contain more carefully supported arguments and proposals.

While women have made considerable progress by increasing awareness and decreasing job and educational discrimination, attitude change about sexual ideology has not kept pace with the goals of the Movement. Women's Studies Programs is one place where these goals can be given exposure.

While the Women's Liberation Movement has been a great force in bringing women into the realm of politics, those who are either in political power, or seeking political power, still have much to do in making women a powerful political bloc.

Maximum mileage has been eked out of the few women elected to office, witness Margaret Chase Smith and Shirley Chisholm. Women were given 44% of the delegate seats at the 1972 Democratic convention, and were allowed hearings before the platform committees of both major parties. Still, one will search the speeches and campaign literature in vain to find any major recognition that the politicians are appealing to women as women. One will find much attention to issues that should concern any citizen (black, white, young, old, union member, businessman or woman, consumer) such as war, taxes, rising prices, etc., but not "women." Many issues concerning women's equality still remain unresolved.

Women should be encouraged to seek elective and appointive posts at local, state, and national levels and in all three branches of government.

Public office should be held according to ability, experience and effort, without special preferences or discriminations based on sex. Increasing considerations should continually be given to the appointment of women of demonstrated ability and political sensitivity to policy-making positions (Bosmajian and Bosmajian 1972 [1963]).

These problems remain with us. No urgency has been reflected by the Johnson or Nixon administrations for the implementation of the recommendations. It is likely that this will only change when a sufficient number of women become "political" as the following statement on women suggests:

We believe that women must now exercise their political rights and responsibilities as American citizens. They must refuse to be segregated on the basis of sex into separate-and-not-equal ladies' auxiliaries in the political parties, and they must demand representation according to their numbers in the regularly constituted party committees — at local, state, and national levels — and in the informal power structure, participating fully in the selection of candidates and political decision-making, and running for office themselves (Bosmajian and Bosmajian 1972 [1966]).

## REFERENCES

ANDERSON, JACK
   1971   President Nixon and women. *Parade* (October).
ATKINSON, TI-GRACE
   1969   Radical feminism and love. *The Feminists.* New York.
BIRD, CAROLINE
   1968   *Born female: the high cost of keeping women down.* New York: McKay.

BOSMAJIAN, HAMIDA, HAIG BOSMAJIAN, *editors*
1972   *"National Organization for Women/statement of purpose, October* 29,
       *1966,"* "Recommendation of President Kennedy's commission on the
       status of women, 1963;" "The Senate holds hearings, the House de-
       bates, and the President receives recommendations," reprinted in
       *This great argument: the right of women.* Reading, Mass.: Addison-
       Wesley.
BROWNMILLER, SUSAN
1970   Sisterhood is powerful. *The New York Times* (March 15).
CHISHOLM, SHIRLEY
1970   Racism and anti-feminism. *The Black Scholar* (January-February).
CUDLIPP, EDYTHE
1971   *Understanding women's liberation.* New York: Paperback Library.
FRIEDAN, BETTY
1963   *The feminine mystique.* New York: Dell Books.
HACKER, HELEN MAYER
1951   Women as a minority group. *Social Forces* (October).
KEARON, PAMELA
1969   Organizational principles and structure. *The Feminists.* New York.
KOMISAR, LUCY
1970   The new feminism. *Saturday Review* (Feburary 21).
MEAD, MARGARET
1971   Address at Barnard College, February 12, 1970. Edited in *Trans-
       Action* (September).
MILLET, KATE
1970   *Sexual politics.* New York: Doubleday.
ROSENWASSER, MARIE J.
1972   Rhetoric and the progress of the Women's Liberation Movement.
       *Today's Speech* (Summer).
TANNER, LESLIE, *editor*
1970   "Manifesto of Lilith; Manifesto of the Redstockings; Why OWL
       (Older Women's Liberation)?; Southern Female Rights Union Pro-
       gram for Female Liberation; and Congress to Unite Women," in
       *Voices from women's liberation.* New York: Signet Books.
TAVRIS, CAROL
1972   Women and man. *Psychology Today* (March).
U. S. NEWS AND WORLD REPORT
1971   Women's political caucus. What it is, what it wants. *U. S. News and
       World Report* (July).

# American Women in Politics:
# Culture, Structure, and Ideology

LUCY GARRETSON

As Lebeuf writes (1971:93): "By a habit of thought deeply rooted in the Western mind, women are relegated to the sphere of domestic tasks and private life, and men alone are considered equal to the task of shouldering the burden of public affairs." Within the home, it is conceded, women hold and wield power, but the general attitude of social scientists and lay persons is that in the "real world" of public affairs, male dominance is both universal and "natural." This paper will explore the assumption that political power is, by definition, male, and the constraints imposed upon American women in politics are a result of this prior assumption.

Data drawn from my own studies in Austin, Texas (Garretson-Selby 1972), and from a study of two women's organizations in Philadelphia, Pennsylvania (Philadelphia Anthropology Collective 1972[1]) will be presented. Additional data concerning debates over organizational structure which took place at the Texas Women's Political Caucus Convention (1972) and the National Women's Political Caucus Convention (1973) will be used. The aim is to explore two related problems. The first concerns the "Traditional" woman, who, when she participates in politics, (defined as male) finds herself in danger of "losing her femininity." The second problem involves those women called "Feminists" in this paper, who attempt to operate in a male sphere without adopting what they define as male organizational structures and tactics.

"Traditional" women are defined here as those who prefer to work for reform within established political channels, and who create hierarchical

---

[1] I am indebted to the members of the Philadelphia Anthropology Collective for permission to cite this paper and to consult an earlier, more extensive, draft.

organizations; that is, they adopt structures which define the exercise and responsibility of power within the group as belonging legitimately to a small set of elected officials. The term Traditional does not imply adherence to conservative political beliefs, nor does the label Feminist necessarily imply commitment to radical leftist positions. "Feminist" here is used to refer to women who believe that the inequality of women is THE central social and political problem in America. Therefore it follows that they would form non-hierarchical organizations, in which decision is reached by consensus.

Not all of the women classed as "Feminist" here organized themselves to deal primarily with politics, but all of them share a belief in the necessity of a total restructuring of American society. Thus, they are concerned ultimately with political structures. Similarly, not all the "Traditional" women are "anti-feminist" in the sense that they are against the aims of Women's Liberation: they acknowledge the need to work for a change in the status of women, but their organizational structures and aims are different from those of the "Feminists."


THE "LOSS OF FEMININITY" THREAT

American women, unlike many women in other cultures, must EARN full social status. Womanhood is not automatically given at a specific age nor does it come with a responsible job. It is won when a woman gets married and has children. True, marriage, motherhood, and adult status are linked in other societies, but hardly ever is the burden put on the individual female to prove her worthiness by "catching her man." A married woman attains the social status of an adult female. In order to be a full-fledged woman, however, she must also have children. As Schneider (1968) has pointed out, the saying, "they're married but they don't have a family" implies that a childless couple is outside the standard Americal social structure, the nuclear family: a woman without children is in some respects regarded as "unnatural."

Once married and a mother, the proper sphere of a woman is her home. She remains "inside" the domestic sphere while her husband works "outside." If a man does not have a job, he will be judged unmasculine, irresponsible, even childish. But holding down a job does not contribute to a woman's socially defined femininity or womanhood. In fact, women who work outside their own homes, even those who perform domestic chores in someone else's home, are often called "girls." Further, a woman who is too closely associated with her job, too successful, or too dedicated, is often labeled "masculine." Thus, any American woman, even if she has married and has children and thus has proved her "femininity," may also "lose her femininity."

The ambivalent situation of the capable woman has been amply documented (Komarovsky 1946, 1950; Bernard 1971; Horner 1972). The hesitation shown by many American women to flout this cultural prescription has been seen as "the motive to avoid success" (Horner 1972). As Horner writes: "The aggressive, and by implication, masculine qualities inherent in a capacity for mastering intellectual problems, attacking difficulties, and making final decisions are considered fundamentally antagonistic to or incompatible with femininity" (1972:158). The findings of Costantini and Craik (1972) that women politicians express ambivalence about their own aggressive and leadership qualities, and that they generally play the typically feminine expressive role even in their political dealings, illustrate Jessie Bernard's observation (1972:90): "A woman could drink, swear, and swashbuckle like a trooper, but if she performed the stroking function she could be considered feminine." To avoid "losing her femininity" then, a woman can play a supportive role in which she chooses not to use her capabilities to the fullest, so that her achievements will not equal those of a man and will not threaten his dominance or her vision of her "femininity."

## "TRADITIONAL" VERSUS "FEMININIST" GROUP STRUCTURE

We have seen that women who step into the public arena must minimize and redefine the threats which their actions pose to their culturally defined femininity, and we have noted one way in which they may do so. In this section, some other strategies for coping with women's ambivalence toward achievement and power will be illustrated. The strategies of two Traditional groups, the Philadelphia chapter of NOW and the Liberal Women of Austin, Texas, will be contrasted with those of two Feminist groups, the Women's Center in Philadelphia and the Community Group in Austin. Aspects of the structure and ideology of these four organizations will be examined, in particular, the ways in which these groups handle, or fail to handle, power relations within their own organizations, and the ways in which conflict is handled.

The Community Group in Austin and the Women's Center in Philadelphia are ideologically and structurally much alike. Both explicitly deny that power within the organization exists (Philadelphia Anthropology Collective 1972; Garretson-Selby 1972). This denial results from their rejection of stereotyped sex roles, and their desire to create a new identity as women, not as second-class men. Male standards and behavior are rejected. Thus, since men organize themselves hierarchically, thereby creating leaders who have more power than the general membership, the women in these Feminist groups feel that women should avoid any semblance of hierarchy. In the Community Group and the Women's Center there are no permanent officers, no by-laws. There is a commitment to consensus as the only valid decision-making process. The idea is to avoid what the Women's Movement people have called "a male ego-trip." The following statement applies to both groups: "The assumption was that 'power' itself was an evil which, if not recognized, would cease to exist" (Philadelphia Anthropology Collective 1972:11). This theoretical denial of the existence of power persisted despite the fact that in both groups some women, in fact, exerted more influence than others and could be identified by observers as leaders.

The denial that power exists is a tactic that is not confined to feminist groups. Rather, it can be seen as one that is available to American women in general. Blood and Wolfe (1960) found that "dominant" wives often insisted they really didn't want decision-making power within the family (the criteria of dominance in this study), but had it forced upon them by their husbands' incompetence or weakness. Blood and Wolfe argue that, in fact, the husbands of "dominant" wives were "'no good' or incapacitated" (1960:45). It can be argued that the dominant wives pictured their husbands as feeble or incapable in order not to be put in the uncomfortable position of appearing to be powerful. As with the Feminists who label all power "male" and then consider power nonexistent in an all-female organization, the women of the Blood and Wolfe study appear to believe that if they admit their "dominance" they would be admitting to "masculinity."

Traditional women's groups, in contrast, while they acknowledge legitimate authority within the organization, may want to deny the power the organization wields on the "outside." The Liberal Women of Austin present such a case. Five years ago, this group was well organized, maintained a sizeable mailing list, screened and endorsed candidates for public office, and had considerable influence in the city government. The group was run by its president. While the monthy meeting was open to any member who wished to attend, new ideas or strategies had little chance of implementation if the president did not approve of them. Her authority was unchallenged, and her exercise of power considered legitimate by the membership.

On the other hand, the power the organization had in the city was well masked. Unlike most political organizations, the Liberal Women did not exaggerate or boast of the size of their membership. In fact, the actual number of names on the mailing list was a secret, known only to the president and secretary of the group. The members of the organization also did not take public credit for the firing of a city manager, an event in which they had considerable influence. The Liberal Women appeared to be a study group, similar to the League of Women Voters. However, when challenged, the president quietly and privately would recount the organization's accomplishments, its political triumphs and failures. By NOT advertising their strengths, the Liberal Women were employing a strategy of denial of power exerted OUTSIDE the organization, much as Feminist groups had denied the existence of power WITHIN the group. Thus, the Liberal Women could retain their "feminine" self-image by pretending to be ineffective, while the truth was that the Feminist groups often WERE ineffective because they refused to adopt any permanent structure.

Both Traditional women and Feminists felt that conflict within the groups should be avoided. For the Traditionalists, it was feared as destructive; for the Feminists, it was coded "male" and was therefore to be minimized. To avoid conflict, each type employed a different set of strategies.

Like the Liberal Women, the Philadelphia NOW minimized conflict by keeping authority centralized and absolute. Despite some ideological pressure toward consensus procedures, the Philadelphia NOW was organized and run so that the president of the chapter, or the governing board (open to officers or to committee heads) unilaterally handed down all decisions. Furthermore, the woman who founded the chapter insisted that a single slate of officers be presented at election time, because she felt that divisiveness was the result of competition (Philadelphia Anthropology Collective 1972:10). When a dissident group presented an alternative slate, the alternative names simply did not appear on the ballot. When the membership complained about an editorial written by a board member, the president announced that this particular member would no longer write editorials. Both within the Liberal Women and Philadelphia NOW, dissident factions had little choice. They could agree to agree with the president, or they could cease to participate in the organization, which in fact occurred when those who presented the alternative slate in the above example dropped out. Conformity of opinion within the organization was enforced by a direct use of the president's power.

In contrast, there were no such formal structures to impose conformity on the women of the Community Group or the Women's Center. During the formative periods of these groups, there was lively discussion, open conflict, or opposing views. However, over time, the commitment to consensus, designed to maximize participation of all the members, resulted in a tendency for discussion to be muted. A notable lack of willingness to voice objections to the prevailing opinions was found among the Women's Center members (Philadelphia Anthropology Collective 1972). In Austin, disagreement produced deadlock: the need for consensus led to constant splintering and withering away of the group during its first year. The organization became more and more homogeneous: women who did not "fit in" gradually drifted away. In some instance there was overt action taken against individuals whom the group members felt were too different or controversial. In one case, a united verbal attack on a woman who opposed abortion drove her away permanently. In another instance, a radical woman who expressed interest in becoming active in group projects was excluded when no one would tell her when or where meetings were to be held. The ideology espoused by the Community Group held that all women are "sisters," but in practice "sisterhood" was severely restricted.

Conformity was imposed on the Feminist groups by the requirement that consensus be reached and by the ideological rejection of aggression as "male." The Traditional groups avoided conflict for pragmatic reasons. The resultant lack of factions with both Feminist and Traditional organizations was very apparent. In fact, there was no case in which the women who were in the minority during a serious disagreement were observed to stand and fight. Open and continued disagreement would seem to be threatening both from the Traditional and Feminist point of view. Solutions to the Traditional problem, how to remain "feminine," and to the Feminist problem, how to reject male values and standards, both involved at some level denial of the exercise of power and thereby gave rise to mechanisms for sublimating conflict.

## THE WOMEN'S POLITICAL CAUCUS

The Women's Political Caucus, which in 1973 included a national organization as well as state and local chapters, began at an organizing conference held in July, 1971. It is the youngest of the organizations discussed here, and it differs in one obvious and immediate way from the groups discussed above: it was formed in order to involve women more fully in the political process at all levels of government and its members are openly interested in acquiring and using political power. They do not, like the Women's Center, define power out of existence, nor do they wish to play

a behind-the-scenes role like that of the Liberal Women. During the
conventions discussed below, there was no sign that conflict was being
avoided. As one caucus reported after the National Convention, "We
made the Democratic Convention sound quiet as a library" (PWPC
*Newsletter* 1973:1). Yet the subject matter of these debates illustrates
Traditional and Feminist viewpoints, and sheds light on the central
problem faced by the caucus members: how to organize.

A distinctly Feminist tone was heard in the Statement of Purpose adopted
at the 1971 organizing conference: "We recognize... that women have
a clear community of interest, and we therefore put forth... the following
issues as guidelines to the kinds of concerns we believe women must have
AS WOMEN [emphasis in the original], not as imitators of the traditional
male style and male politic." Clearly, the call is for an organization that
would be political, but political in a uniquely female way. The problem
has been that no one is precisely sure how, exactly, "female" politics would
differ from "male" politics. The continuing tension between caucus members who would like to see the caucus tightly structured and hierarchically
organized in a Traditional style, and those who favored an organization
more closely patterned after the Feminist model, is related to the underlying problem: how to organize AS WOMEN.

Feminist and Traditional women (as well as conservative and radical
women, in a political sense) who became members of the Women's Political
Caucus at the national, state, or local levels, subscribed to some degree to
a belief that women are more compassionate than men, more humane,
that women's political solutions would involve more cooperation and less
competition for power, that a woman-run government would eliminate
wars. The belief in the non-aggressiveness of women is consistent with
both Traditional and Feminist philosophy. Traditional women embrace
cultural definitions which define women as less aggressive than men;
Feminist women reject "male" aggression. Yet, the women who joined
the caucus were not afraid of conflict in general, and they acknowledged
that in the political arena aggression in some form is necessary. This
pragmatic acknowledgment creates problems for both Traditional and
Feminist women. In order to win elective office and thus to win real
political clout, one must raise money, organize effectively, be prepared to
issue vigorous public statements and to fight for one's position. The debates which will be discussed illustrate a see-saw between the desire to
create an highly efficient organization modeled after traditional political
party lines, and the desire to innovate, to create new organizational forms
which would be distinctly female.

## DEBATES OVER STRUCTURE OF TEXAS AND NATIONAL
## WOMEN'S POLITICAL CAUCUSES

Since no by-laws had been adopted at the organizing conference of the National Women's Political Caucus in 1971, state and local caucuses adopted a variety of structures and ideological positions. In Austin, Texas, in November of 1971, an organizing meeting similarly adopted no by-laws. Instead, an Interim Policy Council was elected, whose job was to organize a state convention so that a permanent state organization might be set up. At the convention in a Dallas suburb in March, 1972, a committee appointed by the Interim Policy Council drew up a proposal for a set of by-laws, which was presented to the convention for modification or approval.

This set of by-laws had a clearly Feminist bias. It was proposed that the ultimate authority of the state caucus was to be vested in the membership, open to all women of Texas. A president would be elected, but she would have no function other than spokeswoman for the caucus. It was suggested that the Policy Council be the executive arm. In an attempt to limit the authority of Policy Council members, it was suggested that they be subject to immediate recall by their constituencies and that all authoritative posts within the Policy Council rotate, each member serving a term of three to six months. No caucus dues would be charged. In this way it was hoped to encourage participation of minority women and poor women, and to prevent caucuses from more prosperous locales from having more power as a whole and in the Policy Council than those from less prosperous ones. This set of by-laws was challenged by a counter set, proposed by a Dallas-Fort Worth Group, who espoused a more Traditional structure. They proposed dues set at five dollars a person, permanent officers, and a strong presiding officer.

In the ensuing debate, there were two blocks of women who emerged as the most vocal. The Chicanas, some of whom were full-time organizers for La Raza Unida,[2] represented a radical political position, while the Dallas-Fort Worth women, active in party politics and well versed in parliamentary procedure, represented a conservative viewpoint. The Chicanas supported the Feminist set of by-laws, while the Dallas-Fort Worth block argued for their own counter set. Debate over the question of dues threatened to break up the convention. Walk-outs by both factions were

---

[2]   La Raza Unida is the name of the political party of Chicanos (Americans of Hispanic or Mexican descent, particularly those who live in the Southwestern region of the United States). In Texas, the party has achieved some success in local races, and has won for itself a place on the state ballot.

prevented only by the impartial and skillful rulings of the temporary chairwoman. A compromise leaving the payment of dues to the option of local caucuses was made possible by the more conservative, Traditional women's willingness to listen to the Chicanas' argument that money is not always the prime ingredient in political achievement and their plea for cooperation between Chicana and Anglo women. It was clear that most women at this convention were willing to entertain the possibility that a Feminist organization might work. A Policy Council was set up, but local caucuses were left autonomous. With some modifications, the original by-laws were adopted.

At the National Women's Political Caucus Convention, held in 1973 for the purpose of drawing up a set of permanent by-laws, the central issue proved to be the question of state and local autonomy. Traditional versus Feminist ideology, or political conservatism versus radicalism, were not so clearly apparent in the debates over structure. Yet, if the arguments — plans and counter plans — are examined closely, affinities to earlier divisions between Traditional and Feminist women emerge.

The prolonged debate at this convention was over a proposal for centralized control of the caucus, submitted by some New York City delegates (the proposal was not supported by all New York City or State delegates). These delegates proposed that the caucus be organized around Congressional Districts rather than around existing local or state caucuses. The plan proposed that the country be divided into roughly equal regions composed of equal numbers of Congressional Districts. Each region was to have five votes on a National Policy Board. On the surface, it looked like an equitable plan, which would ensure local participation (since each Congressional District in which a caucus was organized would be entitled to one delegate to the next National Convention), and would keep caucus jurisdictional disputes at a minimum. The plan, however, was violently opposed by those who called themselves the States' Coalition. They pointed out that a Congressional District organization would mean that larger states would have more than one vote in the Policy Board, while smaller states would have only a fraction of a vote. They felt the plan both unfair and impractical. First, it would undermine the power of the state and local groups. Second, while organizing around Congressional Districts might seem reasonable to a New Yorker, it seemed cumbersome to women from states in which a single Congressional District might take in a hundred-mile-long stretch of country. Further, it was felt that unless the Policy Council members, 75% of them at least, were elected directly by members of state caucuses, too much control would accrue to the Policy Council and there would be no direct control exercised by state or local caucuses upon Policy Council members. Thus, even some large states, notably Pennsylvania and Texas, voted against the Congressional District plan, even though it would have given them an advantage in the Policy Council over smaller states.

The rejection of the Congressional District plan was seen by some of the original organizers of the caucus as a triumph for a conservative viewpoint, stigmatized as an unwillingness to move beyond a parochial, state-bound political view. However, in view of the evolution of the Women's Political Caucus, and the main issue — how to organize as women — the judgment that the vote represented a conservative triumph is arguable. The defeat of the plan was in part motivated by a feeling that the "super stars," women like Gloria Steinem and Bella Abzug, who had been instrumental in forming the caucus, should step down. These women proposed and argued for the Congressional District plan. The vote also reflected a distrust of the Washington, D.C., staff, whom many delegates felt had shown themselves to be unsympathetic to local political problems. The Convention made clear its admiration for strong individuals: it gave Bella Abzug a standing ovation the day after her defense of the Congressional District plan had been shouted down. Yet, the convention delegates manifested suspicion of centralized authority and control. Their rejection of a standardized structure, and their embrace of the principle of local control, can be seen as a reflection of the Feminist viewpoint; for them to accept the Congressional Distrcit plan, to give up local autonomy, would have been a failure to innovate, to continue to seek organizational structures which were truly and uniquely female in nature. It remains to be seen whether the loose structure finally adopted can be effective in achieving political power for women in America.

CONCLUSION

We have looked at some ways in which women in America define and handle power within their own political groups, in an effort to maintain their "femininity" or to avoid copying "male" associational patterns. It is clear that both Feminist and Traditional women are hampered in their political pursuits by their own definitions regarding feminine and masculine behavior. Clearly it is not yet self-evident that American women will find ways to overcome the constraints imposed by their society and to participate fully in the game of political power.

We in the social sciences have likewise been hampered in our research on women in the public sphere, because of our assumption that political power, by definition, is a male prerogative. By focusing on the internal structure of women's organizations, an attempt was made to avoid comparisons between men and women and their exercise of power, and to explore the relationship between women and power in its own terms. The attempt has been only partially successful. Underlying most of the assumptions presented are comparisons with men's political organizations and the relationship of men to power. An awareness of our implicit assumptions about the nature of public power may permit an examination of human behavior AS IT IS. It is hoped that in this way we can transcend the limitations imposed by our own cultural definitions in future studies.

## REFERENCES

BERNARD, JESSIE
   1971    *Women and the public interest: an essay on policy and protest.* Chicago: Aldine-Atherton.
BLOOD, ROBERT O., DONALD M. WOLFE
   1960    *Husbands and wives: the dynamics of married living.* Glencoe: Free Press.
COSTANTINI, EDMOND, KENNETH H. CRAIK
   1972    Women as politicians: the social background, personality, and political careers of female party leaders. *Journal of Social Issues* 28:217–235.
GARRETSON-SELBY, LUCY
   1972    "The nature of American woman: a cultural account." Unpublished doctoral dissertation, Austin, Texas.
HORNER, MATINA S.
   1972    Toward an understanding of achievement-related conflicts in women. *Journal of Social Issues* 28:157–175.
KOMAROVSKY, MIRRA
   1946    Cultural contradictions and sex roles. *American Journal of Sociology* 52:184–189.
   1950    Functional analysis of sex roles. *American Sociological Review* 15: 508–516.
LEBEUF, ANNIE M. D.
   1971    "The role of women in the political organization of African societies," in *Women of tropical Africa.* Edited by Denise Paulme, 93–120. Berkeley: University of California Press. (Originally published 1960.)
THE NATIONAL WOMEN'S POLITICAL CAUCUS
   1971    *Statement of purpose.* (Reprinted in *The National Women's Political Caucus Convention booklet.* 1973.)
PHILADELPHIA ANTHROPOLOGY COLLECTIVE: MINDA BORUN, DIANE FREEDMAN, MOLLY MCLAUGHLIN, GINA OBOLER, LORRAINE SEXTON
   1972    "Power and participation in feminist organizations." Paper presented at the 71st annual meetings of the American Anthropological Association, Toronto.

PHILADELPHIA WOMEN'S POLITICAL CAUCUS
1973   *Newsletter*, February.
SCHNEIDER, D. M.
1968   *American kinship*. Englewood Cliffs: Prentice-Hall.

*Social Trends*

# Social Trends: Introductory Notes

ROUNAQ JAHAN

This section focuses on the changing role and status of women. What seems evident very quickly is the uniqueness with which each society integrates these changes. Another impression is how difficult it is to make generalizations about the role and status of women on a cross-cultural basis with so little research available to guide us.[1] Nonetheless, we can perceive some trends and begin to suggest where and how these changes are taking place. In some instances, attempts to explain why such changes are happening are even possible.

Changes in the structure of the economy, urbanization, and the spread of literacy and education — the general process of modernization — are common to all the cultures described. Some specific effects of these changes include new migration patterns, changes to occupations outside of the family, varied and dramatic modifications of attitudes, legal directives to equalize male and female benefits and new fertility patterns.

Migration, as Buechler has pointed out, has important economic ramifications for Spanish women. Earnings abroad provide new options for women and a degree of emancipation. When they return to Spain they are able to invest their earnings in small scale business or land, which in turn, elevates their position, status, and power roles within the community. The years away from home, besides improving economic circumstances, appear to reduce fertility and birth rate. Migration has a very different, very destructive effect on the social patterns in Uganda (Namboze) when the

---

[1] One reason for the paucity of material has been the inaccessibility of females to male ethnographers. Notable exceptions are few but important. Margaret Mead and John and Beatrice Whiting have attempted to temper this one-way view by using the male/female research team. — *Editor.*

young women leave the more rural areas and move to the more urban sectors for education and work. The ideal value that bearing children is the ultimate fulfillment of womanhood comes into conflict with a changing social system, disrupting the traditional mating patterns and leading to high rates of illegitimacy. In this case, the cultural traits of access to education, urbanization, and social values are changing at different rates.

Another type of change occurs in women's place and role outside the household range. Manisha Roy compares family patterns and role changes among Hindu and U.S. middle-class women, and Marilyn Hoskins describes changes in the economic patterns of women in North and South Vietnam. Both studies seem to indicate that the traditional Asian female role within the family is specifically defined while the role outside the family is not yet specific.

Women in these cultures can adapt or adjust more easily to this new setting. In this respect, women have greater role flexibility than do men. Men's roles outside the family are formally structured. As the economy changes they face difficulty in adjusting to new conditions.

A sense of security within the family facilitates the simultaneous performance of these two roles. I suggest in my paper on the status and role expectations of women in Bangladesh (see Jahan 1975) that women in Bangladesh and in Vietnam are allowed to adopt a role outside the family, and are granted equal status easily because this role does not conflict with the behavior expected of a woman performing the traditional family role. She gets full support from her family because she is said to be working "for the good of the family."

Two additional factors seem to make this role transition easier for these women than for Americans. The first is the availability of support for child care by other women within the family. Second, the acceptance of the motivation of the working woman is viewed as family-serving, not self-serving. No conflict of interests exists. Furthermore, when females do enter the professions, formerly male occupations, their male colleagues already hold a culturally determined distinction between a woman as a person and a woman as a possible mate or sex object. Women's sexuality is firmly based in the family and women are accepted in their own right. A woman's family would have no reason to fear sexual involvement or withhold help. This is very different from the problem of professional women in the United States, where women in the public scene are considered sexually available.

Occupational choices of women are another category of change. Large numbers of women are seeking careers. As would be expected, the trend is to choose traditional women's careers. But, the interesting thing is that what are defined as traditional careers for women differ from culture to culture. For example, in the United States, nursing and secretarial jobs tend to place women in a dependent and inferior position in relation to dominant males, i.e. doctors and executives. In cultures where male/ female physical contact is looked down upon, women go into teaching and medicine and not into nursing (which would put them in intimate contact with men) nor into secretarial jobs which would open them up to questionable spacing near males.

In Southeast Asia, business and commerce are traditionally women's work and, in Africa, trade and marketing occupations are regarded as traditionally belonging to the female. That is where women move when they assume extra-domestic work. Such trends in occupational choices have been fairly predictable except in some socialist countries where a rapid change for women to traditionally male economic occupations has occurred.

We are reminded that of the five U.N. member-nations currently denying the vote to women, four of them are Muslim countries (Lord). The persistence of this pattern stems from the pervasiveness of religious precepts coupled with a low socioeconomic level of development. However, change is occurring, and one major source through which it is funneled is education. Egypt introduced compulsory primary education for women in 1923, whereas Tunisia only introduced it in 1958. The effects are apparent in the far greater visibility of women in the public sphere in Egypt than in Tunisia.

This fits comfortably into a pattern noted for Japanese women prior to World War II (Raphael 1962).[2] Case studies indicated that two generations of educated women were necessary for a dramatic change of behavior from domestic roles into the public professions. The first educated class of women had to wait until they were the controllers of their daughters' fate. The Vassar-trained graduate was forced back into the traditional family pattern, but she, in turn made sure her daughter was able to fulfill her educational goals and become a working physician, a journalist, etc.

Minority status seems to outweigh religious edict in respect to cultural change. Two studies point to minority groups as the initiators of new behavior. The innovators in Lord's paper are the Roman Catholic women. In India, the Muslims and Christian groups appear to move first in the dominant Hindu society according to Kurian and John.

Finally, we are witnessing a reduction in the great gap between wo-

[2] Paper prepared for Seminar in Ethnographic Sources – Latin American Literature, Charles Wagley, Columbia University, entitled "The effects of American education on the returning Japanese woman."

men's legal and socioeconomic status. In many cultures, women are not granted legal equality, and even where they are, they often cannot fully exploit these rights because of their weak political position. Olga Vidláková's paper on Czechoslovakian legal patterns and mine (Jahan) on Bangladesh women reveal this gap between law and practice, but document signs of change.

Where nuclear family patterns predominate, children suffer from a lack of parenting. This is partially due to the time-consuming daily work schedule of mothers and the inability of men to maintain the expected level of achievement in their professions when they participate part-time in child rearing. Vidláková suggests that the laws be altered to take into account the special demands on women during their reproductive period. She suggests a PREFERRED status for working women. This is a new step, eagerly awaited.

## REFERENCES

JAHAN, ROUNAQ
1975   "Women in Bangladesh," in *Women cross-culturally: change and challenge*. Edited by Ruby Rohrlich-Leavitt. World Anthropology. The Hague: Mouton.

# The Eurogallegas:
# Female Spanish Migration

JUDITH-MARIA HESS BUECHLER

One effect of the women's liberation movement in the social sciences is that for scholars, both men and women, females have become a legitimate subject for research (Wolf 1973). Many of the more recent studies attempt to disclose the discrepancies between image and reality of women's roles in the developing world (Sweet 1967; Pescatello 1973) to explode popular myths (Hammond and Jablow 1973), and to evaluate the effects of social change in women's present situation and future prospects (Boserup 1970; J. M. Buechler 1972: Friedl 1972; González 1975; Sweet 1967). This paper addresses itself to the general image of the "passive/submissive, nonworking Spanish woman" and to the effect of international migration on Galician women in particular.

Migration accounts for the curious paucity of young men and especially young women in the total Spanish labor force statistics according to María Angeles Durán (1972). This has occurred because of the constraints on working women in Spain, the scarcity of jobs, the work conditions, and the nonsupportive social system. So, for many women, work abroad becomes the only remunerative employment available. Durán claims that contrary to Spanish Department of Emigration figures — (unreliable in this case) thirty-five to forty percent of all Spanish working women work outside the country. The proportion is even higher for single women and for women with at least some prior experience in service occupations. Within Spain, in Galicia in the northwest, even according to official records, more than seventy-five percent of the women work (1972: 124). It is, moreover, the region which has always had the highest rate of

Research (1972–1974) is supported by the Swiss National Science Foundation.

migration (Beiras 1970; Congreso Regional de la Emigración Gallega 1971; García Fernández 1965; Buechler and Buechler 1975).

My research on female activities included the study of migrants from one parish, a neighboring town and the provincial capital of the province of La Coruña as well as migrants from that area in Geneva, Berne, and Thun in Switzerland. It confirms the importance of female labor migration and clarifies the process involved. In addition, the simultaneous focus on the place of origin and the place of destination sheds light on "the process of adaptation to urban living as a matter of individual choice among a whole series of options, including that of a return to specific opportunities in the rural areas, rather than the fitting of a rural individual into a structured 'network' of relationships determined by the urban context alone" (Salisbury and Salisbury 1972:70). As we shall see, Galician women utilize a number of different strategies in coping with their poverty. They can work at home as subsistence farmers growing a few cash crops, add a small enterprise to farming or establish one in a town or city, or obtain unskilled employment in Switzerland, Germany, France or England.

In the parish studied, women work as homemakers and as farmhands. Beside their domestic chores within and around the homestead of childcare, housekeeping, food preparation, laundering, feeding of animals, milking, raising calves for sale and working at horticulture, they also till the fields, herd and go to local markets accompanied by kin and hamlet neighbors. Beginning in the 1960's with the rise of emigration to industrialized central Europe and wage labor for men in Galicia and elsewhere in Spain, women have become more burdened with agricultural work than before. They have had to take over operations previously performed by men, such as cutting of *tojo* or broom from the forest for litter and manure. They also have had to take on the accounting for suddenly they were "taking responsibility for one of the essential instruments of management" (Mendras 1970:88).

The absence of a major part of the labor force through emigration, which also included the landless who previously had worked as field hands for wages, has been in part compensated for by labor saving devices of both a technological and organizational nature. For instance, within homes, cash remittances from migrants are invested in butane gas stoves, processed foods, refrigerators for those homes which also serve as stores and bars, and, in a very few households censused, in washing machines. Outside the home, land which could no longer be tended was put to pasture or into crops which require less intensive care. Tractors, the province of young men, are now hired to aerate the soil, for plowing and lumbering, whereas in the past most of these tasks were performed by a small group of hamlet neighbors aided by a yoke of oxen and later by cows. In some areas in the region, land is being concentrated and cooperatives organized.

These changes are but mixed blessings for women. On the positive side, the new household aides are accompanied by higher standards of cleanliness, nutrition and childcare. On the other side, they also require more work. Further, the new farm equipment is used by men who manage and control the cooperatives. In these new cooperatives women are employed as very poorly paid hired help. They also continue to milk the family cow and work the small plots, subsistence activities which have continued along with modern agricultural practices.

The major contribution of Galician women to the economy remains the export of labor. They, like women in many other parts of the world (Salisbury and Salisbury 1972; Cole 1973; Sweet 1967; Boserup 1970) make it possible for OTHERS, primarily men, to engage in wage labor which is often associated with migration. By increasing their efforts at home these women are able to manage small scale farming, herding, and commercial enterprises in the absence of a large proportion of the men (Boserup 1970: 79). In Galicia, one strategy for women is to perform a holding operation at home for their migrant husbands who choose to return to their land. Even those migrants who intend to engage in wage labor upon their return find it economically advantageous for the woman to stay at home, work a small plot and raise some chickens, pigs and a cow, while the man commutes to a job, especially because female employment possibilities are scarce in Spain and those that do exist are poorly paid. A woman can contribute more to the family budget by providing food and performing other domestic services.

Another strategy is for women to add trade, commerce and services to their agricultural work, or to gain clerical and professional expertise. In fact, migrant fathers are beginning to invest a sizeable portion of their earnings in their daughters' education, and both fathers and husbands contribute to small enterprises like restaurants or beauty parlors which the women run from their homes.

Since a major form of investment in the land and property where small scale businesses are established is in the control of women, their social position is upheld. In Galicia, as in Greece (Friedl 1967, 1972) this is most evident in matters concerning the control and use of land and the decisions about marriage. Since inheritance is bilateral and the youngest daughter often obtains the parental homestead, uxorilocal residence is common. But, even in the public sphere especially regarding community welfare, "propertied" women are assuming an active part. Some women, who have been abandoned by husbands who migrated to the Americas, particularly Cuba and Uruguay earlier in the century and/or those whose husbands and sons are temporarily absent elsewhere in Europe, now often act in their own right in church and civil matters. Others use male kin as proxy. For example, some women now bid publicly for the honor of sponsoring a community feast either personally or through male intermediaries. Galician women have also become more aware of local politics. In the absence of men, they now run the bars and restaurants and learn from the public discussions held there. And, since they are sometimes household heads they are often consulted by local leaders. Even the priest and the agricultural extension workers use women as the communication channels to gain support for improvement projects. Furthermore female household heads now often represent their family's interests in court, in schools, and in welfare agencies.

At no time in the last few centuries could Galicia accomodate all its members. Those who did not have adequate land or who aspired to a higher standard of living have always used emigration as the only viable alternative. Today, men, enterprising single women, "unmarriageable girls" (mostly those with illegitimate children), newly married brides, and in rare cases women with disabled husbands continue to seek "a new life" abroad.

In 1972 in Thun, Switzerland, in a sample of 262 Galicians, 74 (or 28 %) were females whose average age was 28. Sixty-four percent of these were married; all but one of the married group was accompanied by her husband. Thirty-six percent were single. More than half of the whole sample had annual (or "permanent") work permits. The remainder had seasonal work permits which allowed them to remain and work, legally, in Switzerland for only 9 months of any calendar year. (The 1973 figures registered only a slight increase on all counts.)

These migrant women are highly valued for their domestic services, earning capacity, and thrift by Galicians and Swiss alike. Unlike Galicia, where female work is hard yet independent and of equal prestige, work in the host country is routine and low ranked. They work predominantly in service occupations, in hotels, restaurants, and hospitals, where their ability, cooperation, and background of hard work more than compensated for their lack of education, foreign language skills or training. These disadvantages account for the narrow range of jobs, but it is also in part due to their own preference for "feminine work" in the so-called "helping" occupations where they feel they can work in protected situations with little contact with men.

Ironically, the Swiss bias against their own women working outside the home, and the resultant labor shortage, favors foreign female labor so that sex discrimination in work conditions seemed nowhere apparent. In fact certain occupational flexibility is possible for married women with small children. In some instances schedules have been adjusted, children accompanied their mothers, and occasionally childcare facilities were provided.

In general, however, the mobilization of foreign female labor necessary for the attainment of Swiss economic goals is not associated with the provision of adequate social services. Family health insurance is absent for those members left at home. Few childcare centers exist and housing is inadequate in all but a few cases. Those few job training or educational opportunities which are available are not well attended, because the women are unwilling to invest time and effort in programs abroad which have no long term financial return in Galicia.

In spite of the foregoing reservations, the migration situation DOES provide both single and married women with the possibility of a degree of emancipation and the opportunity for a certain kind of independence. Generally, single women migrate with a kinswoman or friend and move into the home of a relation upon arrival in Switzerland. Work and leisure time activities, such as dances, rapidly involve them with persons from other parts of Galicia, diverse regions of Spain, from Italy and to a lesser extent Switzerland, which considerably broaden their horizon. In the case of married women, the female role becomes less restricted in areas of decision-making, household chores, natality, childcare, and social life. As wage earners, they are more involved in decisions about housing, jobs, and investment. Household chores are more frequently shared. Men who had migrated alone often took care of their own daily needs for food, housing and laundry so that when their wives joined them, they continued to help when work schedules conflicted.

Gallego migrants, like Blacks in Midwestern cities (Stack 1975), West Africans, and West Indians in London (Goody 1975) distribute "their parental responsibilities socially." Mothers and fathers may work alternate shifts and take turns caring for infants. They may also share the responsibility with kin and non-kin living in the same apartment or apartment building, or leave their children in day care centers or with Swiss "baby sitters." The difficulty of getting adequate lodgings and a permanent work permit — both preconditions for bringing children to Switzerland — forces many migrants to leave children behind in the care of maternal grandparents. Since circumstances both in Switzerland and in Galicia are such that no more than two children can be cared for adequately if both parents are away working, the control of natality is an important factor in migration. In this case it seems to be the exigencies of migration to central Europe rather than "the city as a locus for values and means" (Scrimshaw 1975) which brings about family planning.

Migration has also led to changes in interactional patterns between the sexes. Unlike Galicia, where social life in public places tends to be sex segregated — men congregate with other men in bars — Gallego couples spend more of their leisure time with each other in the privacy of their own quarters or at the homes of friends. As for Galician women, although they are not entirely politicized by the migration experience, they have nevertheless become more aware of those aspects of the superstructure which have direct implications in their own lives. For instance, they are aware of the neglect of Galicia as a region on the part of the Spanish central government, and they are concerned about those Swiss policies which discriminate against migrant labor.

I have been concerned with an unexplored area in the social anthropological literature, namely Galician migration. I have taken individual options into consideration and considered the real behavior and alternatives of women in one poor region of Spain. Contrary to others (Schwarzweller, et al. 1971), who conceive of migration as a system maintained in equilibrium by the interaction of a donor subsystem and the recipient or host system, I view migration as a process, as an individual choice, among rational interlinked options within the present day economic constraints and legislative controls of both the migrant and the host areas.

REFERENCES

BEIRAS, J. M.
1970    *Estructura y problemas de la población gallega Grafinsa.* La Coruña.
BOSERUP, E.
1970    *Woman's role in economic development.* London: George Allen and Unwin.
BUECHLER, H. C., J. M. BUECHLER
1975    "Los Suizos: Galician migration to Switzerland," in *Migration and development.* Edited by Helen I. Safa and Brian M. du Toit, 17–29. World Anthropology. The Hague: Mouton.
BUECHLER, J. M.
1972    "Peasant marketing and social revolution in the state of La Paz, Bolivia." Unpublished doctoral thesis, McGill University.
COLE, D.
1973    Bedouins of the oil fields. *Natural History* 82(9).

CONGRESO REGIONAL DE LA EMIGRACIÓN GALLEGA
1971   *Problemática de la emigración gallega.* Oficina de relaciónes con los gallegos en el Exterior La Coruña.

CRONIN, C.
1970   *The sting of change: Sicilians in Sicily and Australia.* Chicago: University of Chicago Press.

DURÁN, M.
1972   *El trabajo de la mujer en España.* Editorial Tecnos Madrid.

FRIEDL, E.
1967   The position of women: appearance and reality. *Anthropological Quarterly* 40 (3):97–108.
1972   "Migration and decision-making: a Greek case." Mimeo.

GARCÍA FERNÁNDEZ, J.
1965   *La emigración exterior de España.* Barcelona: Ariel.

GONZÁLEZ, N.
1975   "Types of migratory patterns to a Dominican city and to New York," in *Migration and urbanization.* Edited by Brian M. du Toit and Helen I. Safa, 209–223. World Anthropology. The Hague: Mouton.

GOODY, E.
1975   "Delegation of parental roles in West Africa and the West Indies," in *Socialization and communication in primary groups.* Edited by Thomas R. Williams, 125–181. World Anthropology. The Hague: Mouton.

HAMMOND, E., A. JABLOW
1973   *Women: their economic role in traditional societies.* An Addison Wesley Module in Anthropology 35.

MENDRAS, H.
1970   *The vanishing peasant: innovation and change in French agriculture.* Cambridge, Massachusetts: MIT Press.

PESCATELLO, A., *editor*
1973   *Female and male in Latin America.* Pittsburgh: University of Pittsburgh Press.

SALISBURY, R., M. SALISBURY
1972   "The rural-oriented strategy of urban adaptation: Siane migrants in Port Moresby," in *The anthropology of urban environments.* Edited by T. Weaver and B. White. S A A Monograph. Washington.

SCHWARTZWELLER, HARRY K., et al.
1971   *Mountain families in transition.* University Park: Pennsylvania State University Press.

SCRIMSHAW, S.
1975   "Families to the city: a study of changing values, fertility, and socio-economic status among urban in-migrants," in *Population and social organization.* Edited by Moni Nag, 309–330. World Anthropology. The Hague: Mouton.

STACK, CAROL B.
1975   "Who raises black children: transactions of child givers and child receivers," in *Socialization and communication in primary groups.* Edited by Thomas R. Williams, 183–205. World Anthropology. The Hague: Mouton.

SWEET, L.
  1967  "The woman of 'Ain ad Dayr'," in *Appearance and reality: status and role of women in Mediterranean societies. Anthropological Quarterly* 40(3).
WOLF, M.
  1973  Half of China: a report on a conference. *SSRC Items* 27(3).

# Attitudes towards Reproduction in a Rapidly Changing African Society

JOSEPHINE M. NAMBOZE

Becoming a mother in most African societies is regarded as a woman's birthright, so that sterility is likely to have social, cultural, and emotional repercussions. The birth of a child can sometimes help to stabilize a marriage and, in a polygamous society, a barren woman may be devalued as compared with the other wives.

Because of the importance attached to reproduction, lack of children may in some societies lead to the break up of a marriage and return of a dowry to the husband by the woman's parents. The woman is then free to marry again. If, however, the man is very fond of the woman, he may not divorce her but would still marry another women in order to have children. A wealthy man can always afford to pay the dowry (in areas where this is essential to the marriage) and would marry several wives while a poorer man would have fewer wives. If a woman is educated it is not often easy to divorce her because of childlessness; in this case the man would look for a child outside the marriage.

If childless, a woman would always try to seek medical help, often from the traditional herbalists who, though reputable, often charge exhorbitant fees. The interesting thing is that it is the woman who always seeks treatment. The man does not often think he can be at fault, and in many cases he might have already proved his fertility by having had children elsewhere. With the increase of westernized medical facilities many women are utilizing these services, and in cases of monogamous marriages the man often comes along for investigations as well.

So much importance is attached to reproduction that in a study conducted by the author (Assaél, et al. 1972) at an antenatal clinic about nine miles outside Kampala, the capital of Uganda, of the 100 women interviewed 85% volunteered the information that they were using native medicine as well as seeking Western-type medicine! The native medicine they used fell into the following categories:

1. Herbal baths mainly to refresh themselves and to prevent "ebigere" which is known in the medical language as puerperal insanity. It is believed in this community that this disease is due to the promiscuous activities of the mother or the father either before or in the course of their marriage.
2. Some mothers were taking a mixture of clay and herbs mixed in water mainly to prevent the effect of salt on the baby which appears as septic spots particularly during the neonatal period, to ensure that the pregnancy proceeds well, and to keep the mother and foetus in good health.

## MAJOR SOCIAL CHANGES

In the past and up to the present day many parents wished their daughters to become pregnant and deliver only after they got married. It was a great disgrace if a girl married AFTER becoming pregnant and more so if she delivered while still "in the parents' compound." In some communities she would even be an outcast. At present some parents would still put some pressure on the man responsible for the pregnancy to marry their daughter, as her chances of marrying somebody else would have been greatly minimized. In some parts of Uganda the man in question would have to pay a fine to the girl's parents, and then pay a dowry, i.e. if he were going to marry the girl.

One of the greatest social changes is that the number of girls who become pregnant before marriage is on the increase. This includes both girls of school age and working girls. In the remote rural areas such girls, with a few exceptions, are no longer so harshly treated, although some of them after discovering that they were pregnant panicked and ran away from the parents' home to a home of a relative. In urban and periurban areas parents are becoming more tolerant. The practice of putting pressure on the man to marry the pregnant daughter is on the decrease. Disappointed as they may be, the parents usually look after their daughter until she delivers, after which they would look after their grandchild while their daughter continued with her education if she were still attending school. Alternatively she would look for a job, or return to her previous job if she were already employed. What the parents would expect from the father of their grandchild is some financial assistance in caring for their grandchild, and if the father of the child should decide to marry their daughter they would be all the more pleased. Some of the school girls get pregnant because they don't know the consequences of their sexual activities. Others are tempted by more mature men who promise them attractive gifts.

As more and more girls are becoming educated, many of them qualify for well-paid jobs with good housing and can really lead a good life. Such girls may have steady boyfriends who promise to marry them after a certain period; a few of these girls may become pregnant. In some cases the boyfriend may desert the girl after learning that she is expecting a baby. Then the girl panics and may even attempt to abort. A few may just forget about the boyfriend and support themselves throughout pregnancy, look after the baby afterwards, and if they are lucky meet somebody else and get married.

On the other hand there are some working girls who wait for some time to get married and after reaching a certain age they give up hope. Since it is the desire of almost every woman in this part of the world to have a baby, these girls finally decide to have a child or two of their own. They look after themselves and their babies well, often supporting them throughout life. This gives them an incentive to work. This seems to be one of the major social changes, for such girls. There seems to be no stigma attached to the pregnancy.

There is a different class of girls with no special training who may go to town to look for employment. In the course of this move, she may meet a man who befriends her. This is fairly easy to do in towns since the percentage of men is often higher than that of women. The 1969 Census figure for the city of Kampala revealed the following percentages of men in the given age groups.

| Age group in years | Percentage of men |
|---|---|
| 15–19 | 50.4 |
| 20–34 | 61.0 |
| 35–49 | 63.2 |
| 50–64 | 58.4 |
| 65+ | 52.8 |

As a result of the friendship the girl may become pregnant but by this time the man might have already disappeared. Usually he is very difficult to trace because of the multiplicity of ethnic groups and the use of different languages which makes communication difficult. The poor girl may then be left on her own throughout pregnancy and after delivery she may have no financial support whatsoever to look after herself and the baby. She may have a housing problem as well since she would be more likely to be staying with a friend whose accommodation would now be too small for the three of them. This is unlike the rural area where the extended family system of African society would enable her to find a home. The ultimate solution for some of these destitute girls would be to abandon the baby. Cases of such abandonment are very much on the increase throughout the country. Various child care agencies are looking after such homeless babies but the need for their services is much greater than the facilities they can afford to offer. Some of the girls in the situation already described may have no alternative but to take the baby to the maternal grandparents in the rural areas where they run the risk of suffering from the maternal deprivation syndrome described by Bowlby. The mother then looks for a job and after finding one she may yet find another boy friend. Thus, the process of serial loose ties then continues. Of course some lucky girls in the course of this may find a permanent partner and may settle down in marriage.

In this paper, an attempt has been made to explain the attitudes towards reproduction in a rapidly changing African society. The desire to have a child as the ultimate fulfilment of womanhood has been emphasized. Similarly, the effects of urbanization and industrialization on childbearing and child rearing have been touched upon. The challenges are numerous at this stage, but much effort is being made to face them and solve them.

## REFERENCES

ASSAÉL, M. I., J. M. NAMBOZE, G. A. GERMAN, F. J. BENNETT
  1972  Psychiatric disturbances during pregnancy in a rural group of African women. *Social Sciences and Medicine* 6:387–395.
BOWLBY J.
  1952  *Maternal care and mental health* (second edition). Monograph series 2, W.H.O., Geneva.
REPUBLIC OF UGANDA
  1969  *Report on the 1969 population census*, volume one: *The population of Kampala City.*

# The Concepts of "Femininity" and "Liberation" in the Context of Changing Sex-Roles: Women in Modern India and America

MANISHA ROY

The theoretical assumption underlying this comparative analysis is that women in every society are socialized and enculturated toward a set of roles. However, the roles are not always amenable to change over time. Some institutions which function as socializing agents change at different paces. Some lag behind, clashing with the values of other faster moving institutions. Many women in both modern India and America find themselves caught in this unbalanced situation. When this occurs they must make compromises between the economic, social and familial demands on them and their personal aspirations. Some cultures offer less scope for such compromise than others and the source of this difference can be found in the sociocultural history of a society and in the pattern of female socialization for adulthood. Change in roles within the milieu of each culture, changes within that culture and the many factors influencing any given individual have been rendered somewhat controllable by focusing on only two crucial concepts in the role change of modern woman in two countries, India and America.

The two concepts — "femininity" and "liberation" (or freedom) — were used as a heuristic device to contrast differences and effects in the socialization process of women in these two cultures, and to show the deep-seated and far-reaching implications in various sociological, economic and psychological aspects of women's roles. It is suggested that the values and

Although the Indian data used in this paper came from one particular state, Bengal, the premises and conclusions made in this study overlap greatly with those of other parts of India. I wish to thank Gunhild Bisztray of University of Chicago for a very encouraging discussion and help on the library research leading to formulating my ideas in this paper.

ideologies expressed in language and its connotative usage have a reciprocal and enduring impact on human behavior and thought on both cognitive and affective levels. Thus, cultural notions such as "femininity" or
"masculinity" or "individualism" contribute toward the formation of an
individual's self-image. This is especially true in the case of the self-conscious, literate, middle classes of the cultures described here.

As we will see below, the use of these value concepts helps clarify a
number of puzzles encountered by both Western and Indian observers. My
intimate contact for a decade with American culture as an anthropologist
and an Indian woman and my life-long contact with my own culture has
led me to believe that these concepts are valuable indicators, operators and
predictors in the realm of women's roles in both private and public arenas.

## METHODS AND DATA

The observations, analysis and conclusions reached in this study are based
on field work in urban West Bengal (India) and urban Southern California
between 1965 and 1970. The socioeconomic group spanned the broad
category of the middle class with a Hindu literate cultural background in
Bengal and a white Judeo-Christian literate background (at least four
years of college education) in California. In addition to the anthropological method of participant observation plus both unstructured and structured interviews, I used a number of published materials in sociology,
psychology and literature. In the case of both cultures so-called soft data
offered by literature, and mass media of various kinds formed a larger
part of the background material. Though often fictionalized and exagger-
ated, the radio, television and the popular journals have been extremely
valuable supplementary sources of information in this research. The age
of the women studied ranged from 5 to 70, with the majority around 30. I
also interviewed men although my primary concern was with women.

## THE CONCEPTS

Let us delimit the cultural meaning and connotation of the concepts of
"femininity,"[1] liberation and freedom first for the Indian culture and

---

[1]    The term in classical Sanskrit that comes closest to the lexica lmeaning of the English term "femininity" is *nārītva* a compound of *nāri*(woman) + *tva* (a suffix meaning
"the content of", "related to"). The word has an ideal connotation and is often used
in formal writing or speeches to refer to Indian womanhood. The etymological mean-

then for America. In Bengali the term "femininity" has none of the implied connotations that the Sanskrit word *nārītva* has, such as the ideal feminine virtues of docility, obedience, self-sacrifice, etc. These qualities are desirable in a women but not oppositional, that is, feminine versus masculine. This lack of opposition between masculine and feminine attributes contrasts strongly with the American meaning of "femininity" with the implicit "non-masculine" emphasis.

Further, in Bengal, a woman is not more desirable or admirable because she is more especially feminine. She is not more or less feminine. She is feminine simply by virtue of being a woman. Once a woman, she may be more or less gentle or demure even as she may be more or less pretty, taller or shorter. Some of these qualities are as desirable and becoming in men as they are in women depending on a man's role or the context of his behavior. Therefore, the concept *'meyelī'* (feminine) does not embody a set of attributes which constitutes a clear-cut identity connected only with a female and desirable in the eyes of men and the society at large as occurs in America.

In India a woman's femininity does not depend on her ability to attract the opposite sex with sexual and personality factors determined by male standards (Roy 1975). In other words, the physical attributes designed to attract the male do not constitute a major part in the cultural definition of femininity. What is stressed are indicators/signs (*lakshman*) — both physical and mental which indicate she will successfully play out her future female roles. Hence a prospective bride is evaluated on indicators which promise the successful fulfillment of the daughter-in-law, wife and mother roles. What makes a woman feminine and attractive depends on what point she is in her life-cycle and how well she is playing her roles. A little girl is attractive because she plays her role of daughter and of sibling ably. A young woman is attractive because she is an able wife and daughter-in-law (sister, sister-in-law, etc.), a good neighbor and friend of both sexes.

The implications of such cultural notions are clear. The behavioral adjuncts change with changing roles and age. So loss of specific physical attributes that occur as one ages is not threatening to women. Parenthet-

---

ing (related to women) mentioned above is nearly lost in common usage. In modern Bengali this term is hardly used to refer to a woman. The Bengali word (common usage) "femininity" is *meyelī*, a compound of *meye* (girl, daughter or woman) + *lī* (a case ending for adjectives meaning "related to" "in connection with"). In real usage the word is used either to mean "effeminate" (pejorative when referred to a male) or feminine in a very neutral sense such as *meyelī* clothes, *meyelī* jewelry, *meyelī* talk and so on.

ically it might be valuable to mention that the concept of femininity just outlined is somewhat changing in urban India where the model of a woman is beginning to be a mixture of movie star, novel heroine and westernized city woman. However, the majority of Bengali population (even men) has not yet integrated these modern western notions sufficiently to support the emergence of such ideas (Roy 1973). A modern woman tries to strike a compromise by compartmentalizing[2] her "modern role" from her "traditional roles." For example, a female physician may behave very much like a masculine woman (in the American sense) in her clinic and swing back to a "feminine wife" or a "daughter-in-law" at home as she changes from her work clothes to her domestic sari.

A further behavior, aggressiveness (as expressive of independent thinking and behavior) is used in America today as a negative attribute when applied to women. It seems as if the American concept of femininity in both the traditional and modern senses excludes such attributes as "aggressiveness," because it is a masculine trait. Aggressiveness is quite acceptable in a Bengali woman, provided her particular role calls for it. For example, a woman over forty who is a matron-mother may rule over her children, her husband and even her neighbors and still not be called aggressive or a "bossy female." She is allowed this seemingly "unfeminine" behavior because she has reached a status in her life-cycle where this is acceptable. A young woman can act aggressively providing she is socially clever and capable of using the right symbols and expressions to assert her authority in the right context. *What really matters in Indian society is how well a woman acts out her role(s) vis-à-vis other roles in a given context.* And she is socialized by her family to acquire cues for relevant behaviors and the culture supports and reinforces such behaviors. Socialization and ideology seem to be in harmony.

The roles a woman is socialized into are mostly ascribed roles determined by birth or marriage. Thus her self-concept is framed in the context of her roles. She is not a person if she is stripped of her roles. Her personal gratification or frustrations are also connected with her role as daughter, wife, mother or grandmother, rather than as woman. If she is unhappy, she tries to find explanations in her actions and behavior, in her roles or in things over which she has little control. She is not encouraged to delve into her own psyche or to have self-doubts. This is possible be-

---

[2]    Milton B. Singer (1972) first used this term in the context of Indian cultural change to demonstrate how compartmentalization is used as an adaptive strategy to cope with the incongruity that may be generated by simultaneous "traditional" and "modern" practices. An actor achieves a compartmentalization of two spheres of conduct and belief that would otherwise collide. The shift between the two may be symbolized by shift in clothes, language and even behavior which two or more settings may demand.

cause the Indian culture offers less confusion between role-expectations and the real contexts of behavior. Even in a somewhat changing socio-economic scene a woman can count on cues from her traditional roles to help her combine behavioral and affective contents. For instance she can extend the role patterns of behavior rather than create new ones, as when a woman treats her male office colleagues as she would her male cousins. In Bengali society, cousins cover a range of various emotional components and, since the nature of modern roles themselves is fluid, such extensions are feasible and often necessary.[3]

The discontinuities in cultural conditioning that Ruth Benedict talked about seem to appear more often in America than in India. For example, in modern America a married woman is ascribed a number of roles, each role implying certain privileges and obligations. Conflict may arise if a woman claims the privileges of more than one role without accepting the corresponding obligations, which her early socialization may not have included.

An example from my field notes indicates how a Bengali woman may visualize herself in her roles. A woman of forty relates the following:

At the age of forty looking back I often try to think how my life has been. I was born in a happy family with my father and uncles always spoiling me. When I did well in my school work, my grandmother always warned me not to do too well, because the books would not tell me how to be a good daughter-in-law and a mother. She meant I would be a lot better off if I paid heed to her and watched other women do their duties. I felt like rebelling at that time. But when my family began to negotiate for my marriage at the age of 19, even before I finished my B. A. I did not rebel and in fact I even welcomed the idea of getting married. For the first five years of marriage I used to feel very home-sick for my father's house. I felt frustrated with my husband. Gradually I became close to my husband's family and began to sympathize even with my husband. In a big household he could not possibly pay much attention to me. Then I discovered compensations in marriage. I was so delighted for example, to have my first son. He took me away from everything including my husband for about 5-6 years. He filled my life. Only then I began to understand what my grandmother used to mean... Yes, I missed my friends and my cousins and those carefree days of my school and college; but this is life and I would not like to go back to those days anymore. Of course, life does not go on the same way always. I was very unhappy when my son had to go to England for his higher studies; I felt my whole life was empty. But I adjusted to the situation. At least I had a son. What could I have done without one? I know gradually he will go even further away. He will marry and, who knows, perhaps his wife would not like the idea of staying with us. Suppose he marries an English girl! I think of all this. But then I am getting old and it is good for me to think of Him, the God, and get involved

---

[3] I discuss this aspect of role-overlap and compositeness within a Bengali family in another paper (Roy 1973).

in *pujā* and meditation. Ten years ago I used to laugh at this suggestion, now I see why my widowed aunt spends seven or eight hours in her *pujā* room... No, I do not have regrets. God gave me a husband who is alive and a son who is good and respectable. What else should a woman need?

Or, to quote from a life-history of a 50 year old articulate and sensitive informant:

I am beginning to think at the age of 50 that something is wrong with life itself. We plan to be happy and do all sorts of things that our mothers and grand-mothers and fathers taught us. I tried my best to be a good wife, a daughter-in-law and a good mother. I enjoyed doing it most of the time but often I felt tired and did not see much point in anything. I found out, for example, that my son no matter how much he loved me would go away someday and would love his wife. This is the way life is. But this knowledge could not make me accept it totally. I am often convinced that we women are born to suffer.

These two views are not that much in contrast with the attitude of a 30 year old modern woman, a college professor who is also married and has three young children:

Well, there are moments when I wonder about what I really wanted and what happened to me. But then, who can plan about life? In a sense, I ought to feel quite happy and smug compared to my class-mates. At least I have a good job in a respectable college with a principal as a boss who is not impossible to get along with. At home, I must admit, my mother-in-law is quite understanding about the time I spend outside home. Because she knows that unless I add to the family income, things are going to be difficult. Also, I have a feeling she prefers that I am not around all the time. She can feel important in her son's household and do things she likes such as bossing the maids around. Besides, the children love her. That solves the baby-sitting problem. As for my husband, frankly, I don't have time to worry about him. During the first years of our marriage I used to grumble about his frequent business trips and his apparent neglect of me and the family. Now I think it's even good not to have him around that much. We meet everyday but hardly have time to be close or intimate. He is a kind and distant person. And I feel proud that I have a husband who allows me to work and does not demand much. Considering all, I have to say that life could be worse.

All these women seem to express the common theme that none of them is confused as to their roles nor would they consider stepping out of their present role(s) — which in India means stepping out of life. They all accept the pain and the plan of life as given and as resulting from a combination of uncontrollable factors. By the same token they also have experienced occasional happiness and satisfaction, again resulting from a combination of factors not necessarily under their control.

A series of published sociological studies explore the current sex-role stereotypes and self-concepts of college students in America. Findings from the first research (D. M. Broverman, et al. 1968) show that 74 male and 80 female college students indicated more frequent high valuation of stereotypically masculine than feminine characteristics. Among some bipolar items the positively valued masculine traits formed a cluster of related behaviors which entail competence, rationality, assertion, independence. The feminine traits formed a cluster of related behavior entailing submissiveness, warmth, expressiveness, dependence, impulsiveness, minimum logic, etc. The results from another research conducted by the same team in 1972 showed similar notions still persist. For example, responses to the sex-role questionnaire from 599 men and 383 women showed that stereotypic masculine characteristics are still valued more than the stereotyped feminine characteristics.

Since feminine traits are negatively valued it would follow that women would tend to have more negative self-concepts than do men. A woman is faced with a contradiction. Since having masculine traits is more desirable in this culture, if she wishes to be feminine she risks being an inferior human being. On the other hand, if she adopts the desirable masculine traits in order to become more acceptable, she gives up the socially sanctioned "nice feminine woman" which may damage her self-image. This double-bind partially results from a notion of "femininity" based on traits and attributes which reflect the demands of an industrial economy which values competition rather than the emotional needs of an individual. Further, this concept of "femininity" fosters ambivalence and an increasing polarization between the two concepts masculinity and femininity, yielding a hostile sex-struggle in personal as well as public spheres of male-female interaction.[4] Bengali culture has not as yet developed indigenous symbols to express a changed attitude about the concept of "femininity" among the youth, as appears to be the case in contemporary middle-class America.

Data collected in 1942 and 1943 (Komarovsky 1946) of 153 undergraduate students showed that while there were a number of permissive variants of the feminine attributes for women of college age (such as being good sport, glamour girl) they always were expressed with reference to the male sex-role. As a school girl, a woman may have been encouraged to compete with boys intellectually, but from adolescence on she was expected

---

[4] Findings from Broverman, et al. (1970) do not show any indications to support the current belief that such polarization is being reduced, at least among the youth of the university campuses. The rhetoric on the campuses stressing a neutral attitude toward homosexual/lesbian movements may not reflect the attitudes of the wider culture as much as the wishful thinking of small groups of individuals. The effect of the clothes and hair-style of today's youth tends to blur the male-female distinction.

to underplay her intellectual ability — a decisively masculine trait — and prepare herself to be more feminine and consequently attractive to men. This conflict between two types of sex-roles that women were encouraged to internalize may clash with educational roles as well as family roles. Whereas in early childhood a girl is encouraged to prepare herself for a desexualized modern role, in college she is definitely discouraged from doing so. The goals set by each role are mutually exclusive and the fundamental personality traits each evokes are diametrically opposed. One significant side-effect of such contradictory socialization is expressed very aptly by Jessie Bernard in her study *American family behavior* (1942). She points out that women after marriage often discover the fallacy of the sex stereotypes. They also discover that their husband, the sturdy American male, often cuts an inferior figure in intimate, interpersonal relations and familial crisis situations. These discoveries are doubly traumatic, for as a wife, a woman cannot express these feelings to others. As a consequence she either learns to delude herself perpetually into an acceptable inferior status of wife or falls into another pattern of behavior of babying the husband — an inversion of the cultural stereotype. A third alternative is to face her situation and run the risk of breaking a marriage (which is also culturally not acceptable).

I was studying both men and women in southern California during the summer of 1970, at various stages of the dissolution of their marriages. Some of the autobiographical data illustrates the problem of socialization mentioned above. Many informants perceived their childhood and adolescence socialization as directly connected with their marital maladjustments. One woman, aged 32, with a B. A. degree from a well-known midwestern university, born of white Protestant parents related the following:

When I was five or six my mother told me many times that I had to play with certain kinds of toys and behave like a little lady. I was given toys which looked like miniature kitchen and bedroom stuff. I often played with the girls next door and we imitated our mothers in our games – mostly doing housework. By the time I went to school my first IQ test indicated that I was far above average in intelligence and my parents made a big thing out of it. I was encouraged to read a lot and do well in Math and Science. When I was 14 or 15, unlike many of my friends' mothers, my mother did not seem to bother too much over my dating situation. I grew up without much emphasis on clothes, cosmetics, etc. I went out with my dad a lot watching baseball games... I went to a college away from my home town and that's where for the first time I faced difficulty with my self-image as a girl. I was doing well at school winning scholarships from the very beginning, but suddenly the whole atmosphere made me aware that doing well at school was not enough. My dorm friends constantly talked about boys and sex and future marriage. A few of my friends from high school still corresponded with me and we all agreed that we would like to go for graduate school and never get married. None of us except one, whose mother was a community college professor, got direct encouragement from home. With my parents, it was odd; because they never said anything one way or the other, except for my mother, who began to write letters to me in my junior year, the main theme of which was consistently the same advice regarding making myself more attractive to boys. I hardly ever dated till my junior year. I met my future husband one Saturday evening in the library; he told me he was impressed by my seriousness. My husband was in his second year of graduate school in physics when we got married and, despite my desire to go to graduate school I decided to take up a job so that we could settle down and have a little extra. We both agreed that I would go back to school after he finished his Ph. D. After two years I became pregnant with our first child – not an unplanned one. I wanted to be a mother at that time. We had two other sons within the next four years. My rationale was that once I had them all, I could go back to school when they grew up fast. When my third son was a year old we moved to California with a better job for my husband. Meanwhile I stopped working. I noticed my husband did not mind my being a full-time housewife and mother at all. We began to drift apart. In his new job he hardly had time to do anything with me or the family. I began to feel very weary and hemmed in. I loved my kids, yet I felt as if I had to get out. I was not quite sure what bothered me most. I felt cheated. The worst thing was that my husband did not understand it at all. He accused me of being too much of an intellectual. We began to argue a lot, and then fight and gradually life together became unbearable... Suddenly I realized I should not have been married. I felt I was married to a stranger and I appeared a stranger to myself. I craved to go back to my third year of college and do it all over again. I wish I were free to do what I wished – anything, something else, I do not quite know what.

This woman's statement shows the results of a process of conflicting socialization and indicates an awareness of a very crucial notion of self consciousness and a sense of lack of freedom. When real life experience cannot feed into the positive self-image of a woman she begins to feel hemmed in. The need for "liberation" or "freedom" is also very intricately and subtly connected with a woman's identity as a female and the cultural image of femininity.

In the rapidly changing technological world of America, change in life style also precipitates change in values and ideas. However, achievement in technology and science does not necessarily mean freedom of choice in personal life, although it does mean a greater choice in the availability of certain roles. But, although the western industrial revolution, by increasing the productive capacity has brought material comfort within the reach of the majority, the process through which this has been achieved has generated tensions and frictions.

Human beings in a technological civilization often live in a state of isolation. Many values take on meanings predominantly in economic terms.

The individual's consciousness of freedom appears to be confined at a level of economic consumption and there is a lack of cognizance of the individual's innate potential. The very promise of individual freedom that one expects from technological progress becomes subverted by its own vicious circle of progress and material gain at the cost of individual psychic sacrifice. This predicament is visible in many aspects of the rising consciousness among women. For over a century, since the beginning of the industrial revolution, women's routine-work at home formed the infra-structure of the modern industrial economy. They have also become the most flexible and vulnerable group of consumers induced by advertisement to react not only to goods but also to education and even such intangibles as a new brand of "love" (Henry 1963). Values emanating from such a life-style often clash with the new inner aspirations and psychic needs of women. When she talks of liberation an American woman is perhaps craving for a liberation which may be available to her Indian counterpart despite and perhaps because of an underdeveloped economy where there is less freedom of choice but also less conflict. Anne Roiphe (1973) in her review of the television series "An American Family," a candid production of an American family over seven months, poignantly says,

I feel badly that I can do so few things for myself with my own hands, that I am a consumer and my children, like me, buy before they build. I have no household gods, or any other kind, to keep me civilized, and... I feel often as if I have been set too free. Culture, if it means anything, must mean the binding of the individual into the social fabric. My threads are all undone...

And,

I wish we could return to an earlier America when society surrounded its members with a tight sense of belonging, of being needed. Maybe it's better to be... tribal and ethnocentric than urbane and adrift.

However, one must remember that even the concept of liberation varies according to the socioeconomic, educational and cultural backgrounds. When an upper-middle-class housewife is hemmed in by her home and successful husband, her lower-class counterpart in the slum aspires for the same comfort which will liberate her from her hand-to-mouth existence. At the same time, the middle-class, university educated, self-conscious woman is fighting for her liberation against discrimination in a job market on the one hand, and against her own internal conflict regarding her self-image, on the other.

CONCLUSION

The crux of the problem presented above, then, is to show a need for a comprise between individual needs (both psychic and intellectual) and social needs. It seems, in Bengali society, that such a compromise is offered by minimizing the possibility of the development of a self-conscious personality among women. This is done by making the self-image of a woman coincide with socially prescribed and culturally supported roles. In America, on the other hand, the conflict between socially prescribed roles and individual self-image is becoming sharper as more women and men are trying to release themselves from previously defined social roles.

By drawing data and observation from two very different cultures, I am not suggesting one is better than the other. Comparison, a bias of a social analyst, is desirable only because it highlights the problems. While I try to remain an "objective" analyst, in understanding some problems with which modern women struggle, I close this paper with a very subjective notion. I strongly believe that there is nothing teleological or inevitable about the predicament that modern women face today. Despite all the historical and economic antecedents, individuals are free to change the course of history. Thus, I am convinced women will achieve the goal of liberation that their inner beings are craving for, if they understand the situation in proper perspective, and act.

REFERENCES

BENEDICT, RUTH
    1938    Continuities and discontinuities in cultural conditioning. *Psychiatry*, 161–167.
BERNARD, JESSIE
    1942    *American family behavior*. New York: Harper.
BROVERMAN, D. M., *et al.*
    1968    Sex role stereotypes and self-concepts in college students. *Journal of Consulting Psychology* 32:287–295.
    1970    Sex role stereotypes and clinical judgements of mental health. *Journal of Consulting Psychology* 34:1–7.
HENRY, JULES
    1963    *Culture against man*. New York: Vintage.
HOLTER, HARRIET
    1970    *Sex roles and social structure*. Oslo: Universitetsforlager.
KOMAROVSKY, MIRRA
    1946    Cultural contradictions and sex roles. *American Journal of Sociology* 52:184–189.

ROIPHE, ANNE
1973   An American family: things are keen but could be keener. *New York Times Magazine*. February 18.
ROY, MANISHA
1973   "Bengali women as respect objects: an analysis of male-female relationship in contemporary urban west Bengal." Paper read at the Ninth Annual Conference on Bengal Studies. New York.
1975   "The Oedipus complex and the Bengali family in India," in *Psychological anthropology*. Edited by Thomas R. Williams, 123–134. World Anthropology. The Hague: Mouton.
SINGER, MILTON B.
1972   *When a great tradition modernizes: an anthropological approach to Indian civilization*. New York: Praeger.

# Vietnamese Women:
# Their Roles and Their Options

MARILYN W. HOSKINS

How can the conflict between the mystique of the oppressed female described in Vietnamese literature and verbalized by Vietnamese women be understood in light of the equally common belief that they are the real power in the country? How can traditionally demure wives adjust to a rapidly changing society without apparent redefinition of roles? How is it possible that women are becoming more active in Vietnamese society and are profiting by an improved status within the political and economic systems in both the North and South without meeting the prejudice and resentment of males so frequently found in the Western world? Raising instead of answering these important questions are many generalizations about the roles and options of the Vietnamese women. These generalizations frequently conflict, are often inconsistent in themselves, and are seldom based on research.

My interest in Vietnamese women began in 1963 when I worked with a UNESCO project studying goals and values of Vietnamese in rural communities. It grew during the next several years as I lived in Saigon and did an ethnographic study of a lower socioeconomic Saigon urban quarter (Hoskins and Shepherd 1970; M. Hoskins 1971). I studied women — but not apart from the rest of the family. In reviewing the research, including my own, it became apparent that the role Vietnamese women play in mediating and reacting to culture change must be understood if we were to answer the above questions. I therefore isolated some of these frequently raised questions, looked into some reasons for the inconsistent conclusions, and attempted to evaluate the available material.

One major reason for the inconsistent conclusions by authors is a confusion between actual behavior and cultural values which are imposed from outside. The Vietnamese have been the repository of forces from other civilizations for centuries as far back as the India-influenced Cham and Khmer people who occupied much of Viet Nam before the Vietnamese. An even more important influence came from the Chinese who ruled Viet Nam for approximately 1000 years (111 B.C. to A.D. 939) and who established the first legal code and national governmental structure. Eighty years of French rule, ending in 1954, with its Westernizing influence, have also had a great effect. Conflicts between the indigenous practices and the imposed patterns create confusion in evaluation if these historical perspectives are not kept in mind.

Another major source of confusion comes from making generalizations based on behavior appropriate in specific situations. For instance, a Vietnamese wife will often use formal respectful language and an attitude of deference toward her husband, but she may run the family business, handle the money for the family, and refuse to give him the extra spending money he requests. One author may describe the subservient role of a woman from her demeanor and another sees only her dominance in economic affairs. Neither realizes that both behavioral complexes are part of the total female role and that all roles are actually a composite of a variety of roles, (Gross, McEachern, and Mason 1958; Linton 1936) even when, as in Viet Nam, the domestic family roles of daughter, wife and mother, and the public societal roles including occupational activity and social leadership have developed somewhat differently.

Confusion comes also from the lack of attention during the last several decades to the role and status of women in this rapidly changing society. Even books specifically about women and change hardly mention the Vietnamese woman, e.g. Ward (1963) and Boserup (1970). An attempt has been made to fill this gap by using historical records and legal codes to establish the setting, selected folk stories for information on indigenous patterns, social science research done during the French occupation up to the present, and comments in the local press and national journals by Vietnamese women about their current roles and role options.

HISTORICAL AND LEGAL SETTING

Anthropologists and historians report that up to the last century before the Christian era, Vietnamese practiced slash and burn rice agriculture and had a matriarchal or bilateral kinship system (Huard and Durand 1908; Le Thanh Khoi 1955; Buttinger 1962). About the beginning of the Christian era the Chinese overwhelmed Viet Nam and incorporated it into

China. There followed a deliberate and thorough program of sinicization which included the introduction of the plow and buffalo and with it a sedentary agrarian life (Buttinger 1962). The Chinese supported by Confucian ideology created laws which permitted male domination of women These laws allowed women no power over their dowry and no access to inheritance or other property. A woman was also bound to her husband for life and upon his death was not permitted to remarry (Cadière 1905; Lusteguy 1935). These concepts were codified in China during the Ch'in Dynasty (259–210 B.C.) and later imposed on the Vietnamese by their Chinese administrators.[1] This era came to an end when the Vietnamese gained their independence in A.D. 939 after almost 1000 years of Chinese domination.

The next recorded legal code was initiated by Emperor Le Thanh Ton (1459–1497). It was more humanitarian and progressive than the previous Chinese Code, combining more equalitarian and local customs with some of the Chinese legal precepts (Nghiem Xuan Viet 1963). It declared women equal to men in almost every respect, including inheritance of family property and freedom to marry without parental consent. It also placed a time limitation on engagement periods that protected girls from being engaged by their families in infancy (Le Thanh Khoi 1955).

After Le Thanh Ton's reign, the country fell into intermittent periods of war and civil strife and was only restored to peaceful unity by Emperor Gia Long in the early 1800's. He established the Gia Long Code of 1812 which again incorporated Chinese patterns, withdrawing women's rights to make contracts or control property (Philastre 1909). However, where the Gia Long Code contravened well-established customs, especially in family matters, it was ignored. For example, parents left their daughters property in wills, and if the matter happened to come to court the presiding mandarin usually decided the case by local custom (Nghiem Xuan Viet 1963). The Gia Long Code was the structure, but not necessarily the practice, in Viet Nam when the French began to exert increasing control over the country in the mid-1800's. They annexed South Viet Nam as a colony, made North and Central Viet Nam protectorates and ruled the country for approximately eighty years.

At first, the French were confused by the Chinese-patterned Code and sought to enforce it, not realizing its violation of established Vietnamese custom (Nghiem Xuan Viet 1963). This had the temporary effect of strengthening male legal dominance, especially of men in the upper classes.

---

[1] In practice, however, they were frequently modified to fit the Vietnamese family pattern whereby most family problems were settled within the family councils where women traditionally had a more equal voice (J. Hoskins 1971).

Later French efforts to eliminate some practices which they believed were unjust to women, such as divorce and child marriage, were unsuccessful (Pham Huy Ty 1957).

When the Vietnamese again regained the opportunity to make laws for themselves, the ruling powers in both the North and the South declared men and women equal. The first constitution enacted by the South Vietnamese government in 1956 declared men and women equal in dignity, rights, duties, pay, and ability to vote and hold public office. In 1967, the South Vietnamese government established a new constitution retaining these rights. It also emphasizes the importance of the family:

The State recognizes the family as the foundation of society. The State encourages and supports the formation of families, and assists expectant mothers and infants. Marriage must be based on mutual consent, equality, and cooperation. The State encourages the unity of the family *(Constitution of the Republic of Viet-Nam 1967)*.

The government of North Viet Nam promulgated its current constitution in 1960. It also gave women equal rights with men in political, economic, cultural, social, and domestic areas, and stressed the importance of the family. It sanctioned equal pay for women, paid leave before and after childbirth, and supported the development of maternity hospitals, day-care centers, and pre-schools (Fall 1965).

Although the ideals expressed in these constitutions are not always fulfilled, the governments have gone a long way toward giving women legal equality. This is often represented as a revolutionary departure from past practices, but the earlier codes which gave women no legal rights were reflections of pressures from the Chinese and French, not the indigenous practices that tended toward more equality (J. Hoskins 1971).

FAMILY ROLES

Traditional folk tales and contemporary anthropological studies describe Vietnamese women as the power within the family structure. This is the case in all the twenty-six stories that mention women from four well-known collections of folk tales (Le Huy Hap 1963; Pham Duy Khiem 1959; Sun 1967; Schultz 1965). It is also true of descriptions written in the early 1900's by French anthropologists and oriental scholars (Huard and Durand 1908; Cadière 1905; Lusteguy 1935). More recent rural studies (Hickey 1969; Hendry 1964; Donoghue 1961a, 1961b), and urban studies (Hoskins and Shepherd 1970; Slusser 1965; Slote 1966; Bourne 1970) bear this out. In all these sources there is, with only minor variations, a picture of the powerful roles of women in the family. When a woman fulfils her part in the family, she strengthens that group which is her source of power as well. In this setting, it is the group welfare that is most important, not the individual. The individual does not ask herself if others make her happy, rather if she and others are fulfilling their roles within the family structure. As long as she lives up to her role, she can count on the power and support from the family. If she fails to do so, power and support are withdrawn.

*The Role of Daughter*

Both the traditional and contemporary source materials emphasize the daughter's value as a member of the family. Although sons are essential for carrying on the family line, daughters are also desired and their actions can enhance or ruin the family name.

The role of daughter, both in myth and in present day descriptions, is to be virtuous, marry well, and have children. The concept includes both "shyness" and "chastity." Shyness describes a quiet calmness, an indirectness, an avoidance of conflict, a polite formal respect shown elders and authorities as well as ancestors, and the control of aggressive feelings. This is well illustrated in the folk story, "The girl from Lim village."

More than ten generations ago, there dwelt in Lim village a very beautiful girl. Orphaned of her mother as a small baby, she lived with her old father in a tiny house at the end of the village. She was betrothed to a young man in the next hamlet, and the wedding was to take place in the near future. One day on the way home from the market a man came toward her and started to speak. His presence embarrassed her for she was a proper and shy girl from a very traditional family and had never been in such close contact with any man other than her father and her fiancé.

The father coming upon the couple standing together misunderstood the situation and severely reprimanded the girl and the man. The girl stood respectfully in front of her father. Her shyness prevented her from defending herself. Unfortunately, the man was a roguish mandarin who then arrested the father and daughter.

The mandarin tried in vain to seduce the imprisoned girl, often resorting to violence. Each time she attempted to end her life, rather than give herself to the man who had caused misfortunes to her family. The king, hearing of the situation, demoted the mandarin and impressed by the girl's virtue, presented her and her father with gold and precious embroideries. The father and daughter returned to the village with honor and wealth (Le Huy Hap 1963).

This story also illustrates a second aspect of virtue, that of chastity. In this case, chastity precludes even speaking to men outside the family. Chastity is related to virginity but may also mean keeping one's "heart pure" so that if a demand of loyalty to the family impels even the sacrifice of virginity, it can be done without the loss of honor. This is vividly illustrated in the most famous Vietnamese epic poem.

...This story concerns a young maiden endowed with all spiritual and bodily graces; an elite, who when placed between love and filial devotion, deliberately chose the harder way; she sold herself to save her father, a victim of an unjust calamity. And from that day, she passed from one misfortune to another until she sank into the most abject depravity. But, like the lotus, in the midst of this mire, she always preserved the pure perfume of her original nobility... (Nguyen Du in Le Huy Hap 1963:iii).

To benefit the family, a daughter is expected to marry a man with the highest possible status. The uniting of families in marriage includes uniting the ancestors in heaven and tends to combine the power and wealth of the two families.

In a study of the role of the family in transmitting culture, Leichty (1963) studied attitudes toward their families of a number of Vietnamese school children. She found Vietnamese children oriented toward family expectations, their main concerns being their future roles as adult members of the family group. Families retain their cohesiveness and their emphasis on traditional family roles by fostering the attitude that the family gives life and sustenance and one can only repay one's debt by assuming an expected role in the family structure. In rural areas, one frequently hears Vietnamese telling toddlers that they must not nurse for too many years or they will build a debt they cannot repay.

*The Role of Wife*

A wife is the center of the household. It is she who is constantly caring for the family, influencing the husband, caring for the finances, and doing whatever benefits the family group. Her role is to pay formal respect to her husband, to his family and ancestors as well as her own, to continue her virtuous way of life so that she brings no shame to either family, and to produce children, especially sons. A husband has great freedom to come and go at will. This leaves the woman major authority within the family. Like daughters, wives use indirect persuasion and exert "gentle pressure" to control their husbands, and this can sometimes include threatened or real attempts at self-destruction.

The folk story, "A woman's wit," shows correct behavior on the part of the wife who finds an unusual way to prove her point.

An elder brother is married to a wise woman. She is aware that her husband is generous to friends but stingy to his family, especially his younger brother. Several times she quietly and politely points out to her husband that his brother is loyal and the friends are "fair-weather" friends, but her husband does not listen. One day this wise woman tells her husband she accidently killed a beggar who surprised her, and has hidden the body in a cloth sack. She urges her husband to get some friends to help bury the sack where officials will not find it and arrest them, bringing shame to the family name. The husband goes to "friend" after "friend" but finds only his brother willing to help. The "friends" actually report the case to the authorities in hope of a reward. When the authorities come and dig up the sack, they find the carcass of a dog. The wife explains to the judge how she planned this incident to prove to her husband that friends may come and go, but brothers cannot be replaced. The judge commends the wife's virtue and cleverness and dismisses the case. The husband sees his error and the family is united (Le Huy Hap 1963).

In a newspaper interview Tran Thi Hoai Tran (1971), assistant professor of law at the University of Saigon, explains that Vietnamese women have never needed a woman's liberation movement. Dr. Tran says that Vietnamese women have always been trained to capitalize on their "femininity," using the soft approach to get their way in the family. She states that the soft approach is very effective, and claims that although a Vietnamese woman would not ask her husband to do housework and although sho shows her husband formal respect, she still manages to get what she wants. Although the Vietnamese woman's overt behavior is formally submissive, she is frequently called "the general of the interior" because she makes most of the family decisions. Researchers have noted that the Vietnamese woman also has the ability to operate independently of her husband to a degree that would amaze many American women (Bourne 1970).

*The Role of Mother*

The role of mother is the least described of all. In the twenty-six folk tales, mothers play a part in only seven and never as the main character. The mother-daughter dyad is never a major element of the stories as is the father-daughter dyad. Parent worship and role idealization operate in such a way that even Vietnamese themselves have a difficult time characterizing mothers as having human personalities and characteristics (Bourne 1970; Slote 1966).

While the traditional ideal for the man points to the scholar-poet or the warrior-politician as the road to honor, wealth, and power, women have a family-centered road to similar honor, wealth, and power. This role is a continuing one for the women, with the goal for the daughter to become a successful wife, so that she can repay her family for what they have done for her by increasing their wealth and power through the combined family status. The goal for the wife is to have a strong family and to become a mother. Once she is a mother, she has helped fulfill her obligations as daughter and strengthened her position as wife.

## OCCUPATIONS

Throughout Vietnamese folk literature, women have pursued gainful occupations to support their families. Women in folk tales worked with their husbands or ran the family farm or business when the husbands were away meditating or studying for the mandarin examinations, fighting bravely in some war, or attending to a political assignment in a province far away. When women took up medicine or trade, it was usually in connection with a family business. Historical studies show women working to support their families in a wide variety of occupations, but these were not always the most prestigious. The Chinese gave the highest position to scholar-mandarins, a middle status to warriors, and gave merchants a low position. During the time of Chinese control, women were frequently merchants, seldom warriors, and were forbidden to participate in the scholastic mandarin exams. However, there are historical heroines famous for military or literary skill.

The French undermined the power of the mandarin-scholar by establishing French schools, many of which were open to girls, and by introducing alternative paths to power and wealth formerly monopolized by the mandarins. In South Viet Nam the positions of high governmental officials are still considered very prestigious, but so is teaching, owning a business, and practicing a profession — all open to women. Wealth is an important determinant of class though it can only give a "grade B" status at the highest levels if not accompanied by education and familial qualifications. Money itself can give a family upward mobility as well as opportunity for its children to get the education necessary for a more stable place in the higher class (Slusser 1965). This new evaluation of status away from the mandarin system does not indicate the society is any more materialistic and less intellectual. It is merely a change in the path to wealth and power, and this change has made the path more available to women.

French colonial rule had different effects on families of different economic classes, and it increased inequality between the sexes in certain sectors of the population. New rules allowing larger land holdings created more foreclosures on small farms. In the rural context men and women had worked more or less equally, but when workers were forced from their own land, they went into the newly established factories and plantations where wages were not equal. In 1931 average daily wages in some areas of Viet Nam were nearly twice as much for men as for women (Turley 1972). Although the constitutions of both the North and South declare wages are ideally the same, women of both areas complain that this is not the actual situation. In 1971 in South Viet Nam, average daily wages paid to skilled women workers were still approximately two-thirds those paid to men and for unskilled work women received from three-forths to four-fifths the wages of unskilled men laborers (*Viet Nam statistical yearbook, 1971* [1972]). These averages do not reflect different wages for identical work for the most part, but the fact that more advanced and skilled positions are held by the men. Although equivalent statistics are not available for the North, women in both areas stress the difference in wages is frequently tied to lack of education and training for women.

When the French left in 1945, they vacated a number of higher level jobs in commerce, in the professions, and in the civil service. Due to the manpower shortage and the availability of educated women, many women had the opportunity to enter higher level jobs.

Within one generation Vietnamese women, passive and subservient at home, have entered business, politics, and the professions in larger numbers and with great success. Vietnamese husbands expect docile wives, yet they work on a basis of equality with professional women. Francis Hsu reports that this has also been true among Chinese women. About Chinese in contrast to American attitudes Hsu says:

In the Chinese pattern, sex being relegated to particular areas of life, does not pervade every aspect of life... The American woman is, in male eyes, never separated from the qualities of her sex... and he is resentful because she brings with her the advantage of her sex in addition to her professional abilities. The Chinese woman's sexual attractions belong to her husband or fiancé alone... Once she has achieved a new occupational or professional status, the Chinese woman tends to be judged in male eyes by her ability and not by her sex (Hsu 1972:56–57).

Hsu goes on to point out that China has never known the concept of "chivalry" through which psychological distances between males and females are accentuated. This same result occurs in Viet Nam with situation-centered, formalistic roles taking precedence over individual interests.

Most rural South Vietnamese women help with the rice production and retain well-understood and valued economic roles working along with their husbands. In a study of one rural village, approximately a third of the women held part-time jobs, usually in rice production or commerce, but only wives with no financial support from their husbands held full-time jobs (Hickey 1969; Hendry 1964). Inflation has made it difficult for urban South Vietnamese families who depend solely on a salary income to retain their standard of living, and women of all classes have felt pressure to get jobs. Urbanization has been rapid in South Viet Nam partially due to the pressures of war, and many families have moved to the urban areas without the extended kin group. Even when family groups have moved from the rural to urban areas, they have frequently had to find housing in separated areas and live in nuclear households. This has had the dual effect of relieving wives from much of the daily responsibility for service to the extended kin group and yet taking away the many hands that helped with housework and babysitting. Women complain that servants are becoming more difficult to find and many solve this problem by taking a niece or other young girl from the country. Others have "adopted" older homeless women who work for room and board (Hoskins and Shepherd 1970). The government has recognized this problem and has made an effort to establish day-care centers and pre-schools though there are waiting lists for all such facilities.

Newspaper articles written by women in the South in the 1960's and 1970's stress the desire to work and to justify this employment in family terms (*The Vietnam Observer; Miet-My; Viet Nam magazine;* Chiem T. Keim 1967). Some reasons these women give for working are that it makes one a more mature, interesting, and understanding wife; it keeps women from acquiring vices caused by idleness; it helps dutiful daughters-in-law get away from nagging mothers-in-law; and, it helps families in this time of inflation keep up or improve their standards of living. One article ends, "So we can see why working not only makes a woman's life independent but also effectively preserves her family's happiness" (Chiem T. Keim 1967:69).

In the North there has been strong governmental pressure toward getting women educated especially for technical and para-professional jobs. In articles translated from the Northern press during the 1960's and 1970's, women write that their status in the working world has improved though employers are not living up fully to their legal obligations to give lighter work loads to pregnant women and to provide baby-care centers, etc. (*Women of Viet Nam* 1972; Mai Thi Tu 1963; Chiem T. Keim 1967). In these articles, women urge other women to fight for their occupational rights, to get better training for higher jobs, and to work hard to help other women, other workers, and the nation's economy. They too are urged to justify their employment in family terms, but differently than the terms stressed in the South. They too are urged not to disregard the family, but unlike the South Vietnamese women, they are urged to expand the definition of the family to include the community. One article, for example, entitled "On the way in the fight for women's equality with men" concludes, "On the road to socialism, not only is our life — the women's life — better, but our interests are also wider. At the present time a number among us regard co-op and factory work as their own family's tasks" (Chiem T. Keim 1967:41).

The development of incongruent values and the effects of Westernization probably created the most stress on girls in the elite families who bridged the gap between Confucian tradition and French education and have since entered the professions. Mme. Le Kwang Kim, a well known pharmacist in Saigon, describes vividly what it was like in 1940 to be an eighteen year old traditional upper class girl, and some of the changes that happened to her and to many girls in this situation. In 1940 like other higher class Vietnamese, she had a great deal of contact with the ruling French, she attended the only available school, a French-run boy's college. Coming from a Confucian background, she and her small group of co-ed friends rarely spoke to their male classmates. The girls were chaperoned to and from school. The classwork, all in the French language, dealt with French subjects. One evening, while writing an essay on Voltaire, her father came into her room and announced that the following day she would return her books to the school. Her father continued:

"Your mother and I, with the approval of your grandparents, have arranged a marriage for you with the sixteenth son of Madame H. The young man is one of the most eligible *partis* in the country. They are Catholics and have asked that you should become one, and therefore you will do so. It is of no importance since, as a girl, you would not have to be responsible for the cult of the ancestors. Your brother will undertake this honorable duty. The day after tomorrow you will attend instruction at the Cathedral of Saigon" (Le Kwang Kim 1963: 463–464).

Le Kwang Kim describes how she accepted these decisions which had been made for her. As she had seen the "Great Family" care for and support its members, she trusted its system would take care of her.

At that time I was not an independent person responsible for my own future. I was only the grand-daughter of the Great Nobleman of Binh-y, daughter of his second son, existing not on my own account but in relation to my family (Le Kwang Kim 1963:464).

Le Kwang Kim was caught up in the confusion caused by the violence beginning in 1945. Many of her friends who had led secure lives found them shattered with the disappearance of prosperity. Her "Great Family" and that of many others had shrunk to the nuclear family due to death, loss of land, and enforced mobility caused by war. Mme. Kim found herself a widow with a two year old son and younger brother to raise, a mother to support, and an inadequate education. She describes this as a time when many young women saw an alternative to living solely within the family — that of becoming more independent in newly opening jobs and occupations as the country began to organize itself without the French.

To marry again was out of the question; it was not considered fitting for a woman to marry twice. Was my reluctance to marry due to a desire to show myself worthy of my mother-in-law, that indomitable woman who, though widowed, was bringing up her children alone? No, I think rather, though I was unaware of it at the time, that the fact of being able at last to take my life and my future into my own hands, having no longer either father or husband in authority over me, liberated me from my bonds, so that I intended to preserve my new-found freedom at all costs (Le Kwang Kim 1963:468).

Selling her jewelry, she traveled to France where she studied pharmacy. Returning to Viet Nam seven years later, she found the changes amazing. There was a two way pull. Not only had things become "Westernized," but at the same time people were returning to traditions of the past, as if conscious of a need to rediscover themselves. Writing in 1963, she said that times were still changing rapidly and that the adjustment had not been altogether comfortable. She felt it would be some time before the Vietnamese would become integrated again and know, as they had known in the past, what their roles and options were, and what to expect of those around them.

## LEADERSHIP

Vietnamese women have exerted leadership throughout history, but almost always through their family role and the men around them. The most famous folk heroines in both the North and South are the Trung sisters or the *Hai Ba Trung*. In A.D. 34 Viet Nam, then called Giao Chi, was ruled by a Chinese governor noted for his tyranny and for forcing the proud Vietnamese to assimilate Chinese culture. This governor executed Tri Sach, an influential Vietnamese land-owner and literary man of the time. His widow, Trung Trac and her sister Trung Nhi, sought to avenge his death, raised an army, and, riding elephants at its head, fought the

Chinese. Exercising great military skill, they defeated the Chinese. Though their reign was short, they have remained enduring national heroines of the Vietnamese.

The occasional examples of female leadership in descriptive studies show women are almost invariably leaders due to the positions held by their husbands. For example, in one rural community the wife of the village chief organized a women's militia, but she did not serve in a leadership capacity (Donoghue 1961b). In looking at leadership in an urban community, I found that when women had no men in the family they would work through other women whose husbands could take the recognized leadership for a project, while the women designed, organized, and saw that their project was completed (Hoskins and Shepherd 1970).

Only recently have women begun to conceive of a leadership role apart from the family role. Women have traditionally had equal votes with men in family councils and the current governments of both the North and South have recognized their potential leadership and have given women equal votes in national elections. For almost twenty years, women have been declared politically and socially equal to men and for that length of time they have held elective and appointed leadership positions in both governments. Articles from the South indicate, however, some ambivalence on the part of women to define leadership roles outside of their relationship with their family or the strengthening of their husband's political role. A group of interviews of prominent women by the journal *Xa Hoi Moi* [Modern Society] shows a range of opinions from those who said women were too emotional and sentimental to be good politicians to those who believe that from long practice in getting along with their mothers-in-law women had a gift for diplomacy which would be crucial in politics. One female professor said women needed to participate actively in politics to protect their own interests, while a female mayor said that most women should stay home and become better informed voters (Chiem T. Keim 1967). In an article entitled "Women and ther new responsibility," the author summarizes a theme common in the newspapers, that women's first duty is to their family and if they become active in society they must guard against "libertinism" or losing their traditional virtue of shyness and chastity. "...If the family is no longer firm and respectable, then women will be the ones to suffer most... If a woman fails to be a deserving wife and mother, then she cannot possibly perform any valuable work" (Chiem T. Keim 1967:26).

Articles from the northern press also indicate the ambivalence of women toward leadership positions. A number of females were nominated for the national assembly, but, despite pressure from the party, women lost seats in the 1971 election. The party has also appointed a number of female vice-chairmen of co-operatives, many of whom have resigned. The newspaper articles discussing these failures to take leadership say that the old system taught women they were inferior and that women must gain confidence. They urge women to get better educations and urge husbands to take pride in wives who show community leadership. As in the articles on occupations, women are urged to extend their attitude of responsibility from the family to the community and country.

## CONCLUSIONS

The most important conclusion from this wide variety of material deals with the relationship between the domestic and societal roles of women. Well-defined and relatively stable domestic roles have been the power base for Vietnamese women, while traditionally loosely-circumscribed societal roles offer them flexibility and options to take advantage of current changes in society. In addition, this conclusion gives insight into the three questions asked at the beginning of this article. For example, we can now see the roots of the conflict between the mystique of the oppressed female described in Vietnamese literature and verbalized by Vietnamese women and the equally common belief that they are the real power in the country. The "powerless Vietnamese woman" was an ideal imposed by other cultures, particularly the Chinese; it was not the indigenous pattern. Closer evaluation of historical and legal documents reveals that in actual practice women always had a strong position in the family. The family roles women play in Viet Nam are predetermined, with positions and behavior closely prescribed. Women continued to play a powerful role within the family, while maintaining the stance of outwardly submissive behavior at the appropriate times. Women emphasize the family but are free to participate in any outside activity that furthers it as long as she brings no embarrassment to the kin group.

   In practice, this freedom, along with the feeling that commerce is a natural field for women, has given her great opportunities to participate in the economic structure of the country. The French developed an economic structure which made new positions available for women at various levels, but they also encouraged the concept of unequal wages for men and women. Though women now own many commercial enterprises, other women still work for wages and incomes lower than men. The laws in both the North and South, however, are encouraging more sexual equality. Women are also filling some leadership positions in the North and the South and though not yet any top positions, they are being encouraged to work toward assuming these roles.

This type of analysis had shed light on our second question of how traditionally demure wives adjust to a rapidly changing society without apparent redefinition of roles. The answer includes an awareness that wives are not challenging domestic roles, for the most part, and as a matter of fact their roles have always included the mandate to do whatever was necessary to support the family unit. Dr. Bourne, a psychiatrist studying values of Vietnamese says:

The Vietnamese man is facing increasing difficulty in adapting his traditional role to the rapid changes in this society. Disintegration of the old culture, which began under the French, has accelerated precipitously under American influence. The Western emphasis on productivity, materialism, and personal security based on emotional dependence on the nuclear family is much closer to the traditional expectations of the Vietnamese woman than the Vietnamese man (Bourne 1970:220).

In other words, traditional values put women in a very good position to function within the changing Vietnamese society.

Our final question asked how it was possible for women to become more active in Vietnamese society and profit by an improved status within the political and economic systems in both the North and South without meeting the prejudice and resentment of males so frequently found in the Western world. Historical developments and wartime conditions have created openings for women which they can fill without changing their domestic role regarding the separation of sexual behavior and of aspects of life concepts. The previous quote by Francis Hsu offers further insight into the answer. Sex is limited to specific situations and does not dominate other aspects of daily male-female relations outside of these situations. Therefore, educated females do not challenge the male ego when working with them on a professional basis. And, traditionally women are expected to be concerned about the material well-being of the family, so for a wife to bring an income into the family funds is not a challenge to males.

As to the future, the material raises a number of questions. With legal rights in marriage, property, voting, education and economic opportunity assured in both North and South Viet Nam, what role will the Vietnamese woman play in the future? Throughout history the women of Viet Nam have participated in wars, commerce, music, arts, teaching, and medicine, whenever family position and obligations permitted or required it. However, there is only so far that a woman can go, especially in leadership positions if her activities are tied to her husband's position. The traditional role, which includes strengthening the family, offers women the rationale for participating in the political and economic systems, especially for the educated middle and upper classes. However, new opportunities for leadership are unrelated to the position of the woman's husband and many would require a commitment beyond that of supporting the husband's status.

There are other important questions to raise such as what will happen to the forces in society which have been pushing women to take a more active role in the economic and leadership positions in their country when the crisis of war lessens? Will men returning to the labor market create a surplus which will reverse the trend that presently encourages women to participate actively? Will the lessening of nationalistic fervor also lessen the desire to have women participate actively in politics? What effect would the possible future reductions of inflationary and urbanization pressures have on the woman's role? And finally, if there is a partial return to extended family living, will the women affected be asked again to spend most of their time fulfilling roles within the extended kin group?

The future of women in Viet Nam appears to depend on whether or not they wish to or can redefine their power base. In the North the government is encouraging woman to make the "duty of the family" ideal include "duty to the community." In the South the path may be through an emphasis on individual achievement within the social structure. Currently many women are participating in the socioeconomic systems of their country but still primarily to improve or solidify the position of their family. Much of the future of Vietnamese society will depend on whether this element of consistency continues to underlie women's perception of their external roles, or whether they will exercise their options to redefine their power base as they participate more fully in the power and economic structures of their country.

## REFERENCES

BOSERUP, ESTER
    1970  *Women's role in economic development.* New York: St. Martin's Press.
BOURNE, PETER G.
    1970  *Men, stress and Vietnam.* Boston: Little, Brown.
BUTTINGER, JOSEPH
    1962  *The smaller dragon: a political history of Vietnam.* New York: Frederick A. Praeger.
CADIÈRE, LEOPOLD
    1958  *Croyances et pratiques religieuses vietnamiens* (second edition). Saigon: Imprimerie Nouvelle d'Extreme Orient. (Originally published 1905.)

CHIEM T. KEIM, *translator*
1967   *Women in Vietnam; selected articles from Vietnamese periodicals, Saigon, Hanoi, 1957–1966.* Honolulu: East-West Center.

Constitution
1967   *Constitution of the Republic of Viet-Nam.*

DONOGHUE, JOHN D.
1961a   *Cam An: a fishing village in central Vietnam.* Saigon: Michigan State University.
1961b   *My Thuan: the study of a delta village in South Vietnam.* Saigon: Michigan State University.

FALL, BERNARD B.
1965   *The two Viet-Nams: a political and military analysis.* New York: Frederick A. Praeger.

GROSS, N., A. W. MCEACHERN, A. W. MASON
1958   "Role conflict and its resolution," in *Readings in social psychology* (third edition). Edited by Eleanor E. Maccoby, T. M. Newcomb, and E. L. Hartley, 447–459. New York: Holt.

HENDRY, JAMES B.
1964   *The small world of Khanh Hau.* Chicago: Aldine.

HICKEY, GERALD C.
1969   *Village in Vietnam.* New Haven: Yale University Press.

HOSKINS, JOHN A.
1971   "The Vietnamese legal system." Lecture presented to the Viet Nam Training Center of the Foreign Service Institute.

HOSKINS, MARILYN W.
1971   *Building rapport with the Vietnamese.* Washington, D. C.: U.S. Government (AGDA-A M OPS-IA-SO).

HOSKINS, MARILYN W., ELEANOR SHEPHERD
1970   *Life in a Vietnamese urban quarter* (second edition). Carbondale, Illinois: Southern Illinois University.

HSU, FRANCIS L. K.
1972   *Americans and Chinese* (second edition). Garden City, New York: Doubleday Natural History Press.

HUARD, PIERRE, MAURICE DURAND
1954   *Connaissance du Viet-Nam* (second edition). Hanoi: Ecole Française d'Extreme-Orient. (Originally published 1908.)

LE HUY HAP
1963   *Vietnamese legends.* Saigon: Khai-Tri.

LE KWANG KIM
1963   "A woman of Viet-Nam in a changing world," in *Women in the new Asia.* Edited by Barbara B. Ward. The Netherlands: UNESCO.

LE THANH KHOI
1955   *Le Viet-Nam: historie et civilisation.* Paris: Editions de Minuit.

LEICHTY, MARY M.
1963   The role of the family in transmitting culture. *Viet-My* (83).

LINTON, R.
1936   *The study of man.* New York: Appleton-Century.

LUSTEGUY, PIERRE
1953   *The role of women in Tonkinese religion and property* (second edition).

Translated by C. A. Messner. Yale Human Relations Area File Press. (Originally published 1935.)

MAI THI TU
1963   "The Vietnamese woman, yesterday and today," in *Vietnamese women*. Hanoi: Democratic Republic of Viet Nam.

NGHIEM XUAN VIET
1963   "La technique juridique du credit immobilier en droit." Unpublished thesis for the Doctoral en Droit, University of Saigon.

PHAM HUY TY
1957   Law and society in Vietnam. *Studies in the law in Far and Southeast Asia*. Washington: The Washington Foreign Law Society and George Washington University Law School.

PHILASTRE, P. L. F.
1909   *Le code annamite*. Paris: Ernest Leroux.

SCHULTZ, GEORGE
1965   *Vietnamese legends*. Rutland, Vermont: Charles E. Tuttle.

SLOTE, WALTER H.
1966   *Observations on psychodynamic structures in Vietnamese personality*. Arlington, Virginia: Advanced Research Projects Agency.

SLUSSER, MARY
1965   *Characteristics of the people of Indochina*. Washington, D.C.: External Research Division, Department of State.

SPINDLER, LOUISE, GEORGE SPINDLER
1958   Male and female adaptations in culture change. *American Anthropologist* 60:217–33.

SUN, RUTH A.
1967   *Folk tales of Vietnam: land of seagull and fox*. Rutland, Vermont: Charles E. Tuttle.

TRAN THI HOAI TRAN
1971   "Quiet persuasion used; Viet women use feminity for liberation." *Daily Egyptian*, Southern Illinois University. August 6.

TURLEY, WILLIAM S.
1972   "Women in the Vietnamese revolution." Paper presented to Panel on Vietnamese Communism, Convention of the Association for Asian Studies, New York, March 27–29.

*Viet Nam government organization manual, 1957–1958*
1958   Saigon: National Institute of Administration.

*Viet Nam magazine*
1970–1972   Volumes three, four, and five. Saigon: Vietnam Council on Foreign Relations.

*Viet Nam statistical yearbook, 1971*
1972   Saigon: National Institute of Statistics.

VO HONG PHUC
1960   The role of women in Vietnamese society. *Viet-My* 4 (winter).

WARD, BARBARA, *editor*
1963   *Women in the new Asia; the changing social roles of men and women in South and South-East Asia*. The Netherlands: UNESCO.

*Women of Viet Nam*
1972   Hanoi: Viet Nam Women's Union I–IV.

# Changing Roles of Women
# in Two African Muslim Cultures

EDITH ELIZABETH LORD

U Thant, former Secretary General of the United Nations, noted that only five U.N. member-nations currently (1973) deny the vote to women and that four of the five are Muslim countries. There is evidence, however, that the particular prejudice against women which is reflected in a denial of suffrage exists today in countries which are, by color, black, brown, white; by religion, Christian, Islamic, or "other"; by political persuasion, democratic, totalitarian, or monarchical.

One is forced to conclude that generalizations concerning the status of women today are dangerous if they sweep across major categories such as a religion, a continent, or even a country. Change is permeating traditional sex roles world-wide. The study of contemporary dynamics of change among various segments of humanity might well be a more relevant concern of scientists than a mere reporting of gross current statistics, whether by nationality, religion, race, political orientation, or geography.

A review of the literature on changing roles of women reveals a paucity of information on the situation among African women in predominantly Muslim societies. Studies of African women tend to generalize about their changing status without reference to such variables as Christian influence (in Ethiopia and tropical coastal Africa), Islamic influence (in coastal Northern Africa, and animistic influence (in some non-coastal interior countries of Africa). Even within a largely Islamic area, such as Eritrea,

This study was supported in part by National Science Foundation Grant # GF 29954: Principal investigator, Edith Lord; Egyptian research assistant, Rasmeya Aly Khalil; Tunisian research assistant, Kacem Ben-Hamza.

Ethiopia, one finds great differences in the status of Muslim women in population centers such as Asmara and Karen, less than 50 miles apart.

Variables also spill over into the political status of women in African countries. For example, when Nigeria became independent in 1960, three women were elected to the Eastern legislature, while veiled women in the Northern region of Nigeria were — and still are — denied suffrage: Christianity is a strong influence in the former region while Islam predominates in the latter. In the religiously mixed Western region of the Federation, all women, regardless of religious affiliation, were permitted to vote, and reportedly Muslim women, mostly unveiled in this coastal area, voted heavily.

Regardless of these marked differences in the status of women WITHIN this one African country, a Nigerian writer, in 1965, freely generalized about the changing status of African women as follows:

Up to now African women had a clearly defined — and limited — part in our society. It started by their being a disappointment in most cases to their parents, who had almost invariably hoped for a boy! Having got over the shock, father usually reconciled himself by working out how much he would get as bride price when the time came... It is only since our girls and women have been given more education and training facilities that we all realize the importance of women's contribution to the progress of our nation (Obukar and Williams 1965:8).

In a 1957 discussion on problems of female education in a Muslim culture, a Libyan government official stated that one faction in Libya wanted to require girl students to forgo purdah, to lift their veils, as a condition for admission to public schools. But, he reported, he was among the group that convinced education officials that if they could merely induce parents to permit their daughters to attend school, these girls would quickly discover other cultural patterns and would not only break free of purdah, but would also be a force for educating the female adults in their families to look on today's world with uncovered faces. This African government official made the point that he was a devout Muslim; in turning from purdah he was not turning from Islam. Within Muslim cultures, he was convinced, the status of women could be advanced so that their contributions to national development would be comparable to those of women in non-Islamic states.

Marked changes in the status of Muslim women reportedly occurred in the nineteen thirties in the Soviet East where, traditionally: "women had been regarded as scarcely human. They were sold to their husbands in childhood and forced to work as slaves. On the husband's death, the widow legally became the property of the nearest relative along with the domestic utensils, livestock, and other possessions." Reforms and changes in the roles of Muslim women in the Eastern Soviet countries have been called "dramatic" (Halle 1938).

While the evidence so far cited may suggest that most Muslim women in Africa are locked in traditional molds, one need only look at Egypt to alter the stereotype. In 1963, a conference sponsored by the United Nations Educational, Social, and Cultural Organization was held in Lagos, Nigeria, on The Role of African Women in Urban Development. Representatives of most African countries attended, but parts of the conference were dominated by the U.A.R. delegation, which included a physician and other professional women — all Muslims. This fact was somewhat disturbing to a delegate from Muslim Northern Nigeria who publicly stated that she had assumed that all Muslim women in the world were as restricted as those in Northern Nigeria.

There is further evidence that the variation in status of women is as great within religious categories as between them. The modern, "liberated" Roman Catholic African women of Eastern Nigeria stand in contrast to the "castelike inferiority" of women found in Roman Catholic Latin America by R. S. Williamson in a study of role themes. He noted, "Despite the forebodings of demographic pressures, economic stagnation, and political traditionalism, it would seem unlikely that the liberation of women from a castelike inferiority can be postponed forever.... Progress at least is visible in the urban middle class" (Williamson 1970:197).

Countries of North Africa have been, and are, subject to educational, industrial, and sociocultural influences from Europe across the Mediterranean Sea. Yet, they are strongly linked, through Islam, to the East. Current pressures — often equating Muslim with Arab — are being exercised to influence political identification with the Arab states, rather than with a geographical identity as African states. These various influences and pressures affect the roles of women, particularly the changing roles of African Muslim women.

During the summer of 1971, the writer visited Egypt, Tunisia, Algeria, and Morocco. This brief report presents a few highlights gleaned from some of the data collected in Egypt and Tunisia. These data suggest that there are marked differences among numerous variables between Egyptians and Tunisians, particularly with reference to females. Both countries are Islamic, a religion which holds that "Allah has power over all things" (external locus of control)[1] and which provides the basic rules of conduct

---

[1] *Locus of control orientations* (Tillman and Lord 1975). One hundred sixty-six Egyptians, 86 males and 80 females; and forty-eight Tunisians, 30 males and 18 females, completed a culturally modified version of the internal-external control scale

for Muslims including clearly defined roles for women such as nurturance, self-abasement, deference, non-dominance, and subordination to men.[2] Both countries are similar in that they are Mediterranean, North African, Muslim, predominately Arab cultures. They are different, however, in economy, western influence, and education.

Egypt's economy began a steady acceleration in the mid-forties; whereas Tunisia began to accelerate in the mid-sixties. While the 1971 estimated per capita income of Egypt is $240 and that of Tunisia is $210 — not far apart — the Tunisian figure is presumed to have been inflated by the relatively higher incomes of European residents of Tunisia. Since independence, Egypt has increasingly withdrawn from European influence; whereas, Tunisia remains ideologically and culturally (and perhaps economically) somewhat a European colony.

Egypt enacted legislation for compulsory primary education in 1923; Tunisia, not until 1958 (UNESCO 1971). Almost all women in Tunisian secondary educational institutions are enrolled in teacher-training programs; in Egypt, 85% of female secondary school students are enrolled in university-preparatory programs.[3] While women are beginning to take

---

composed of 15 items. The Egyptian sample was significantly LESS externally oriented than the Tunisian sample. In both samples, males were LESS externally oriented than females, and the differences between the sexes was greater in Tunisia than in Egypt.

[2]   *Adjective check list:* The Egyptian and Tunisian samples were compared on eight of the scales of the Gough and Heilbrun Adjective Check List. The Egyptian females exceeded the Tunisian females on measures of Achievement, Dominance, Endurance, and Nurturance. The Tunisian females exceeded the Egyptian females on Abasement and (desire for) Change. There was no significant difference between males on any of the other four scales. Within the Egyptian female sample, 50 employed adults were compared with 30 college students. The adults significantly exceeded the students on scales measuring Achievement and Endurance. The students exceeded the adults on Dominance and (desire for) Change.

[3]   *Roles of educated women:* subjects were given the following directions:

"Educated women today are concerned about their roles in society. Listed below are ten possibilities. Read all ten statements, then write *1* in the space before the statement which you consider to be the BEST CHOICE. Write *2* before the next-best choice. Then write *0* before the statement which you consider to be the WORST CHOICE."

Fifty per cent of the Tunisians selected as BEST CHOICE, "Career, marriage, few children." Fifty-five per cent of the Egyptians also selected this option as BEST CHOICE. However, an analysis of sub-sets within the Egyptian sample discloses some interesting differences between males and females on this measure: "Career, marriage, and few children' was FIRST CHOICE for 82% of adult females, 72% of female college students, 44% of male college students, and 40% of male adults. NEXT BEST choices were widely scatered among all groups. Again, 50% of the Tunisians selected as WORST CHOICE, "No career, marriage, many children." However, 23% selected as worst, "Career, no marriage, no children.' Among the Egyptian respondents, WORST CHOICE selections among college students and male adults were so scat-

more active and varied roles in both countries, the educational and occupational mobility of Egyptian women far exceeds that of Tunisian women, as does the variety of jobs and professions open to women.

The economic and educational development of both Egypt and Tunisia have been paralleled by a movement toward modernization, including modernization of attitudes toward and opportunities for Muslim women. These trends toward attitudinal changes are more marked in women than in men, and they are greater, in general, in Egypt than in Tunisia. However, whereas the development and modernization of Tunisia seems to have included a movement toward westernization, the movement in Egypt appears to have been away from westernization.

Perhaps the most optimistic outcome of this study is the observation that with education, economic advances, and modernization there is a measurable shift from external orientation of control — "Allah has power over all things" — Koran — toward an internal locus of control — "I am the master of my fate." Although maintaining a strong identification with Islam, the women, the youth, and the men of Egypt in particular and of Tunisia increasingly are incorporating attitudes which may result in greater progress, productivity, and — especially for women — increased self-esteem.

## REFERENCES

HALLE, F. W.
   1938   *Women in the Soviet East*. New York: Dutton.
OBUKAR, CHARLES, JOHN WILLIAMS
   1965   *The modern African*. London: Macdonald and Evans.
TILLMAN, WAYNE, EDITH LORD
   1975   Locus of control orientations. *Human Understanding*.
UNESCO
   1963   Conference on education: role of African women in urban devel-development.
   1971   Conference on compulsory education.
WILLIAMSON. R. S.
   1970   "Role themes in Latin America," in *Sex roles in a changing society*. Edited by Georgene H. Seward and Robert C. Williamson. New York: Random House.

---

tered as to preclude a modal response. However, the female adult employees clearly indicated 'no career' as a WORST CHOICE: 40% checked, 'No career, marriage, few children"; 30% checked, "No career, marriage, many children."

# Women and Social Customs within the Family: A Case Study of Attitudes in Kerala, India

GEORGE KURIAN, MARIAM JOHN

This study is an attempt to assess the attitudes of rural women in a Kerala village towards four selected areas of cultural practices: (1) rituals during marriage ceremony, (2) dowry system, (3) aspiration towards children's education and profession, and (4) children's decision-making. The attitudes have been studied in relation to an *a priori* independent variable, the community (i.e. the group such as the Christians, Muslims, etc.) and the generation, and, *post facto* independent variables, the educational and the occupational level to which the respondents belong.

An attitude scale was constructed to elicit the responses of women on these cultural practices. A stratified sample of 60 Christians, 60 Hindus and 30 Muslims was selected. Each community had an equal number from the older and younger generation. The majority of the respondents were educated at least up to primary school in all communities. They were mostly from nuclear families. About one-third of them came from agricultural households, approximately one-third from households whose head had teaching jobs or clerical jobs, and about one-third from the occupational class of semi-skilled laborers.

## COMMUNITY INFLUENCES

The religious community of the respondent was not found to be an influencing factor, except in one area, namely — "rituals during marriage ceremony." Thus it may be said that the three communities show more or less similar attitudes towards the cultural practices, although they belong to three different religious faiths. It is generally believed that religion regulates human conduct and behavior and sets "a limit which has implications for the learning capacity of the society in which it is institutionalized" (Bellah 1965:117). The finding of this study is not in accord with that concept.

The similarity in attitude observed in the three communities may be attributed to a common mode of living in the state of Kerala. Historically, these religious groups have been living together for generations. Christianity came to Kerala as early as A.D. 52, when the apostle Thomas came to India, preached the gospel and converted some of the local inhabitants (Kurian 1961:34–46).

The dominant socioreligious culture in India is that born of Hinduism. Thus, it may be surmised that through the generations of cultural linkage, the essential features of the dominant values and styles of living came to be culturally assimilated into the minority groups who settled in that area.

The three communities of Hindus, Christians, and Muslims living together use one common language (Malayalam) and are exposed to similar literature, which culturally binds the communities together. In India, "these linguistic regions have considerable homogeneity of culture and of family organization, as language makes communication possible and sets limits of marital connection, local folklore and literature" (Tara Ali Baig 1969).

Furthermore, the supportive information shows that these three communities have similar marriage customs. Most respondents had their marriages arranged by the elders of the family, and the choice of marriage pattern was decided by the parents with the consent of the respondent, the dowry payment among these communities being quite similar except in the case of the Hindus where land was given as dowry as opposed to the Muslim and Christian payment in money and gold. This exception in the Hindu community may be explained as a part of the matrilineal traditions which have influenced a number of Hindu caste groups in Kerala.

The table below shows an apparent difference in the forms of dowry payment made in each community. The majority of the older Hindus paid dowry in the form of land, whereas a majority of the younger Hindus paid in money. Among the Muslims, the majority of both young and old paid money and gold; among Christians the majority of both generations paid in money.

Hence, the Muslims and the Christians have retained some of the Hindu cultural customs like their marriage rituals and dowry payments. One important Hindu custom among the Syrian Christians of Kerala

Table 1. The form of dowry as expressed by 120 respondents

| S. Number | frequency interval | Hindu Old | Hindu Young | Muslim Old | Muslim Young | Christian Old | Christian Young | Total |
|---|---|---|---|---|---|---|---|---|
| 1. | Money alone | 2 (6.7%) | 8 (47%) | 3 (20%) | 1 (10%) | 19 (63.3%) | 14 (77.8%) | 47 (39.1%) |
| 2. | Money and land | | | | | 3 (10%) | 2 (11.1%) | 5 (4.1%) |
| 3. | Money, land, and gold | | | 3 (30%) | 1 (10%) | | | 4 (3.3%) |
| 4. | Land and gold | | | 1 (6.6%) | 1 (10%) | | | 2 (1.7%) |
| 5. | Money and gold | | 2 (11.5%) | 6 (40%) | 4 (40%) | 4 (13.3%) | | 16 (13.3%) |
| 6. | Land alone | 27 (90%) | 6 (35.8%) | 1 (6.7%) | 2 (20%) | 1 (3.4%) | 2 (11.1%) | 39 (34.5%) |
| 7. | Gold alone | | | | | | | |
| 8. | No dowry | 1 (3.3%) | 1 (5.7%) | 1 (6.7%) | 1 (10%) | 3 (10%) | | 7 (5.8%) |
| Total | | 30 (100%) | 17 (100%) | 15 (100%) | 10 (100%) | 30 (100%) | 18 (100%) | 120 (100%) |

is the marriage badge (thali) and another among the Muslim "Mapillas" of North Malabar is the matrilineal family organization (Rao 1957:22). Mayer observes that "the Muslims have retained the Hindu custom of inheritance" (1952:29). Perhaps the voluntary adjustments made by the Muslims and Christians have helped them adjust their religious differences.

The survival of the Church in Kerala is very much due to the fact that it developed an indigenous character and adapted itself to local conditions. Though the Christians in Kerala had Syriac liturgy and had much in common with the orthodox churches in the middle east, the Christians as such tried to fit into Indian or otherwise the Hindu social strata. In fact they show features of syncretism (Kurian 1961:35).

The attitude towards "rituals during marriage ceremony" indicated that the Hindus were significantly more conservative than the Muslims and that the Christians were more progressive than both. This conservative attitude indicated by the Hindu community may be due to the fact that since they were the originators of these rituals, and since rituals form a dominant part of their way of living, it was perhaps a way of maintaining their cultural identity. The progressive attitude on the part of the Christians may be related to a degree of progressivism that could compare very favorably with that most progressive Indian group, the Parsis (Kurian 1961:103). The findings of similar attitudes in the three communities for all cultural practices, except the marriage rituals, need further examination, particularly with respect to the impact of religion and the proximity of their living space.

## GENERATIONAL INFLUENCES

Results of the findings regarding the generational differences in attitudes confirm that the younger generation is far more progressive. The results are in accord with an accepted social science theory as stated by Spicer (1952) that each generation behaves differently from the previous generation. Kapadia (1966) has attributed a capacity for changed outlook in family relationships and traditions in young people, which accounts for the major difference between the older and the younger generation.

In the state of Kerala, moreover, the educational level of the young is high because of the increased number of incentives offered by the government as well as private institutions. Therefore, the younger generation are better educated than the older group, creating another difference.

Barnabas (1969) and Mahadeva (1969) claim that there are no major differences between the opinions of parents and their children. This discrepancy between their views and ours may be due to the fact that the two populations examined come from widely different areas, or that the two studies explored different dimensions of these attitudes using different types of questions.

Differences between generations in all four areas showed the highest mean difference in the area of "rituals during marriage ceremony." This was followed by "children's decision-making," "dowry system," and "aspiration towards children's education and profession." This indicates a general shift in the attitudes of the young away from "rituals during marriage ceremony" and the "dowry system." The young group seems inclined to give a great deal more freedom to the children.

What do these findings indicate? First that there is a difference in the attitudes of the younger generation, and second that their rate of change is much faster and hence may be one cause for the widening generational gap. It is, therefore, possible to assume that this difference in attitude in such an important "core" value might lead to conflict between the young and the old. Technological change may be an important and additional catalyst.

## INTERACTION OF COMMUNITY AND GENERATION

The investigation into the interaction between the communities and generations in regard to all four cultural practices taken together uncovered no significant difference between the communities. Further, in relation to each area of the dependent variable, namely "rituals during marriage ceremony," "dowry system," "aspiration towards children's education and profession," and "children's decision-making," no significant differences were found.

These findings may be due to the fact that the homogeneity in these communities may have been a modifying factor in the differences between generations.


## THE INFLUENCES OF EDUCATION

The *post facto* variable, education, appeared to have strongly influenced the attitudes of the respondents. The analysis clearly showed that the more highly educated the respondent, the more progressive the attitude. The university graduates and vocationally trained respondents were the most progressive, then came the matriculates, the primary school attenders, and then the non-educated. This pattern prevailed in all except the response to "children's decision-making." There the matriculates had a higher score than the graduates, indicating that in this area they were more permissive with children.

In Mehta's (1969) study on need achievement in boys, the variables, "low occupation" and "low education of the family" were related to high need for achievement. The less educated in this study who had the highest mean score for progressivism in "children's decision-making," were also from families of low occupational levels, i.e. low socioeconomic status. One might question what the relationship (in this lower socioeconomic group) might be between permissiveness towards children on the part of the parents and the need for achievement as shown by their children.

A further probe into the influence of education shows that the higher the education of the respondent, the greater the progressivism expressed in "rituals during marriage ceremony." However, in the areas concerning the dowry system and the respondent's aspiration towards their children's education and profession, the differences were not so marked. Perhaps the deep-rooted values about the dowry system are due to the long duration of the custom. Possibly the difference in ideas about women's aspiration towards their children's education and profession may be a manifestation of a high value attached to education in planning for children's future welfare at all levels of education.

## OCCUPATIONAL INFLUENCES

The *post facto* variable, occupations, includes farming, teaching, clerical jobs, shop keeping, and unskilled labor. The variance of attitude scores in relation to these occupations has shown no significant differences in total progressivism.

Even though the influence of occupation in all areas of progressivism was not found to be significant, a careful look at the mean shows that individuals from all occupational levels indicate a high aspiration for children's education and concern for their future profession.

## INFLUENCE OF THE GENERATIONS WITHIN THEIR RESPECTIVE COMMUNITIES

When all respondents were grouped together, the interaction of community and generation showed no significant differences. However differences between the two generations within each community did exist. The "T" test demonstrated that mean differences in the total attitudes of the two generations in the Christian community and the Hindu community were found to be significant. The following table gives the "T" ratio for progressivism in each area.

Table 2.  Tests of significance for attitude scores on "total progressivism" in regard to the four cultural factors

| Community | PROGRESSIVISM | | | | |
|---|---|---|---|---|---|
| | Dowry system | Ritual during marriage ceremony | Aspirations on children's education and profession | Children's decision-making | Total attitudes |
| Hindu | 2.08 | 2.53 | 1.55 | 2.27 | 3.41 |
| Muslim | 2.07 | 1.22 | 0.01 | 1.29 | 1.91 |
| Christian | 1.84 | 3.05 | 3.17 | 2.80 | 3.74 |

The mean scores on "total" progressivism in both communities show that the Christian young have a score higher than the Hindu young. Perhaps this is due to the educational differences between the two communities, Christians and Hindus. When a "T" test was computed between the two generations in all communities for all four areas of progressivism, only the Christian community showed significant differences. These significant differences appeared in three areas but not in the area of "dowry system."

This may be due to concurrence in attitudes towards dowry despite other factors such as strong differences between generations in the Christian community where dowry is an almost compulsory practice. People look down on a bride who does not bring a respectable sum as dowry. This is evident even among educated groups. However, modern education and accompanying liberal views are influencing people to question and often show dislike for this system even among some Syrian Christians.

In all areas without exception, the Muslim community showed no significant differences between the generations. Though the older generations of Muslims have shown progressive attitudes there seems to be a tendency to keep the youth from moving away from their own set of attitudes by the older generation themselves. This may be because Muslims, in the locality where the study was conducted, were the minority and may have wanted to maintain their identity.

## INTERCORRELATION BETWEEN THE AREAS OF THE DEPENDENT VARIABLE FOR COMMUNITY GENERATION

As an index of reliability an intercorrelation between areas was calculated for each sub-group.

Table 3.    Summarizations of correlation coefficients (rs) between two generations in each community for the areas of progressivism

| | Community | Areas of progressivism | Rituals during marriage ceremony | Children's education and profession | Children's decision-making |
|---|---|---|---|---|---|
| Hindu | Old n=30 | Dowry system | .26 | .02 | .22 |
| | | Rituals during marriage ceremony | | .27 | −.18 |
| | | Children's education and profession | | | .15 |
| | Young n=30 | Dowry system | .27 | .42 | .05 |
| | | Rituals during marriage ceremony | | .22 | .07 |
| | | Children's education and profession | | | .12 |

| | Community | Areas of progressivism | Rituals during marriage ceremony | Children's education and profession | Children's decision-making |
|---|---|---|---|---|---|
| **Muslims** | Old n=15 | Dowry system | .42 | '34 | .56 |
| | | Rituals during marriage ceremony | | −.24 | .07 |
| | | Children's education and profession | | | .68 |
| | Young n=15 | Dowry system | .45 | .06 | .60 |
| | | Rituals during marriage ceremony | | −.31 | .33 |
| | | Children's education and profession | | | .37 |
| **Christians** | Old n = 30 | Dowry system | .23 | .14 | .05 |
| | | Rituals during marriage ceremony | | .09 | .13 |
| | | Children's education and profession | | | .37 |
| | Young n = 30 | Dowry system | .44 | .19 | .29 |
| | | Rituals during marriage ceremony | | .38 | .25 |
| | | Children's education and profession | | | .20 |

One pattern found was a difference between the old generation of the Muslims (significant at 1% level) and the old generation of Christians (approaching tendency towards significance) in the areas "aspiration towards children's education and profession" and "children's decision-making." This may be explained on the basis of: (1) parents raised in a traditional society aspire for "better prospects" for their children in relation to their own socialization experiences; (2) a heightened awareness of the need for a change in their attitude in relation to the accelerated social changes in the world in which their children live.

## CONCLUSIONS AND IMPLICATIONS

From the above discussion, it is apparent that out of the two *a priori* independent variables, community and generation, it is only the generation variable which significantly affects the progressive attitude of the respondents. The variable "community" was found to influence only one area significantly i.e. "rituals during marriage ceremony." This indicates a variation in an area which seems to be deeply rooted in socioreligious norms. The Christians, being most progressive in this area and being somewhat Westernized, have perhaps adapted themselves more quickly to social change.

The younger generation is comparatively better educated than the older and is therefore more exposed to modernizing stimuli. Hence it is possible that education is a very significant influencing factor. This is borne out by the fact that in all areas the *post facto* variable "education" was found to be significant. The higher the education, the more progressive the attitude, except in the area of "children's decision-making" where the matriculates were found to be most progressive. This implies a need for further investigation in other areas of aspiration for children in relation to education of the parents.

The second *post facto* variable "occupational level" did not significantly influence attitudes. In the discussion, an indication was given that this may have arisen due to two possibilities. The categorization was a compound of two criteria, (a) the skilled/unskilled dimension and (b) occupational classification. If instead, the index had been income, perhaps a more reliable result would have been obtained. Further, a composite index of socioeconomic status including education, occupation, income, and residential area, might have been a more effective independent variable than occupation.

In all areas except the "dowry system" the two generations in the Christian community were different due to the earlier availability of modern education. There was no significant difference in the Muslim community. The young educated Christian seems to be in the forefront of adaptability to social change in relation to the parent generation. One might hypothesize that there might be conflicts in values and attitudes in this community more than in others. The Muslim community showed the least differences in responses. Perhaps the protected familial environment and strict socioreligious practices in this community create a common identification in attitudes.

There was no systematic pattern of intercorrelation within the community age-group sub-samples in the four areas, except in the older Muslim generation between areas "aspiration towards children's education and profession" and "children's decision-making."

It should be stressed that, according to the cultural lag theory (Ogburn 1954), all parts of culture do not change at a similar pace. A group may be progressive in some areas and traditional in others.

In the case of Kerala the Christians have the advantage that they have been exposed to modern education. Unlike Muslim and Hindu communities, Christians have been moving away from traditions. This was clearly shown in a study made by the senior author in Kerala in 1968 and 1972. However, with regard to dowry payments, the Christians show little change in attitudes. From the woman's point of view, dowry is received in lieu of land which their brothers inherit. Some of the recent changes in society tend toward giving equal rights to women with regard to inheritance. However, the emphasis on dowry is still dominant. This is a case where the concept of cultural lag seems to apply.

## REFERENCES

BAIG, TARA ALI
   1969   *Assignment children*. Reprint Number 10, UNICEF.
BARNABAS, A.
   1969   *Social change in a North Indian village*. The Indian Institute of Public Administration, Delhi.
BELLAH, R.
   1965   *Religion and progress in modern Asia*. New York: Free Press.
CORMACK, MARGARET
   1961   *She who rides a peacock*. Bombay: Asia Publishing House.
DESAI, I. P.
   1953   *High school students in Poona*. Poona: Deccan College.
KAPADIA, K. M.
   1966   *Marriage and family in India*. Bombay: Oxford University Press.
KURIAN, GEORGE
   1961   *Indian family in transition*. The Hague: Mouton.
MAHADEVA, B.
   1969   *Achievements and aspirations; people in Indian universities*. Jamshedpur: Xavier Labour Relations Institute.
MAYER, A. C.
   1952   *Land and society in Malabar*. Bombay.

MEHTA, P.
1969  *The achievement motive in high school boys.* National Council of Educational Research and Training.

NATRAJ, P.
1965  Mental pictures of college girls of Hindus, Muslims and Christians. *The Indian Journal of Social Work* 26(3):287.

OGBURN, W. F., M. F. NIMKOFF
1954  *A handbook of sociology.*

RAO, M. S. A.
1957  *Social change in Malabar.* Popular Books Depot.

SINGH., M.
1968  "A study of attitudes of rural women towards selected social problems." Unpublished thesis, Department of Rural Community Extension, Lady Irwin College, Delhi.

SPICER, E. H.
1952  *Human problems in technological change.* New York: Russell Sage Foundation.

# Some Remarks on the Legal Equality between Men and Women

OLGA VIDLÁKOVÁ

During the last two years (1971–73) both the Communist Party and the Government of Czechoslovakia have concentrated their efforts on stimulating young couples to have more children. As a result, many recent legal amendments have been made. For instance, there has been approximately a 25% increase in family allowances (effective January 1973) for couples with two, three and four children.

Another way to promote an increase in population is to look at the very delicate question of legal equality between men and women (an issue closely connected with fertility) with a new approach favoring the reproductive stage.

From the legal point of view in socialistic legislatures everything seems to have been done to promote the equality of the sexes. In the Constitution of the ČSSR, similar to the Constitutions of other socialist countries, it is decreed that:

a.   all citizens have equal rights and obligations;

b.   men and women have an equal position in the family, at work and in public activities;

c.   all citizens, women as well as men, have an equal right to work and to earn an equal income for work done, in accordance with its quantity, quality and social significance, etc.

Of special importance is section 27 in the Constitution of 1960, that decrees the basic principles for the social realization of equality between men and women as follows: "The equal position of woman in the family, at work and in public activities is ensured by a special arrangement of working conditions and special medical care during pregnancy and maternity as well as by the development of facilities and services that make it possible for women to apply their abilities to participation in public life." The significance of this section is that it goes beyond the legislative character inherent in the Constitution, and attempts to show the authorities how to apply the Law.

The Acts ensuing from the Constitution, primarily the Family Code (Act 94/1963 C.o.L.), the Civil Code (Act 40/1964 C.o.L.) and the Labour Code (Act 65/1965 C.o.L. ammended by Act 88/1968 C.o.L. and Act 153/1969 C.o.L. and Act 42/1970 C.o.L.) specify that man and woman are to be considered equal.

The Family Code decrees that men and women are equal in marriage regarding family and parental rights and obligations. It also states that a woman need not have the approval of her husband to conclude a working contract. The legal regulation of the mutual liability for maintenance also demands the legal equality of men and women as does the law for the legal settlement of property.

The Civil Code requires joint ownership of husband and wife (Sections 143–151), joint use of a flat by husband and wife (Sections 175–182), joint use of land by husband and wife (Sections 214–216) and equal inheritance (Sections 473ff.).

All property acquired by either spouse during their marriage and that which may be the object of personal ownership is subject to a so-called joint ownership.[1] The spouses have access to the use of all things in joint ownership and mutually bear the costs connected with their use and maintenance. Joint ownership terminates with the dissolution of a marriage.

Similarly the legal position of woman at divorce follows from the pattern of legal equality between man and woman in this society. Thus allowances for maintenance may be claimed by either divorced spouse but only when he or she is unable to provide for himself/herself.

Besides her role in marriage and family life the woman fulfills significant tasks in a broader social sense, namely at work and in public activities. Herewith is laid before the legislature a very difficult task of how to provide for the legal equality of woman.

The Czechoslovak legislation states that equal labor laws are valid for both man and woman. Nevertheless the Labour Code stipulates different working conditions for women in general and pregnant women and mothers in particular.[2] The stipulations mainly concern a ban on

---

[1] Exceptions are possessions acquired by one of the spouses through inheritance or gift and property which serves the personal or professional use of only one spouse.
[2] Chapter VIII, Sections 149–162 of the Labour Code.

certain jobs considered unsuitable for women. These can be divided into the following groups:

a. Occupations banned by the Labour Code — e.g. manual work underground in mining minerals and casting tunnels and galleries;

b. Occupations enumerated in lists issued by the central authorities responsible for individual industries, in accordance with principles laid down by the Government and agreed upon by the Ministry of Health and the Central Committee of the Trade Unions concerned. The purpose is to prevent the employment of women in jobs which are physically unsuitable or detrimental to their physical welfare, in particular jobs which might impede their maternal functions;

c. Occupations banned for pregnant women and young mothers up to 9 months after confinement, which according to medical opinion might detrimentally affect their physical condition;

d. Night-work for women in general, with the exception of occupations listed under Section 152 of the Labour Code.[3]

The pregnant woman and mother up until 9 months after confinement (as per "c" above) has the right to have her employer transfer her temporarily to some other, more suitable work. If this new work pays a lower salary, she is entitled to a "levelling-out allowance" amounting to the difference between her former and her present gross earning, although for only three months.

Pregnant women and mothers caring for one child under the age of one year are protected against dismissal. This protection does not apply in cases of substantial organizational changes, such as liquidation or transfer of the organization or its fusion or partition. The Labour Code contains a special stipulation which obliges the employing organization to respect the requirements of pregnant women or women caring for children when allocating work-shifts. If pregnant women or mothers of children under 15 years of age apply for part-time jobs or a different adjustment of their weekly working time, employers have to grant their requests provided no serious working situation prevents such an arrangement. All these stipulations are conditional. The employing organizations may take advantage of them. On the other hand, research

---

[3] These exceptions include:

a. work which has to be performed at night because normal work was disrupted by natural disaster or other extraordinary circumstances or in case the life and health of people are at stake,

b. processing perishable goods or raw materials in order to prevent their loss,

c. women holding leading or managerial posts or working in medical, social welfare or cultural services, in public catering, telecommunications and postal services, on railways and in public transport and in livestock industry.

confirms the well known fact that especially because it is financially un-profitable very few women apply for part-time jobs.

In my opinion the error lies at the very essence of the so-called "feminine problem." In the beginning of this century, a well known Czech literary critic F. X. Šalda wrote: "The equality between man and woman does not exist by nature but it is a goal for love to create it, if possible."

I believe he was right but today the vague hope "if possible" is no longer sufficient. We are witnessing an immense cultural and social change. The effect of this change on the family and society as a whole can hardly be foreseen. It is coming about for two major reasons. The first is the growing employment of women[4] without which the fulfilment of the challenging targets of economic and cultural construction in socialist society cannot be imagined. The other reason is the growing level and amount of education for women. At present, in Czechoslovakia, approximately 40 per cent of our women study at universities and other institutions of higher learning, 67 per cent in grammar schools and more than 50 per cent at other secondary schools (commercial, technical, vocational, schools of social hygiene, etc.).

We cannot afford to overlook the fact that realistically biological equality between man and woman does not exist. Nor is there an equality in the quality of the tasks performed by man and woman INSIDE the family. The emotional relation of mother to her child differs from that of father to his child. From this follows a more intensive and strenuous fulfilment of the tasks of mother in the family, many of which cannot be performed by father.

Since biological inequality between man and woman does exist, the problem of legal and social equality should not be treated in the traditional way by adapting women to the law of men. In fact, if indeed women have reached a position in society equal to men, legal measures — especially in the sphere of labor laws — are needed which give woman rights to far shorter working hours (in comparison with the working hours of men), longer leaves from work with full pay and the like. Such measures could take into consideration the biological diversity between men and women and the different functions of women in the family ensuing from that biological difference.

It is extremely important to find comprehensive legislative solutions for these problems that will be valid unconditionally and not just temporarily for sporadic periods in a woman's life, such as when she is pregnant.

[4]  In 1970 ČSSR, the employment of women represented 47 percent of the total employment in the national economy.

Otherwise we must bear the blame of discrimination against women *de facto* even if *de jura* no discrimination exists.

As far as I know the problem of equality between man and woman has never been approached in this way in any legislative system. Nevertheless I believe it to be a very serious target for legislators and politicians if they want to ensure equal possibilities for women at work and in public activities without damaging a balanced reproductive behavior of the population. The decreasing birth rates in many European countries in the last few decades, the extended life expectancy of European populations and the penetrating changes in the rates of education and employment of women give us reason and motivation to work for such legislation.

# Biographical Notes

BETTIE SCOTT ALLEN (1939) received a bachelor's degree in Cooperative Extension Education from Southern Illinois University, Carbondale. She has done graduate work in Interpersonal and Political Communication at Southern Illinois University. Currently she is working on a graduate degree in human relations and counseling at the University of Bridgeport, where she is a lecturer in the Department of Journalism and Communication. She has coauthored several articles on interpersonal communication with her husband Jerry Allen. They are currently editing a work on political communication.

JUDITH-MARIA HESS BUECHLER (1938) received her B.A. from Barnard College in 1959, an M.A. from Columbia University and a Ph.D. from McGill University in 1972. She has conducted field research in Bolivia, Ecuador, Spanish Galicia, and Switzerland sponsored by the Canada Council, the Center for Developing Area Studies, McGill University, and The Swiss National Science Foundation. She has taught at Queens College (C.U.N.Y.), Monmouth College, LeMoyne College, and Syracuse University. She is currently teaching at Hobart and William Smith Colleges. Her publications include *The Bolivian Aymara* (coauthored with Hans C. Buechler) and articles on peasant marketing, female entrepreneurship, and social change in Bolivia and Spanish Galician migrants to Switzerland.

ANKE A. EHRHARDT (1940), a native of Germany, received her Diploma in Psychology from the University of Hamburg and her Ph.D. in Psychology from the University of Düsseldorf in West Germany. She came to the

Johns Hopkins Medical School in 1964, where she worked with John Money in psychohormonal research until 1970. She is coauthor (with Money) of the book *Man and woman, boy and girl*, published in 1972. In 1970, she joined the faculty of the State University of New York at Buffalo, where she is heading, together with her husband (Heino F. L. Meyer-Bahlburg, Ph.D.), the Program of Psychoendocrinology at the Children's Hospital. Her main interest is in the area of the relationship of hormones and behavior.

LUCY GARRETSON (1936) received her B.A. from Radcliffe College and her Ph.D. from the University of Texas at Austin. She has written on the social definition of women and men in America, on neo-feminism, on women and social policy, and on American culture. Her main interests are the study of the bio-cultural determinants of sex-linked attributes and roles, and the study of urban America. She is currently teaching in the Anthropology Department at Temple University.

WILLIAM TULIO DIVALE (1942) received his B.A. from the University of California at Los Angeles in 1969, and his M.A. from California State University at Los Angeles in 1971 and is working toward a Ph.D. at the State University of New York at Buffalo. He was Odgen Mills Fellow at the American Museum of Natural History in 1972–73 and received the C. S. Ford Cross-Cultural Research Award in 1973. He is currently Instructor in Anthropology at York College of the City University of New York. His main interest is developing and testing theories cross-culturally which investigate the interaction between warfare, population, and social structure. He has published *Warfare in primitive societies* and has written articles on population control, residence patterns, and cross-cultural methodology.

BETH DILLINGHAM (1927) recieved her B.A. (1949), M.A. (1950), and Ph.D. (1963) from the University of Michigan. She has done field work among the Oklahoma Kickapoo Indians and the Seminole Negroes of Coahuila, Mexico. With Leslie A. White she published *The concept of culture* (Burgess, 1973). She previously taught at Central Michigan University. She is currently Associate Professor of Anthropology at the University of Cincinnati, where she has taught since 1965.

C. P. HOFFER (MACCORMACK) (1933) received her Ph.D. from Bryn Mawr College in 1971. She has done ethnographic field work in Sierra Leone and archival work in Freetown and in London. She was Assistant Professor of Anthropology at Franklin and Marshall College until 1974 and is presently Assistant Lecturer in Social Anthropology at Cambridge University.

MARILYN W. HOSKINS (1934) studied family and child development and nutrition at Southern Illinois University and received her M.S. in this field from Ohio State University and her M.A. in Anthropology from the Catholic University of America. She did research for the U.S. Department of Agriculture on goals and values of young Ohio farm families. In 1962–65 she lived in Viet Nam where she taught research methods in a UNES-CO program at the University of Saigon, did research and wrote on goals and values of rural Vietnamese families, and prepared an ethnographic study of an urban area in Saigon. In 1965–67 she was in Thailand where she wrote a series of articles on Thai women. Since 1967 she has served in Washington as a consultant to the U.S. Government on cultural values of Southeast Asian societies and has published on this subject.

BARRY L. ISAAC (1942) received his B.A. from the University of Kansas and his Ph.D. from the University of Oregon in 1969. He has done field work in central Mexico, Sierre Leone, and among the Prairie Potawatomi of Kansas. His publications include work on culture change, economic anthropology, and peasant societies. He is currently Associate Professor of Anthropology at the University of Cincinnati, where he has taught since 1969.

ROUNAQ JAHAN received her Doctoral degree in Political Science at Harvard University. She is Chairman and Professor of the Department of Political Science at the University of Dacca.

MARIAM JOHN was born in New Delhi, India. She received her Bachelor's degree from Delhi University, and her Master's degree from Lady Irwin College, Delhi University, 1971. She has done field work in Kerala, India. She is at present teaching in New Delhi.

JUDIT KATONA-APTE (1943), a native of Hungary, received her B.A. in Anthropology and is currently a doctoral candidate in the Department of Nutrition at the University of North Carolina School of Public Health. She is specializing in nutrition and anthropology and has done field work in India and in the United States. Her interests and publications focus on medical and nutritional anthropology, methodology, acculturation, and nutritional adaptation.

GEORGE KURIAN was born in Kerala State, India. He received his B.A. degree from Madras University and a Doctor of Literature and Philosophy in Sociology from the State University of Utrecht, Netherlands, in 1961. He has taught in Osmania University, India; Victoria University, Wellington, New Zealand; and since 1966, he has been with the University of Calgary, Alberta, Canada.

His book, *The Indian family in transition: a case study of Kerala Syrian Christians* was published in 1961 (Mouton), another, *The family in India: a regional view* was published in 1974 (Mouton). He has published a number of articles on family studies and social change in India and is the founder and editor of the *Journal of Comparative Family Studies* which emphasizes cross-cultural studies in anthropology and sociology. He is also very active in Asian studies in Canada and was the first Secretary-Treasurer of the Canadian Society for Asian Studies.

LOUISE LAMPHERE received her Ph.D. from Harvard University in 1968; she is currently Assistant Professor of Anthropology at Brown University. In 1965–66 she conducted research on the Navajo Reservation in New Mexico, and has written several articles on Navajo social organization and a forthcoming monograph. In 1971–72 she was a postdoctoral fellow at the London School of Economics, and worked on a pilot study of working-class women in their home and work situations.

ALAN LOMAX is Director of the Cantometrics Project, under the joint sponsorship of the Department of Anthropology and Bureau of Applied Social Research, Columbia University.

EDITH ELIZABETH LORD (1907) received her B.S. from the University of Houston in 1935; M.A., University of Texas, 1938; Ph.D., University of Southern California, 1948; M.A., N. Y. U., 1954. She is now Professor of Psychology (Clinical), University of Miami, Florida, 1968 to present. Previously she held faculty positions at the Universities of Houston, Southern California, Hawaii, and Nigeria and worked as a Human Resources Development Officer, U.S. Department of State, and with foreign aid agencies on African programs. Publications include a book on cultural patterns in Ethiopia, chapters in books on emergent Africa, the abused child, the Rorschach Test, and journal articles in the areas of clinical, cultural, and cross-cultural psychology.

JOSEPHINE NAMBOZE is a Senior Lecturer for the Department of Preventive Medicine, Makerere University, Kampala, Uganda.

LUCILE F. NEWMAN (1930) received her Ph.D. from the University of California, Berkeley, in 1965. She has taught anthropology at Mills College in Oakland, California, and from 1968 to the present at the University of California San Francisco Medical Center. She is currently working to establish a Medical Anthropology Program at that campus. Her research interests are in the area of human reproduction and her publications are on pregnancy, birth, family planning, and abortion. Her current research is on indigenous fertility regulation methods.

NILES NEWTON received her Ph.D. degree from Columbia University Teacher's College in 1952. She has written *Maternal emotions* while at the University of Pennsylvania School of Medicine and has authored and coauthored with her husband, Michael Newton, M.D., many articles on lactation. She is currently Associate Professor in the Department of Psychiatry, Northwestern University Medical School.

ETHEL NURGE (1920) received her B.A. from the University of New Mexico in 1950, M.A. from the University of Chicago in 1951, and Ph.D. from Cornell University in 1956, all in Anthropology. She taught in several university Departments of Anthropology and in 1968 joined the faculty of the University of Kansas Medical School. Her fieldwork includes New York State dairy farmers, Rosebud Sioux Indians, German villagers, and Filipinos in northeastern Leyte. Her current work is on cultural and social factors in sickness and health. In 1975 she plans to return to the Philippines for a study of changes in a Leyte village after twenty years.

DANA RAPHAEL received her B.S. and Ph.D. (1966) from Columbia University in anthropology. She is the author of *The tender gift* (Prentice-Hall, 1973) a work on mothering and lactation. Her research interests include social networks, supportive behavior in animals and human beings, malnutrition and starvation during the perinatal period. She was formerly full-time consultant for Columbia University International Institute for the Study of Human Reproduction where she is working on a comprehensive field guide *The anthropology of human reproduction* to be published in 1975. She is Adjunct Professor in Anthropology at Fairfield University in Connecticut where she lives, married and with three children, and is currently director of the Human Lactation Center.

FRANK POIRIER (1940) received his Ph.D. at the University of Oregon in Anthropology in 1967. He has done fieldwork in Cayo Santiago, Japan,

South India, West Indies, and Micronesia. He is currently Professor of Anthropology at Ohio State University. He has published extensively in the field of ethology and has edited and coauthored many books. He has done field work with Rhesus, langurs, green monkeys, and crab-eating macaques.

JOHN R. K. ROBSON (1925) a British subject, received his medical degree from Kings College Medical School, University of Durham. After practicing medicine in England he moved to East Africa. As a Medical Officer in the Tanganyika Government he began to specialize in nutrition and subsequently received postgraduate degrees in tropical medicine and public health from the Universities of Edinburgh, London, and New-castle. After ten years in Africa he joined the World Health Organization where he was advisor to governments in the Western Pacific and Eastern Mediterranean regions of WHO for five years. During these fifteen years in developing countries, he realized that the prevention and alleviation of malnutrition depends on a knowledge of the remote causes of the problems. Since many of these have been concerned with human behavior, he has collaborated closely with anthropologists. He is the editor of *Ecology of food and nutrition* and the principal author of *Malnutrition: its causation and control*. His present interests are in the field of paleonutrition and indigenous foods.

HENRY ROSENFELD is Professor of Anthropology and Sociology at the University of Haifa and visiting Professor at the Hebrew University of Jerusalem, Israel.

MANISHA ROY (1936) was born in India, received her B.A. and M.A. (1958) in Geography from Calcutta University, and her Ph.D. (1973) in Anthropology from the University of California, San Diego. Her doctoral thesis on the subject of frustrations and compensations of women's roles in upper-class Bengal (India) is to be published by the University of Chicago Press. She has done fieldwork among the matrilineal Khasi tribe of Assam (India), a peasant village community in West Bengal (India) and the middle and upperclasses in Calcutta. She has taught in Calcutta, at California State University and Chicago University. At present she is teaching urban and psychological Anthropology at the University of Colorado, Denver. Research interests include family dynamics and sex-role change in contemporary U.S.A. and India.

ALICE SCHLEGEL (1934), received her Ph.D. from Northwestern University in 1971. Since then, she has taught at Arizona State University and studied under a National Institute of Mental Health Post-doctoral Fellowship. She is presently teaching at the University of Pittsburgh. She is also an editor of *Ethnology*. Her publications include cross-cultural studies and papers on Hopi ethnology.

OLGA VIDLÁKOVÁ (1928) received her Ph.D. from the Charles University in Prague, Czechoslovakia in 1951. She is a research worker in the Institute of Landscape Ecology of the Czechoslovak Academy of Sciences, where she is responsible for the demographic and administrative part of the anthropological studies. Her publications include studies on the relationship between demographic phenomena and living environment, on the Czechoslovak population policy and the role of law in the development of population. She is a member of the Ruling Committee of the Czechoslovak Demographic Association and member of the IUSSP, where she recently participated in the study group on legislation and population in European countries.

SUZANNE FRAYSER WILSON (1943) received her B.A. from the College of William and Mary in 1965, her M.A. in Anthropology from Cornell University in 1968, and expects to receive her Ph.D. in Anthropology from Cornell University in 1974. From 1968–1973 she worked as a Research Assistant at the Cross-Cultural Cumulative Coding Center at the University of Pittsburgh under the direction of George Peter Murdock. Her main research interest has been in connecting reproductive and sexual behavior with population trends, comparative social organization, and theories of illness.

YING-YING YUAN (1945) received her A.B. at Bryn Mawr College and a Certificate in Social Anthropology at Cambridge University. In 1973, she received her Ph.D. from Harvard University. Currently she is a part-time lecturer in Sociology at the University of Zurich. Her research interests focus on friendship patterns, with particular reference to women and children, in complex societies and in situations of social change.

# Index of Names

# Index of Subjects

Abasement, 251–252

Abipon, 83

Abortion: induced (voluntary), 11–12, 25, 27–34, 180, 182, 184, 185; spontaneous (involuntary), 11, 25–27, 32

Achievement, as variable on Gough and Heilbrun Adjective Check List, 252

Adrenal cortex, 7–8, 21

Affectivity, 10, 87–97

Affinality, 59–61

Africa, 39, 114, 125, 126, 133, 135, 136, 166, 168, 205, 211, 215–218, 249–253. *See also* Names of individual countries

Aggression, 13, 14, 15, 16, 20–21, 172–173, 194, 195

Aggressiveness, 222

Ahaggar Tuareg, 167, 168

Algeria, 251

Alliance making, 125, 146, 147–148, 162. *See also* Affinality; Solidarity, female

Alorese, 32

"American family, An" (television series), 228

*American family behavior* (Bernard), 226

Androgenital syndrome, 7–8, 21

Androgens, 7–8, 19–23

Annual Congresses to Unite Women (ANCUW), 182

Apache, 105

Arabs, 139–152, 251, 252

Ashanti, 117–118, 126

Asia, 135, 166, 305. *See also* Names of individual countries

Asmara, Ethiopia, 250

Assiniboine, 32

Attitudes, change in, toward women, 203–204, 205; change in, and women's liberation movement, 184–185; Ugandan, toward reproduction, 215–218; women's ,225–264

Austin, Texas, 189, 197

Australia, 32–33, 133, 136

Authority, 2–3, 103–104, 106–107, 113–114, 115, 117–128, 140, 145–146, 148, 165–175, 189–199; ritual, 155–162. *See also* Matri-patrilocality and authority patterns; Power

Autonomy, female, 11, 121, 125–128, 174–175, 236–237, 244

Bahaya, 39

Bangladesh, 204, 206

Bantu, 60

Behavior: adult, of non-human primates, 13–14, 15–16, 20–21; formalistic, 232, 235, 236–237, 239; submissive, 232, 235, 236–237, 239

Behavorial diversity, 8, 11–12, 22–23, 113

Bengal, India, 219, 220, 221, 222, 223, 225, 229

Bengali language, 221

Berne, Switzerland, 208

Biosocial factors in reproduction, 7–12, 13–16, 19–23, 25–34, 37–40, 43–48, 49–52, 55–61, 65–70, 73–84, 111–113,131–132, 156–158, 178, 203–204, 206, 211–212, 267–271

Birth: control (*see* Family planning);